DINOSAUR KNOWLEDGE GENIUS!

DK | Penguin Random House

DK Delhi

Senior Editor Janashree Singha
Senior Art Editor Vikas Chauhan
Project Editor Abhijit Dutta
Project Art Editor Revati Anand
Contributing Editor Alka Thakur-Hazarika
Art Editors Aparajita Sen, Tanvi Sahu
Picture Researcher Geetika Bhandari
Picture Research Manager Taiyaba Khatoon
Managing Editor Soma B. Chowdhury
Managing Art Editor Govind Mittal
DTP Designers Vijay Kandwal, Rakesh Kumar, Mrinmoy Mazumdar
Production Editor Anita Yadav
Pre-Production Manager Balwant Singh
Production Manager Pankaj Sharma
Jacket Designer Vidushi Chaudhry
Senior Jacket Designer Suhita Dharamjit
Senior Jackets Coordinator Priyanka Sharma Saddi
Creative Head Malavika Talukder

DK London

Senior Editor Georgina Palffy
Senior Art Editor Rachael Grady
Senior US Editor Kayla Dugger
Project Editor Hélène Hilton
Managing Editor Francesca Baines
Managing Art Editor Philip Letsu
Production Controller Poppy David
Jacket Design Development Manager Sophia MTT
Publisher Andrew Macintyre
Associate Publishing Director Liz Wheeler
Art Director Karen Self
Publishing Director Jonathan Metcalf

First American Edition, 2024
Published in the United States by DK Publishing
1745 Broadway, 20th Floor, New York, NY 10019

24 25 26 27 28 10 9 8 7 6 5 4 3 2 1
001-333629-Apr/2024

A catalog record for this book is available from the Library of Congress.
ISBN: 978-0-7440-6984-6

Printed and bound in China

www.dk.com

DINOSAUR KNOWLEDGE GENIUS!

Written by: Dr Chris Barker and Riley Black
Consultant: Dr Chris Barker

DK

CONTENTS

1 PREHISTORIC LIFE

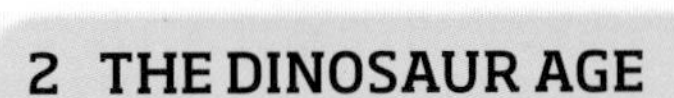

2 THE DINOSAUR AGE

3 REPTILES OF SEA AND SKY

4 RISE OF THE MAMMALS

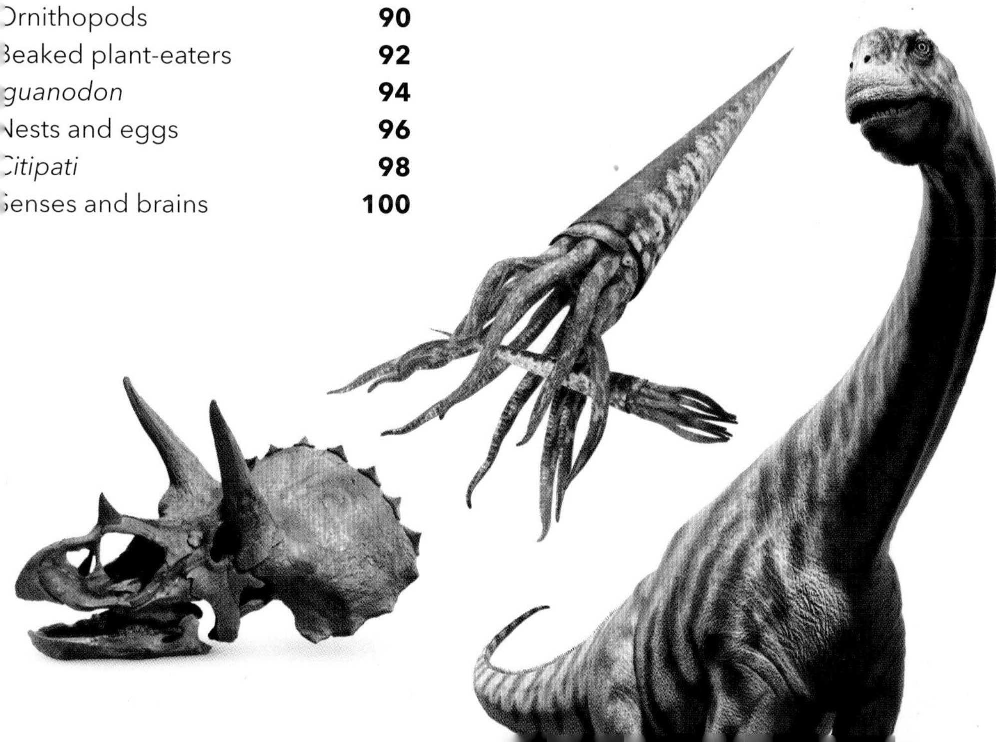

How this book works

Welcome to this fact-packed, quiz-filled challenge. Top up with some new knowledge, then put your brain to the test by matching the picture clues with the answers. Can you tell a *Velociraptor* from a *Diplodocus*? Do you know which tail belongs to which dinosaur? Can you identify the theropods? It's time to find out.

Then the challenge

It's time to test yourself. Take a look at the pictures and the list of answers in the panel on the side and try to match them up. Follow these four steps for the best way to tackle things.

01. First, choose your topic. There are four chapters all about prehistoric creatures, including lots of quizzes. Maybe start with one that you know all about, then move on to something new.

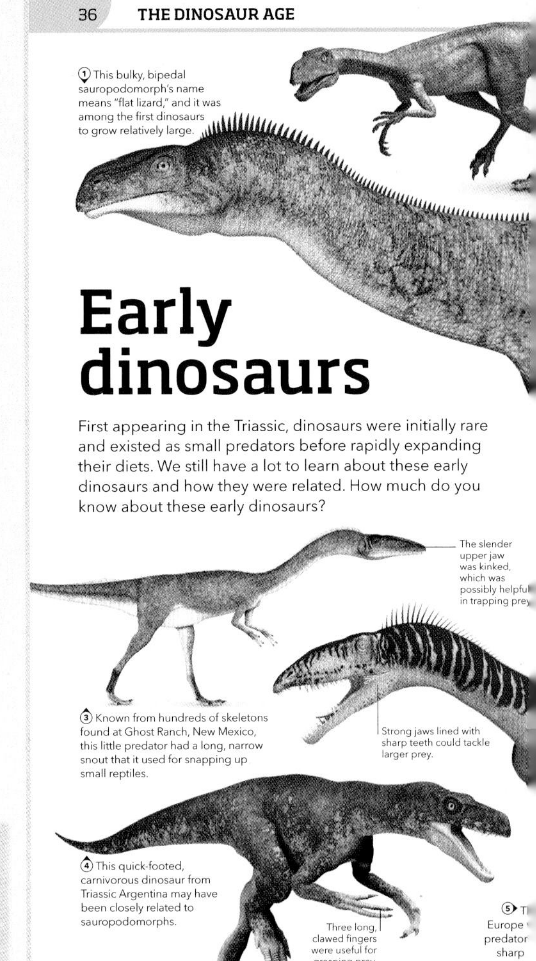

36 THE DINOSAUR AGE

① This bulky, bipedal sauropodomorph's name means "flat lizard," and it was among the first dinosaurs to grow relatively large.

Early dinosaurs

First appearing in the Triassic, dinosaurs were initially rare and existed as small predators before rapidly expanding their diets. We still have a lot to learn about these early dinosaurs and how they were related. How much do you know about these early dinosaurs?

The slender upper jaw was kinked, which was possibly helpful in trapping prey

③ Known from hundreds of skeletons found at Ghost Ranch, New Mexico, this little predator had a long, narrow snout that it used for snapping up small reptiles.

Strong jaws lined with sharp teeth could tackle larger prey.

④ This quick-footed, carnivorous dinosaur from Triassic Argentina may have been closely related to sauropodomorphs.

Three long, clawed fingers were useful for grasping prey.

Facts first

Brush up on the essential information with these fact-packed pages on all the main topics. They will warm up your brain for the pages that follow.

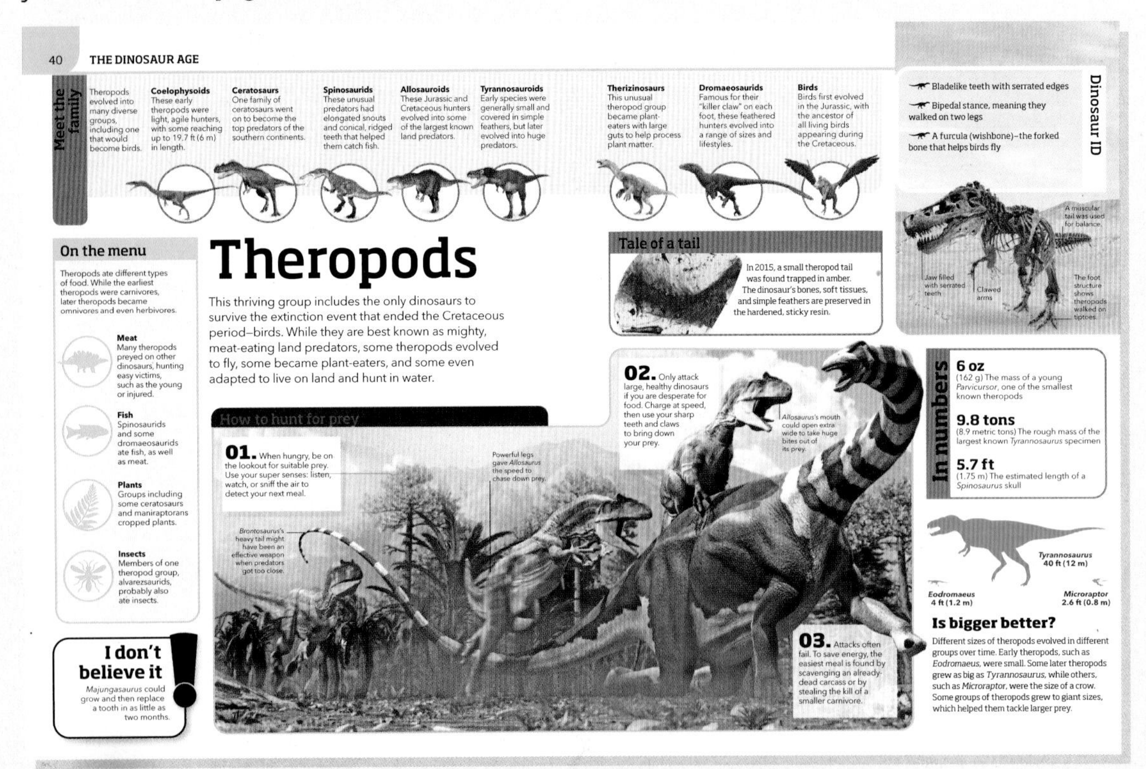

40 THE DINOSAUR AGE

Meet the family

Theropods evolved into many diverse groups, including one that would become birds.

Coelophysoids These early theropods were light, agile hunters, with some reaching up to 19.7 ft (6 m) in length.

Ceratosaurs One family of ceratosaurs went on to become the top predators of the southern continents.

Spinosaurids These unusual predators had elongated snouts and conical, ridged teeth that helped them catch fish.

Allosauroids These Jurassic and Cretaceous hunters evolved into some of the largest known land predators.

Tyrannosauroids Early species were generally small and covered in simple feathers, but later evolved into huge predators.

Therizinosaurs This unusual theropod group became plant-eaters with large guts to help process plant matter.

Dromaeosaurids Famous for their "killer claw" on each foot, these feathered hunters evolved into a range of sizes and lifestyles.

Birds Birds first evolved in the Jurassic, with the ancestor of all living birds appearing during the Cretaceous.

On the menu

Theropods ate different types of food. While the earliest theropods were carnivores, later theropods became omnivores and even herbivores.

Meat Many theropods preyed on other dinosaurs, hunting easy victims, such as the young or injured.

Fish Spinosaurids and some dromaeosaurids ate fish, as well as meat.

Plants Groups including some ceratosaurs and maniraptorans cropped plants.

Insects Members of one theropod group, alvarezsaurids, probably also ate insects.

I don't believe it! *Majungasaurus* could grow and then replace a tooth in as little as two months.

Theropods

This thriving group includes the only dinosaurs to survive the extinction event that ended the Cretaceous period–birds. While they are best known as mighty, meat-eating land predators, some theropods evolved to fly, some became plant-eaters, and some even adapted to live on land and hunt in water.

How to hunt for prey

01. When hungry, be on the lookout for suitable prey. Use your super senses: listen, watch, or sniff the air to detect your next meal.

Brontosaurus's heavy tail might have been an effective weapon when predators got too close.

Powerful legs gave *Allosaurus* the speed to chase down prey.

02. Only attack large, healthy dinosaurs if you are desperate for food. Charge at speed, then use your sharp teeth and claws to bring down your prey.

Allosaurus's mouth could open extra wide to take huge bites out of its prey.

03. Attacks often fail. To save energy, the easiest meal is found by scavenging an already-dead carcass or by stealing the kill of a smaller carnivore.

Tale of a tail

In 2015, a small theropod tail was found trapped in amber. The dinosaur's bones, soft tissues, and simple feathers are preserved in the hardened, sticky resin.

Dinosaur ID

Bladelike teeth with serrated edges

Bipedal stance, meaning they walked on two legs

A furcula (wishbone)–the forked bone that helps birds fly

Jaw filled with serrated teeth

Clawed arms

A muscular tail was used for balance.

The foot structure shows theropods walked on tiptoes.

In numbers

6 oz (162 g) The mass of a young *Parvicursor*, one of the smallest known theropods

9.8 tons (8.9 metric tons) The rough mass of the largest known *Tyrannosaurus* specimen

5.7 ft (1.75 m) The estimated length of a *Spinosaurus* skull

Tyrannosaurus 40 ft (12 m)

Eodromaeus 4 ft (1.2 m)

Microraptor 2.6 ft (0.8 m)

Is bigger better?

Different sizes of theropods evolved in different groups over time. Early theropods, such as *Eodromaeus*, were small. Some later theropods grew as big as *Tyrannosaurus*, while others, such as *Microraptor*, were the size of a crow. Some groups of theropods grew to giant sizes, which helped them tackle larger prey.

No peeking

You'll find the answers matched with the numbers of the correct pictures at the bottom of the page.

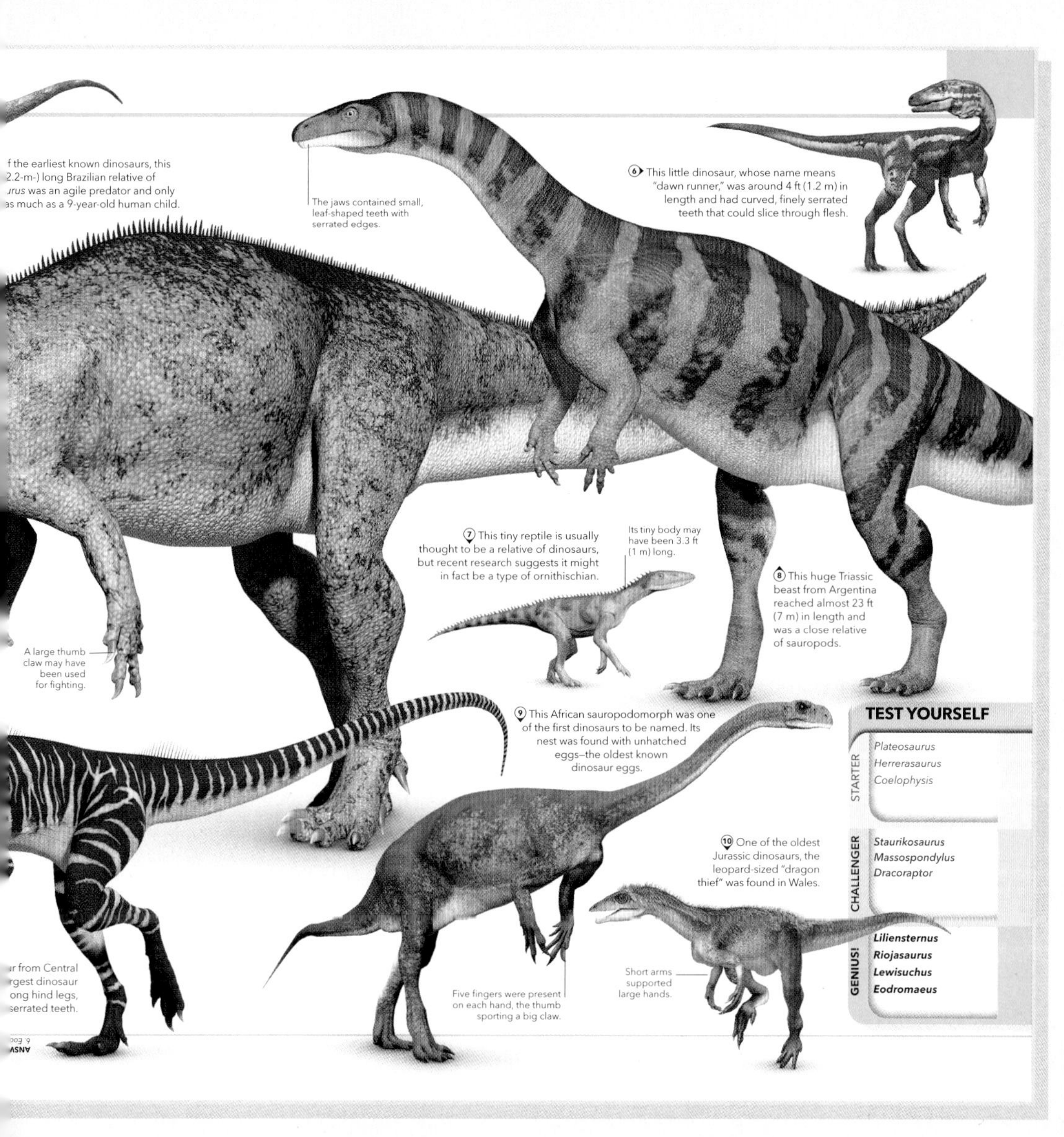

02. When you have chosen a quiz, take a careful look at the pictures. Can you identify all the dinosaurs? The clues will give you extra information to help you work things out.

03. Look at the "Test Yourself" panel and match the words and pictures. Don't write the answers in the book—you may want to quiz again later to improve your score or give it to a friend to see how they do.

04. Work your way through the three levels of difficulty—it's not supposed to be easy! When you think you have got them all, check the answers—they are upside-down at the bottom of the page.

Right choice

There are multiple-choice quizzes, too, further testing your knowledge of some of the most remarkable dinosaurs and prehistoric animals. Can you select the correct answer? How many did you get right?

MYA

"Million years ago" has been abbreviated to MYA throughout this book.

1 PREHISTORIC LIFE

Beginnings of life

Life first appeared in Earth's oceans hundreds of millions of years ago. Myriad plants and animals later evolved in the seas before eventually moving onto land. While most prehistoric life forms are now extinct, many left fossil evidence behind, which is how we know about them.

Timeline of life

Earth was a hostile place when it formed around 4.6 billion years ago. Yet life appeared relatively soon in geological terms. Since then, life has evolved into an astonishing array of forms, including the plants, fungi, and animals that populate our planet today.

Beginning of life

Scientists think life may first have appeared undersea, where volcanic activity heats water in the rocks and makes it shoot up through holes like the one above. The mineral-rich water provides energy for life-forming chemical reactions to happen.

Story of life on Earth

Life has evolved over billions of years from simple bacteria and archaea into a wide variety of complex sea- and land-based organisms. Scientists can chart the process of evolution through geological time–starting with the first signs of life in the Precambrian; through the explosion of new life forms in the Cambrian period; and the emergence of plants, fish, amphibians, reptiles, mammals, and (very recently) humans.

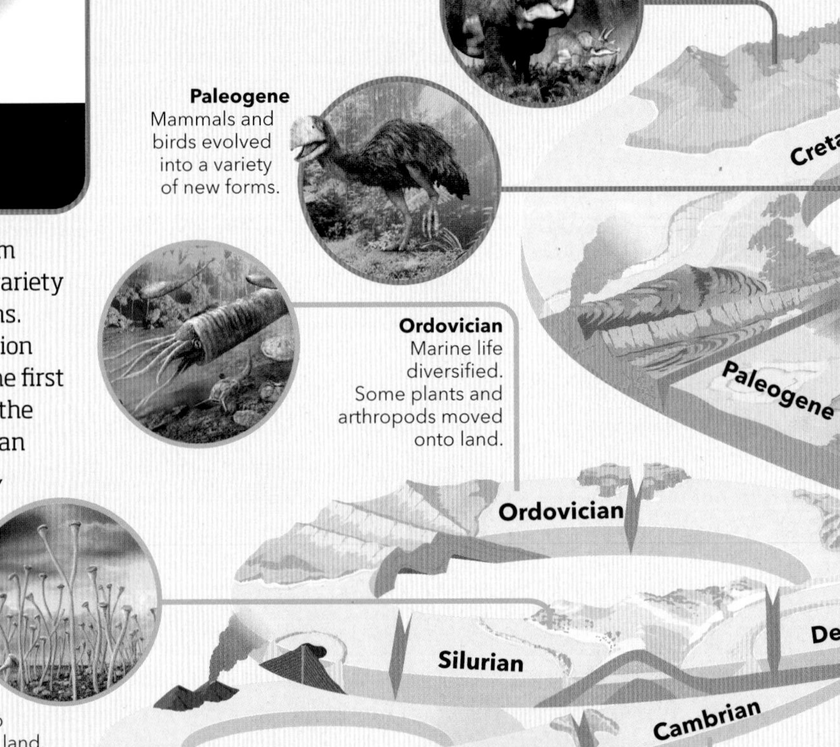

Cretaceous On land, dinosaurs continued to thrive.

Paleogene Mammals and birds evolved into a variety of new forms.

Ordovician Marine life diversified. Some plants and arthropods moved onto land.

Silurian Fungi and land plants that have tissues for conducting water and minerals throughout the plant begin to evolve on land.

Precambrian Microscopic life first evolved around 3.5 billion years ago.

Cambrian Complex plant and animal life bloomed in the oceans.

Devonian Fish were abundant and some evolved into tetrapods, which moved onto land.

Earth's eras

Scientists have learned about Earth's long history by studying its rocks. These contain evidence of major events, such as climate change and extinctions, and fossils of plants and animals.

Precambrian	Paleozoic Era				
	Cambrian	**Ordovician**	**Silurian**	**Devonian**	**Carboniferous**
Much of the rock from the Precambrian eons no longer exists. Scientists don't know why, but they know early life appeared in the oceans.	A warmer climate led to sea-level rise and minerals dissolved in water that formed animals' hard shells.	An ocean covered the north, with a supercontinent in the south. Most life was still in the seas.	The climate became warm and stable, allowing plants and animals to emerge on land.	Life, including plants and arthropods, spread on land, altering the environment.	Vast forests sucked carbon dioxide out the atmosphere, cooling down the planet.
4,600-545 MYA	**542-485 MYA**	**485-444 MYA**	**444-419 MYA**	**419-359 MYA**	**359-299 MYA**

Coming to life

Oxygen is an essential element to support complex life forms, and there was none in the atmosphere of early Earth. However, simple organisms called cyanobacteria began using sunlight, water, and carbon dioxide to make food by photosynthesis, releasing oxygen into the air. As the oxygen built up, it created the conditions for new life.

Forms of life

There are three main branches of the tree of life, but only one contains complex organisms.

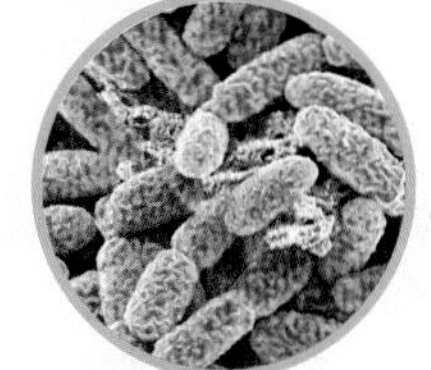

Bacteria
These microscopic single-celled organisms are found everywhere on Earth, including inside us!

Archaea
Roughly the same size as bacteria, some of these single-celled organisms can live in extreme environments.

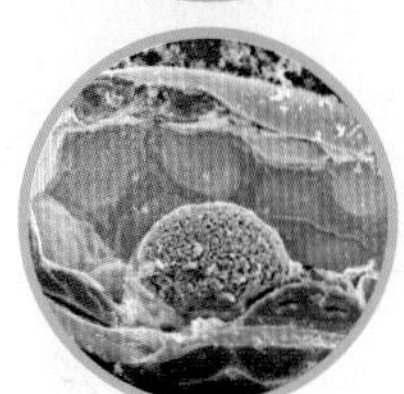

Eukaryotes
This group contains all animals, plants, and fungi, as well as single-celled yeasts and algae.

Triassic
The first pterosaurs took to the sky, while dinosaurs were rivaled by predatory crocodile relatives.

Jurassic
Dinosaurs thrived as competitors became extinct.

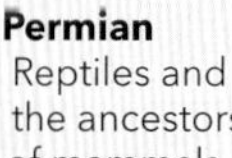

Permian
Reptiles and the ancestors of mammals dominated land habitats.

Carboniferous
Reptiles first evolved in the tropical forests at this time.

Neogene
Hominids, the group containing humans and their close relatives, first evolved.

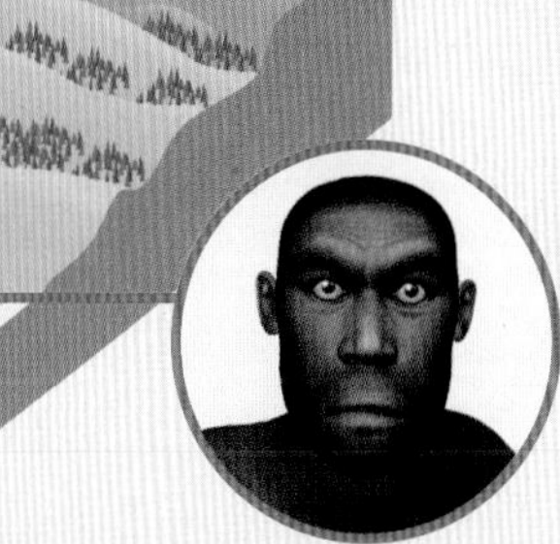

Quaternary
Various human species evolved, including our own.

I don't believe it!

The sudden increase in different life forms known as the Cambrian explosion took place over just 20 million years.

	Mesozoic Era			Cenozoic Era		
Permian The worst known mass extinction ended this warm, dry period, wiping out many species.	**Triassic** Life slowly recovered. Dinosaurs and pterosaurs evolved on Pangea.	**Jurassic** Pangea began splitting into the continents of Laurasia and Gondwana, with lush, tropical climates.	**Cretaceous** Gases from undersea volcanoes enhanced middle-late Cretaceous super-greenhouse conditions.	**Paleogene** Temperatures soared up to 8 degrees above present-day averages by the end of the Paleogene.	**Neogene** North and South America joined together, allowing animals to move between the two continents.	**Quaternary** This period is marked by the ice ages in the Northern Hemisphere and the emergence of humans.
299-252 MYA	**252-201 MYA**	**201-145 MYA**	**145-66 MYA**	**66-23 MYA**	**23-2.58 MYA**	**2.58 MYA-Present day**

Life before the dinosaurs

The era before dinosaurs lived on Earth is called the Paleozoic. It began with a dramatic rise in the number of new species but ended with the largest extinction event yet. During that time, the seas teemed with fish and giant arthropods. Eventually, invertebrates and fish evolved into animals that walked and breathed on land.

1 This Devonian marine arthropod was a trilobite—its body was divided into three parts: head, thorax, and tail. Its unique eyes allowed it a 360-degree view of the underwater world.

2 These "layered rocks" are some of the earliest fossils of life on Earth. The oldest of these rocks were formed 3.45 billion years ago.

3 A distant relative of mammals, this odd-looking Permian omnivore was the size of a bull and probably used its impressive horns to drive away rivals of its own species.

4 This crocodilelike amphibian was a huge Permian predator, measuring 18 ft (5.5 m) in length, that lived in the waterways of what is now Brazil.

5 A Carboniferous relative of dragonflies, this hunter preyed on other insects. It used special spines on its legs to grip prey so they could not escape its hold.

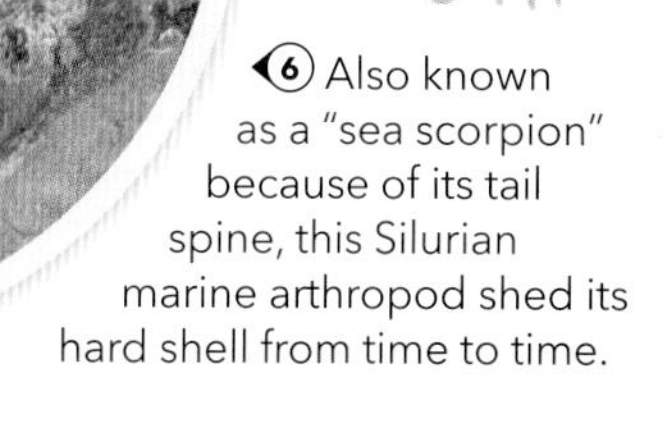

6 Also known as a "sea scorpion" because of its tail spine, this Silurian marine arthropod shed its hard shell from time to time.

Paddlelike back legs helped it walk on the sea floor and swim fast.

TEST YOURSELF

STARTER

Stromatolites
Meganeura
Dunkleosteus

CHALLENGER

Prionosuchus
Arthropleura
Anomalocaris
Estemmenosuchus

GENIUS!

Eurypterus
Endoceras
Erbenochile

7 This giant Ordovician mollusk could reach around 16 ft (5 m) in length. Its soft body lived at the entrance of the shell.

It used its powerful arms to grab prey.

8 The world's largest land-living arthropod, this extinct millipede relative lived in the Carboniferous and weighed up to 110 lb (50 kg).

It measured up to 8.2 ft (2.5 m) long.

Bony, protective plates covered the head.

9 This 13-ft- (4-m-) long oceangoing Devonian fish had a powerful bite that helped it crack open armored prey.

10 One of the largest animals in the Cambrian oceans, this "weird shrimp" reached 23.5 in (60 cm) in length.

Pair of spiky claws, which helped it grasp prey

ANSWERS: 1. *Erbenochile* 2. *Stromatolites* 3. *Estemmenosuchus* 4. *Prionosuchus* 5. *Meganeura* 6. *Eurypterus* 7. *Endoceras* 8. *Arthropleura* 9. *Dunkleosteus* 10. *Anomalocaris*

Evolution and extinction

All the living things we see today are the result of evolution and extinction. Evolution is the process of species and groups of organisms changing over generations. Mass extinctions are rare events when many life forms disappear forever. These two processes have been shaping life since it first appeared on Earth.

The evolution of birds

All living birds are dinosaurs. They belong to a group of dinosaurs known as theropods. Birds share many features with their closest theropod relatives, the dromaeosaurs and troodontids.

Although *T. rex* walked on two legs like birds, it's hard to imagine this giant taking flight!

Fossil feathers are present in various theropods.

36 ft (11 m) long, this ornithomimosaur resembled a massive ostrich.

Arms were fringed with long feathers, similar to bird wings.

Tyrannosaurus

Alxasaurus

Deinocheirus

Citipati

Mass extinctions

Since life began on our planet, there have been five mass extinctions that have wiped out most of life at the time. Known as the "Big Five," these have been caused by a range of factors.

Ordovician (443 MYA)
Climate change caused the planet to cool and sea levels to drop. The waters froze, killing 85 percent of ocean creatures.

Devonian (374 MYA)
Some experts suggest that a lack of oxygen in the seas affected marine life, leading to a mass extinction, but the exact cause is still debated.

Permian (252 MYA)
The worst extinction event ever was probably triggered by massive volcanic eruptions in Siberia. It almost wiped out all life on Earth.

In numbers

13%
Percentage of bird species assessed as being threatened with extinction today.

2.7 million sq. miles
(7 million sq. km) The area of Siberia where volcanic activity occurred, contributing Permian-Triassic mass extinction.

1859
Darwin's book *On the Origin of Species* was published, which led to the theory of evolution being widely accepted

New threats

Some experts think we are in the middle of a sixth mass extinction. More than 42,000 species assessed by a nature conservation group are known to be at risk of dying out. Climate change and human activities such as farming, fishing, and mining are all leading to a massive loss of biodiversity. But if we all work together, there is still time to stop this mass extinction.

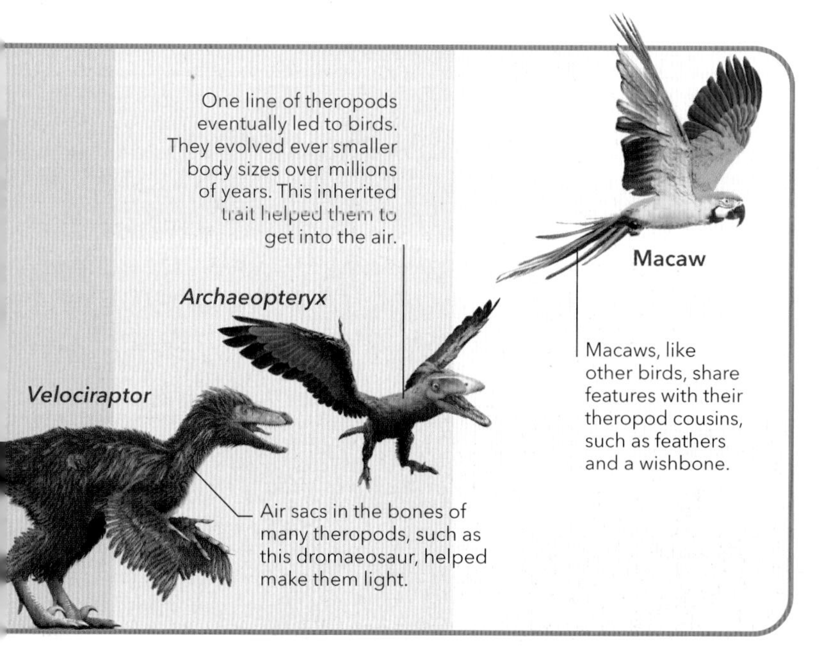

Triassic (201 MYA)
Instead of it being a single devastating event, some recent research suggests that this extinction took place over a longer period of time.

Cretaceous (66 MYA)
Possibly the most famous extinction, it was caused by a meteorite 6 miles (10 km) wide crashing into Earth.

Call of the ocean

The ancestors of whales were four-legged mammals that walked on land. Around 50 MYA, some of them adapted and evolved to live in the sea. Experts have been able to trace the stages of their evolution from land to marine mammals through the fossil record.

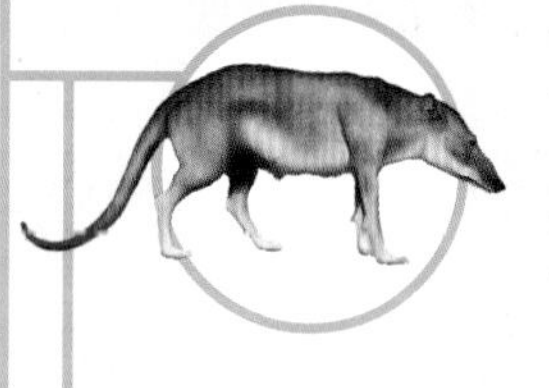

Pakicetus (49 MYA)
This four-legged mammal lived around 49 MYA, possibly hunting prey in and around waterways.

Ambulocetus (47 MYA)
Equally comfortable on land and in water, this predator had short legs and paddlelike hands and feet.

Dorudon (37 MYA)
With flippers and tiny hind legs, this aquatic mammal lived out at sea, feeding on fish and other marine organisms.

Modern whales (40-37 MYA)
With no hind legs, modern whales are highly adapted to life in water but need to come up to the surface to breathe air.

I don't believe it!

More than 99 percent of all species that ever existed are now extinct.

1 The biggest *Dimetrodon* species probably weighed as much as which modern animal?

A. 165 lb (75 kg), same as a snow leopard

B. 660 lb (300 kg), same as a Bengal tiger

C. 1,764 lb (800 kg), same as a polar bear

D. 13,225 lb (6,000 kg), same as an African elephant

2 What did *Dimetrodon*'s diet mainly consist of?

A. Insects

B. Plants

C. Tree bark

D. Other animals

3 *Dimetrodon* had a hole behind each eye socket to which its jaw muscles attached. Which living animal group shares this trait?

A. Mammals

B. Fish

C. Insects

D. Reptiles

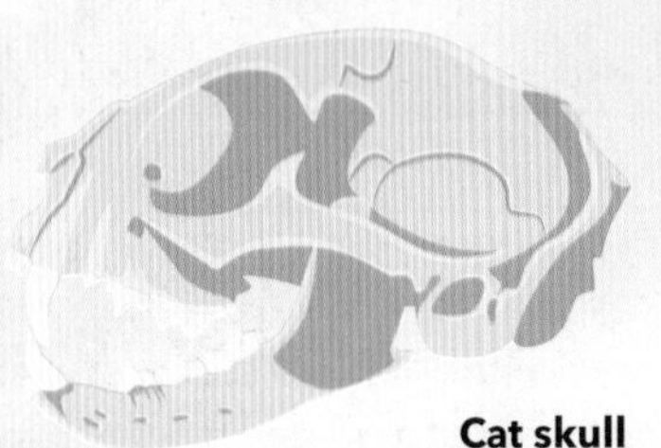

Cat skull

Amphibian *Diplocaulus*, with its arrow-shaped head, was on the menu.

Dimetrodon

One of the first top predators to stalk the land, *Dimetrodon* lived millions of years before the dinosaurs. It grew to be very big, taking on large prey. Later species would develop serrated teeth that helped them kill their prey. Find out more about this strange, sail-backed prehistoric animal!

4 The biggest *Dimetrodon* species measured more than 13 ft (4 m) from head to tail. Its head was large for its body. How long was the biggest *Dimetrodon* skull ever found?

A. 8 in (20 cm) **B.** 20 in (50 cm)

C. 3 ft (1 m) **D.** 6.5 ft (2 m)

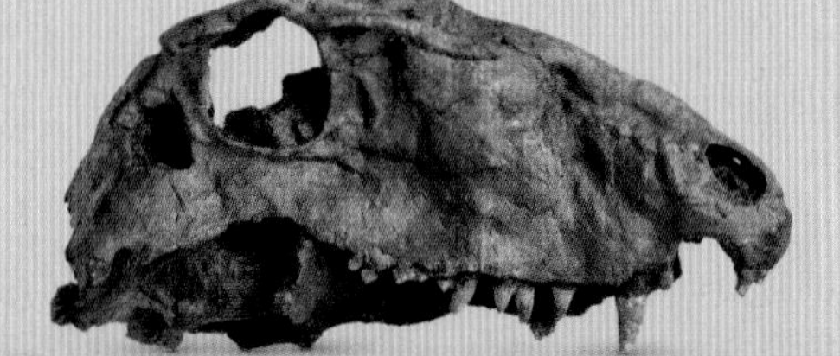

5 *Dimetrodon* had huge, caninelike teeth as well as many smaller ones, which is where it gets its name. What does its name mean?

A. Two sizes of teeth

B. Spike-toothed

C. Crooked teeth

D. Teeth that never fall out

6 *Dimetrodon* was not a dinosaur, but belonged to a group of animals that were ancestors of mammals. What are these known as?

A. Crocodilians

B. Primates

C. Synapsids

D. Arachnids

7 How was the sail on the back of *Dimetrodon* supported?

A. Internal spines made of cartilage

B. Tough skin

C. Rodlike extensions of the vertebrae

D. Muscles on the back

8 *Dimetrodon*'s tail made up around half of its body length. How many bones did it have in its tail?

A. 20

B. 30

C. 40

D. More than 50

ANSWERS: 1-B, 2-D, 3-A, 4-B, 5-A, 6-C, 7-C, 8-C

Fossils

Much of what we know about prehistoric life comes from fossils. These are the preserved remains of plants and animals buried in sand and mud. However, a fossil requires specific conditions to form, which means only a tiny percentage of organisms end up being fossilized.

In numbers

1824
The year the first dinosaur fossil, *Megalosaurus*, was named

3.5 billion years
The age of the oldest known microfossils—tiny fossils of bacteria

26.5 in
(67.5 cm) The length of the largest fossilized poop in the world, belonging to a *Tyrannosaurus*

How to become a fossil

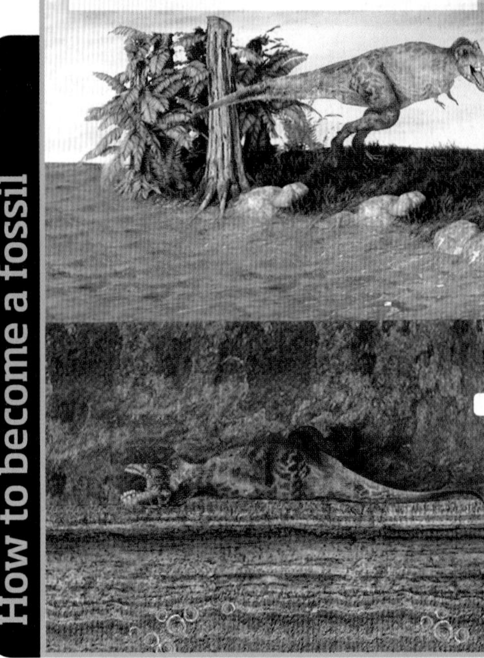

01. For a dinosaur to turn into a fossil, it must die in a place where it will be quickly buried by sand or mud (sediment)—such as in water. Its soft parts decay or are eaten, until just hard bones and teeth are left.

02. A layer of sediment covers the skeleton before it is scattered or decays completely. Over millions of years, layers build up, burying the dinosaur deep underground, and are compressed to form solid rock.

Types of fossils

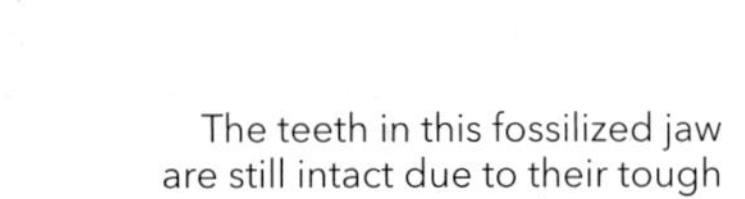

The teeth in this fossilized jaw are still intact due to their tough enamel covering.

Fossils can be of two main types: body fossils, which are the fossilized remains of an animal or plant (such as bones), and trace fossils, which include footprints.

Body fossils
Bones, teeth, and other hard parts of organisms can be buried and absorb minerals from the ground that turn them to stone. Most dinosaur fossils are of this type.

Impressions
When a plant is buried in sediment, an impression of its shape and details may be preserved on the rock's surface.

An insect is trapped in this amber.

Amber
At times, insects and other small animals are caught in tree resin. The resin hardens to become amber and preserves their bodies perfectly.

Trace fossils
Animals may leave footprints on soft sand or mud. If preserved as trace fossils, they can tell us how an animal walked or behaved.

03. Over time, the pressure exerted by the layers above turns the sediment into rock. Minerals seep into the bones and replace them, turning the skeleton to stone, too.

Record of life on Earth

Paleontologists study fossils, such as those of these partially excavated hadrosaurs, to find clues about how life evolved on Earth. However, fossils were only formed if the conditions are right, making them rare. There are lots of gaps in the fossil record, but there is still enough data to study life from lots of different prehistoric periods.

04. Millions more years pass. Wind, water, or ice erode the sedimentary rock, exposing the fossilized skeleton. Fossil hunters are excited to find a new dinosaur specimen!

Fossils up close

New technology means scientists today can study fossils in detail, look inside them, and even construct 3D models of them.

Laser scanning
This scientist is running a handheld laser scanner over the skull of a *Triceratops* so a 3D digital model can be made of it.

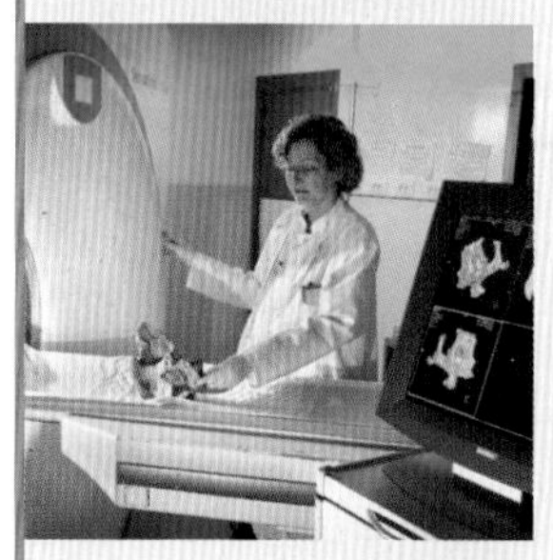

CT scanning
This fossil of the skull cavity of an *Arcovenator* has been put in a CT scanner. Hundreds of X-rays can then be put together to make a very detailed 3D digital model of the fossil.

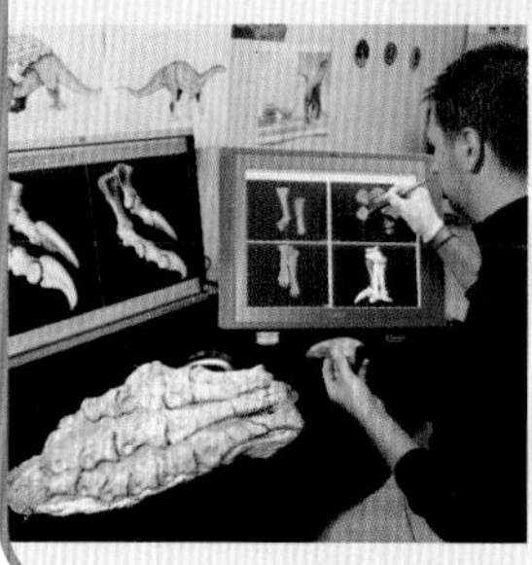

3D imaging
Based on the images made using CT scans, this scientist is digitally separating areas of interest in 3D with the help of special computer programs.

Coprolites
Fossilized droppings, known as coprolites, can tell scientists a lot about the diets or even the digestive systems of the animals that produced them.

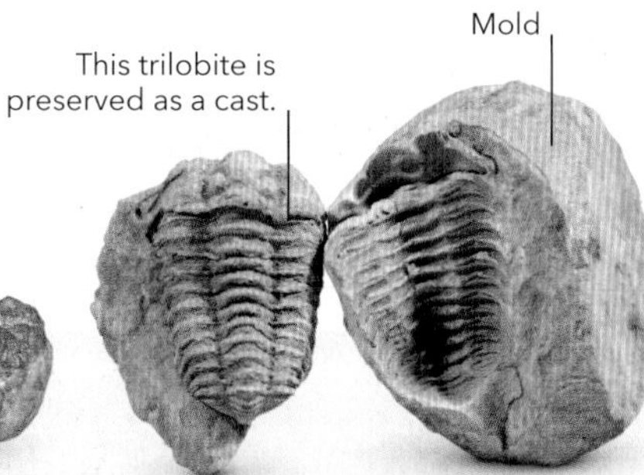

Casts and molds
Sometimes animals leave impressions in mud, which hardens around them. When their body rots away, this can become a mold, filling with sediment to make a fossil cast.

I don't believe it!

Some dinosaurs are so well preserved that paleontologists can study the remains of their internal organs.

TEST YOURSELF

STARTER

Otodus megalodon tooth
Ginkgo leaves
Bison priscus horns
Insect in amber

CHALLENGER

Temnodontosaurus **tooth**
Mammoth tooth
Mantellisaurus **skull**

GENIUS!

Dactylioceras
Trilobite
Micraster

1 This huge, grinding tooth, 6 in (15 cm) wide, belonged to an Ice Age relative of modern elephants.

Large, grooved surface on its molar teeth helped this animal grind down grasses and young trees.

2 This conical, ridged tooth helped the marine reptile it belonged to grip onto prey.

3 Sharks' teeth are some of the most commonly found fossils, but their skeletons—made of soft, flexible cartilage—are rarely found preserved as fossils. This tooth is from the biggest of all sharks.

Triangular upper teeth were perfect for killing prey.

4 This fossilized ammonite—a common mollusk with a coiled shell—is around 2.3 in (6 cm) across.

5 This fossil is of a heart-shaped urchin, related to a starfish and commonly found in chalk beds. The creatures were usually spiny, but the spines often got lost during fossilization.

⑦ This carbonized plant fossil is one of the oldest tree lineages still around today. It would have been a good source of food for some dinosaurs.

Its delicate leaves have earned it the name of "maidenhair."

⑥ This stunning skull is a rare find and part of one of the most complete dinosaur skeletons unearthed in the UK. Single bones are more common. The dinosaur was named after the person who discovered it!

Fossil finds

To hunt for fossils yourself, first research where to go. The best places are usually where sedimentary rock is exposed. Always go with an adult, as these areas can be dangerous, and take safety precautions. Some sites may be protected and you may need permission or permits to collect fossils. Could you identify these specimens if you found them?

These fossilized bone horns would have been covered in nail-like keratin.

⑧ The Paleozoic seas teemed with these arthropods, so they are one of the more common fossils found. They got their name from the fact that their bodies were made up of three main parts.

⑨ The large horns of these Ice Age bruisers were used for wrestling over food and potential mates. They are often the only part to have been preserved as fossils.

These fossils are often found in chalky rocks.

⑩ Tree resin can sometimes trap unlucky insects. When it fossilizes, it preserves their bodies inside.

ANSWERS: 1. Mammoth tooth 2. *Temnodontosaurus* tooth 3. *Otodus megalodon* tooth 4. *Dactylioceras* 5. *Micraster* 6. *Mantellisaurus* skull 7. Gingko leaves 8. *Trilobite* 9. *Bison priscus* horns 10. Insect in amber

Fossil hunting

People have known about fossils and puzzled over them since ancient times. However, it was not until the late 17th century that some Europeans started to collect and study fossils in a modern, scientific sense. Today, the search for fossils and research into prehistoric life takes place all around the world.

Fossil pioneer

In the early 19th century, nearly all scientists were men. Despite this, Mary Anning, an English fossil hunter, made incredible contributions to paleontology by unearthing many fossils of Jurassic marine life. She found a complete ichthyosaur skeleton at the age of 12.

The first dinosaurs

In the early 19th century, scientists found dinosaur fossils but did not know what they were. In 1842, British anatomist Richard Owen realized that the fossils belonged to massive prehistoric reptiles, which he named "Dinosauria." Only three dinosaurs were originally included in this new group: *Megalosaurus, Iguanodon,* and *Hylaeosaurus.*

British geologist William Buckland first described this *Megalosaurus*, or "great lizard," jawbone.

I don't believe it!

A new dinosaur species is named roughly every two weeks on average.

How to excavate a fossil

01. Fossils are hidden all over the world, but you need to know where to dig. This dig site in Portugal was found by someone who noticed bone fragments in their back garden.

02. Carefully scrape away rock and dirt, unearthing the bones. These rocks, which are around 150 million years old, can tell you about the environment at the time of the dinosaur's death.

Various tools are used to remove the rock around the fossil.

In numbers

6th century BCE
When Greek philosopher Xenophanes noticed fossil seashells on land and realized that the land was once a seafloor

1822
The year in which the word "paleontology" was first used

4 years, 337 days
Age of the youngest person ever, Wylie J. Brys, to discover a fossil of a previously unknown dinosaur species

Fossils for all

To create a fair and respectful scientific community, paleontologists are now:

Returning important fossils to their countries of origin

Making sure correct permits are in place when collecting

Making fossils available to all by using new technologies, such as laser scanning, to create 3D digital images

03. Once freed, protect the fossils by encasing them in plaster. Large specimens are taken away by trucks or even helicopters.

04. Transport the fossils to the lab, where they can be studied. Scientists were able to determine that this Jurassic sauropod fossil might be the largest specimen ever found in Europe.

These ribs belonged to a giant sauropod around 82 ft (25 m) long and 39 ft (12 m) tall.

Fossil theories

Throughout the world, people have used and tried to understand fossils long before they knew what they were.

This arrowhead is made from petrified wood.

- Some early peoples used fossils as tools or for decorative or religious purposes.
- Fossils were used in traditional Chinese medicine. They were often sold as "dragon bones."
- As far back as ancient Greece, fossils were thought to be the remains of long-dead plants and animals.

Shen Kuo lived in the 11th century.

- In the 11th century, Chinese scientist Shen Kuo found fossilized bamboo in a place where it could no longer grow. He realized that the climate had changed over time.
- Aztec and Inca peoples described the fossilized bones of giant animals as belonging to ancient beings that had died out.
- In medieval European folklore, some fossils, such as those of urchins, were believed to have protective powers.

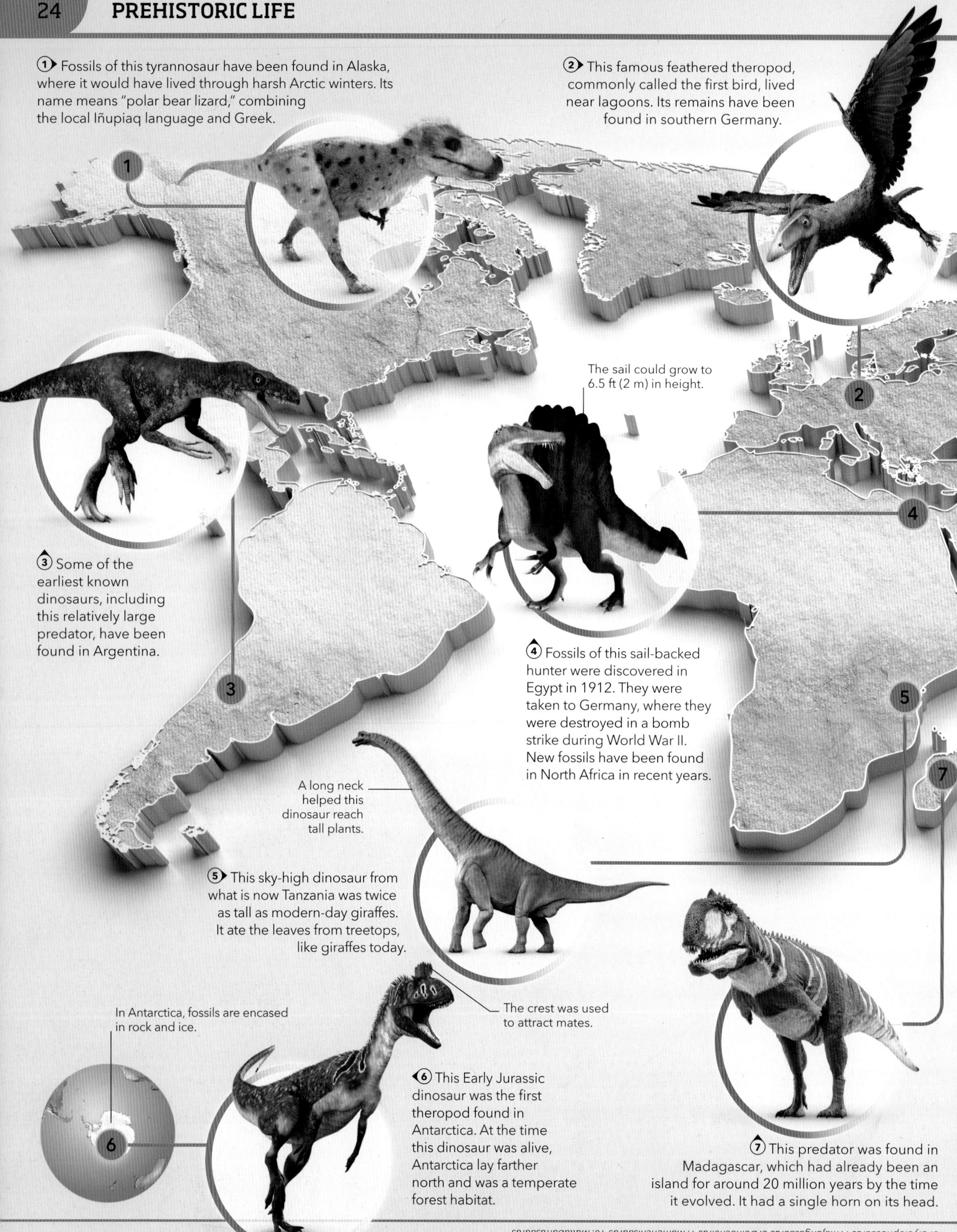

① Fossils of this tyrannosaur have been found in Alaska, where it would have lived through harsh Arctic winters. Its name means "polar bear lizard," combining the local Iñupiaq language and Greek.

② This famous feathered theropod, commonly called the first bird, lived near lagoons. Its remains have been found in southern Germany.

③ Some of the earliest known dinosaurs, including this relatively large predator, have been found in Argentina.

④ Fossils of this sail-backed hunter were discovered in Egypt in 1912. They were taken to Germany, where they were destroyed in a bomb strike during World War II. New fossils have been found in North Africa in recent years.

⑤ This sky-high dinosaur from what is now Tanzania was twice as tall as modern-day giraffes. It ate the leaves from treetops, like giraffes today.

⑥ This Early Jurassic dinosaur was the first theropod found in Antarctica. At the time this dinosaur was alive, Antarctica lay farther north and was a temperate forest habitat.

⑦ This predator was found in Madagascar, which had already been an island for around 20 million years by the time it evolved. It had a single horn on its head.

ANSWERS: 1. *Nanuqsaurus* 2. *Archaeopteryx* 3. *Herrerasaurus* 4. *Spinosaurus* 5. *Giraffatitan* 6. *Cryolophosaurus* 7. *Majungasaurus* 8. *Deinocheirus* 9. *Mamenchisaurus* 10. *Muttaburrasaurus*

Dinosaur discoveries

Dinosaur fossils have been found on every continent, although when dinosaurs walked on Earth, the land masses were different shapes and in different positions from today. Can you guess which dinosaurs were found where?

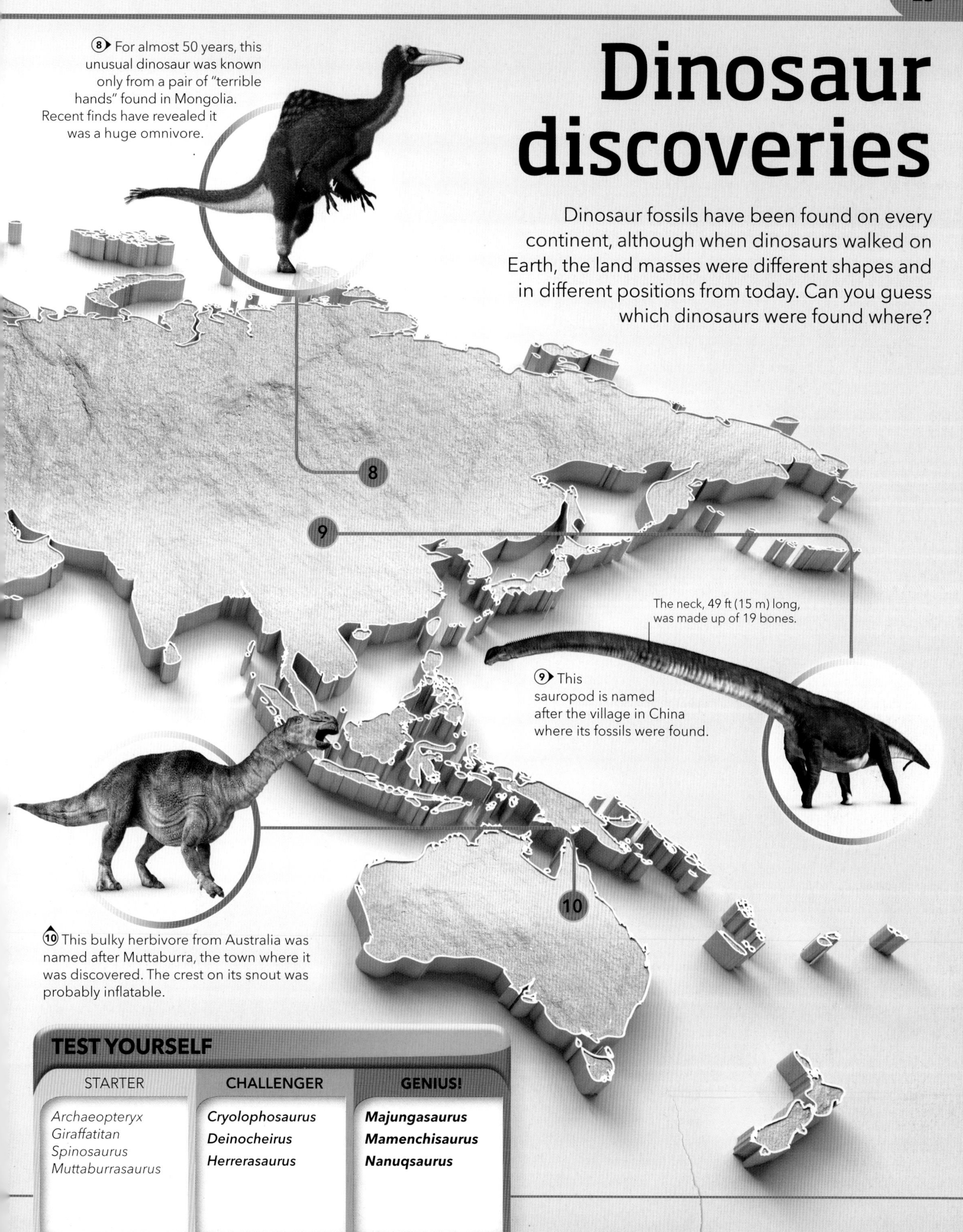

⑧ For almost 50 years, this unusual dinosaur was known only from a pair of "terrible hands" found in Mongolia. Recent finds have revealed it was a huge omnivore.

⑨ This sauropod is named after the village in China where its fossils were found.

⑩ This bulky herbivore from Australia was named after Muttaburra, the town where it was discovered. The crest on its snout was probably inflatable.

TEST YOURSELF

STARTER	CHALLENGER	GENIUS!
Archaeopteryx	***Cryolophosaurus***	***Majungasaurus***
Giraffatitan	***Deinocheirus***	***Mamenchisaurus***
Spinosaurus	***Herrerasaurus***	***Nanuqsaurus***
Muttaburrasaurus		

1 Preserved pigments, or colors, were found in the fossilized skin of this nodosaur. It was probably reddish brown on top and pale below. What were the colors used for?

A. To dazzle predators

B. To deter insects

C. As camouflage

D. To recognize others of its own species

2 The site of the mine where it was found was once an ancient sea. What did the scientists expect to see when they were called to check the fossil?

A. A giant turtle

B. A plesiosaur

C. A crocodile

D. A *Diplodocus*

Borealopelta

In 2011, Canadian miners accidentally discovered a dinosaur fossil. It is one of the best-preserved fossils in the world. The skin was astonishingly intact, with some traces of rusty brown pigments, while the stomach showed the animal's last meal. The fossil's superb condition helped scientists learn that it was a nodosaur, a type of armored dinosaur.

The narrow jaw of *Borealopelta* suggests that it ate only certain types of plants.

3 How do paleontologists think *Borealopelta* ended up in rock under the sea?

A. The carcass floated out to sea and sunk to the bottom.

B. It lived in the sea.

C. It was dragged in by a marine predator.

D. It tried to swim to a different continent.

4 How many hours did it take for the museum preparator to extract the specimen from its rocky surrounding?

A. 100 hours

B. 500 hours

C. 1,000 hours

D. 7,000 hours

ANSWERS: 1-C, 2-B, 3-A, 4-D, 5-C, 6-A, 7-A

Rows of bony armor plates covered *Borealopelta*'s body and made it nearly impossible for predators to bite it.

5 How long did it take to extract the specimen from the mine?

A. Two days **B.** Seven days
C. 14 days **D.** 20 days

6 Which of these plants formed most of its last meal?

A. Ferns **B.** Cycads
C. Conifers **D.** Gingkos

A large spine jutted out from the shoulder region.

7 *Borealopelta* had two 20-in (50-cm) spines jutting out from its shoulders. Traces of pigment suggest they were light in color and stood out from the rest of its body. What were these likely used for?

A. Visual display **B.** Cutting down branches **C.** Shoulder-slamming predators **D.** Digging nests

2 THE DINOSAUR AGE

Rule of the reptiles

The Mesozoic Era was the dawn of a new world. Earth had just experienced a mass extinction, and the surviving plants and animals adapted to form a rich variety of life. Reptiles evolved into a spectacular range of groups, including the most famous: the dinosaurs.

The Mesozoic Era

The Mesozoic Era was a time when continents were shifting and seas were forming. It followed a mass extinction and saw extraordinary new life emerge, including the dinosaurs. This "dinosaur age" lasted for over 180 million years—more than 600 times as long as modern humans have existed—and is divided into three periods: Triassic, Jurassic, and Cretaceous.

The dinosaur age

Triassic period (252–201 MYA)
When this period began, Earth was recovering from a devastating mass extinction. The climate was hot and dry. Land was clumped together in a supercontinent known as Pangea. The first dinosaurs appeared on land, although they were initially small and rare.

Branching out

Archosaurs

A new group of reptiles appeared in the Early Triassic. Known as archosaurs, or "ruling reptiles," these included the ancestors of crocodiles as well as pterosaurs and dinosaurs.

Pseudosuchians

Crocodylomorphs
This group of pseudosuchians includes crocodilians and many of their close relatives.

Avemetatarsalians

Pterosaurs
The first known flying reptiles, pterosaurs are known from fossils found in many parts of the world.

Dinosaurs
The most famous Mesozoic animal group, these reptiles gave rise to the first birds in the Jurassic.

I don't believe it!

Pangea existed for 100 million years before it began to break up, eventually forming the continents we know today.

Armored attack

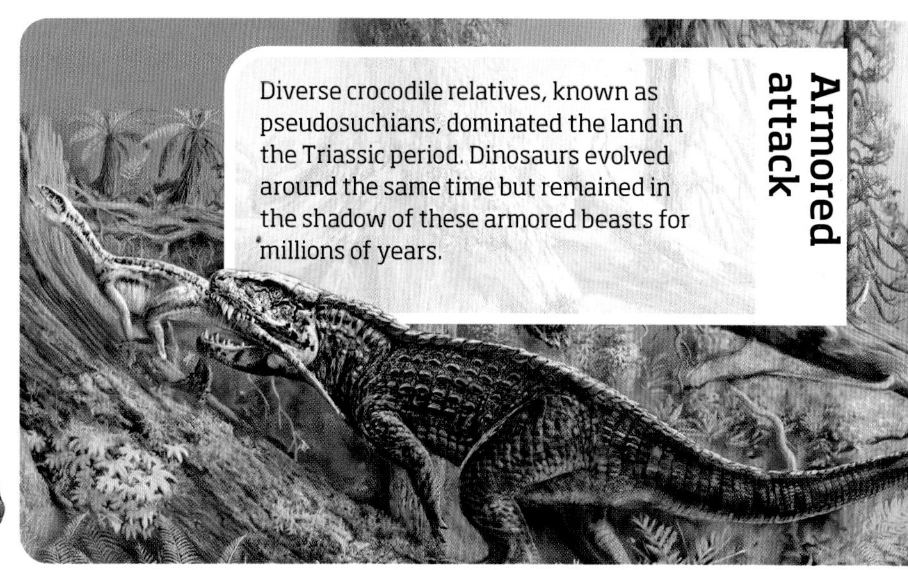

Diverse crocodile relatives, known as pseudosuchians, dominated the land in the Triassic period. Dinosaurs evolved around the same time but remained in the shadow of these armored beasts for millions of years.

Jurassic period (201–145 MYA)
Pangea split into two continents, Laurasia and Gondwana, and the Atlantic Ocean began to form. The climate became cooler, although it was much warmer than today. Many groups of dinosaurs flourished in the new habitats.

Cretaceous period (145–66 MYA)
By the end of the Cretaceous period, the continents had started to move to their current positions. It was a time that saw extremely warm climates and very high sea levels. Dinosaurs continued to thrive until a meteorite crashed into Earth.

Other Mesozoic life

Lissamphibians
This group includes frogs, salamanders, and their extinct relatives.

Flowering plants
Common today, they first appeared in the Early Cretaceous.

Mammals
Small at first, they went on to get bigger and adapt to different habitats and diets.

Beelzebufo

Magnolia flowers

Cronopio

In numbers

70%
Area of the Earth's surface covered by Panthalassa, the huge Triassic ocean.

4.5
How many times more carbon dioxide there was in the Jurassic atmosphere, compared to today's level.

96-107°F
(36–42°C) Temperature range around the equator in the Cretaceous period.

Life in the Mesozoic

At the beginning of the Mesozoic Era, life was recovering from a devastating extinction that wiped out almost everything. The survivors had few competitors and, in the periods that followed, a huge range of new groups evolved—including some that are still alive today.

Jurassic

⑤ This little pterosaur had a long, spearlike beak full of pointy teeth, which it used to snare fish and squid.

⑥ These crinoids (a type of marine animal) were relatives of starfish and sea urchins. Colonies would attach themselves to floating driftwood.

Triassic

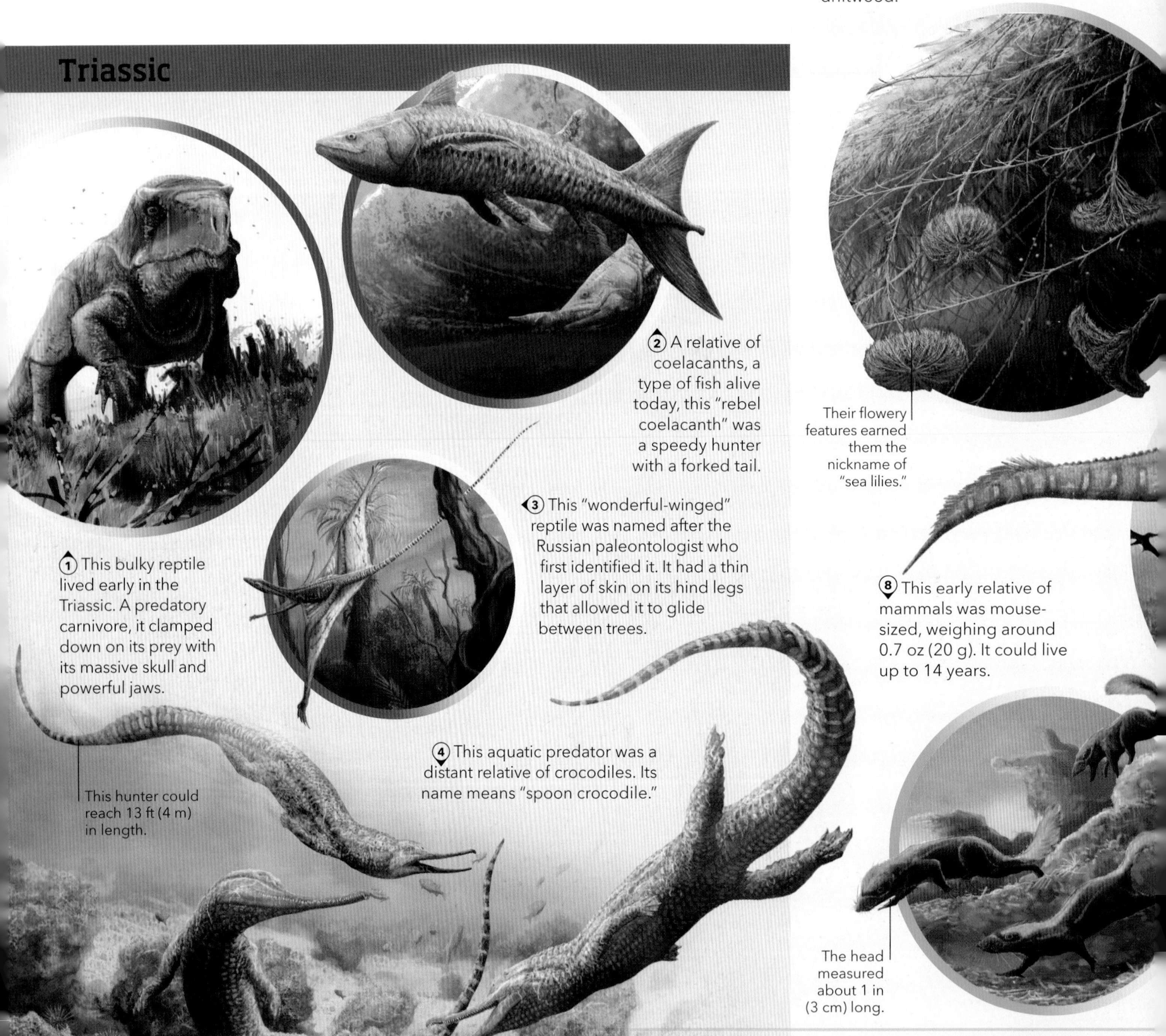

① This bulky reptile lived early in the Triassic. A predatory carnivore, it clamped down on its prey with its massive skull and powerful jaws.

② A relative of coelacanths, a type of fish alive today, this "rebel coelacanth" was a speedy hunter with a forked tail.

③ This "wonderful-winged" reptile was named after the Russian paleontologist who first identified it. It had a thin layer of skin on its hind legs that allowed it to glide between trees.

④ This aquatic predator was a distant relative of crocodiles. Its name means "spoon crocodile."

This hunter could reach 13 ft (4 m) in length.

Their flowery features earned them the nickname of "sea lilies."

⑧ This early relative of mammals was mouse-sized, weighing around 0.7 oz (20 g). It could live up to 14 years.

The head measured about 1 in (3 cm) long.

ANSWERS: 1. *Garjainia* 2. *Rebellatrix* 3. *Sharovipteryx* 4. *Mystriosuchus* 5. *Rhamphorhynchus* 6. *Seirocrinus* 7. *Megalosaurus* 8. *Morganucodon* 9. *Mosasaurus* 10. *Hatzegopteryx* 11. *Cretoxyrhina* 12. Flowering plants

Cretaceous

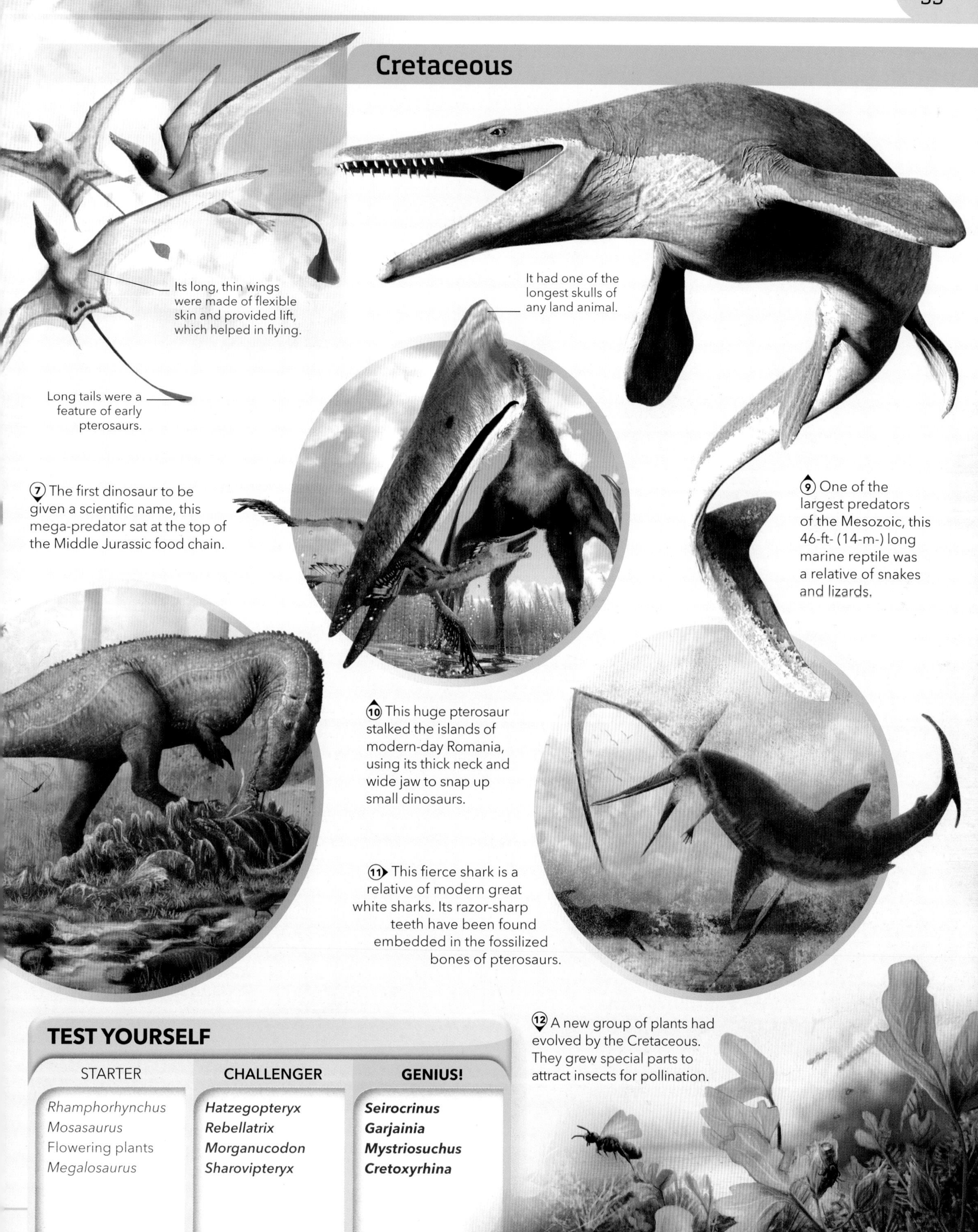

7 The first dinosaur to be given a scientific name, this mega-predator sat at the top of the Middle Jurassic food chain.

9 One of the largest predators of the Mesozoic, this 46-ft- (14-m-) long marine reptile was a relative of snakes and lizards.

10 This huge pterosaur stalked the islands of modern-day Romania, using its thick neck and wide jaw to snap up small dinosaurs.

11 This fierce shark is a relative of modern great white sharks. Its razor-sharp teeth have been found embedded in the fossilized bones of pterosaurs.

12 A new group of plants had evolved by the Cretaceous. They grew special parts to attract insects for pollination.

TEST YOURSELF

STARTER	CHALLENGER	GENIUS!
Rhamphorhynchus	***Hatzegopteryx***	***Seirocrinus***
Mosasaurus	***Rebellatrix***	***Garjainia***
Flowering plants	***Morganucodon***	***Mystriosuchus***
Megalosaurus	***Sharovipteryx***	***Cretoxyrhina***

What is a dinosaur?

For tens of millions of years, a unique group of reptiles—dinosaurs—roamed our planet. Their name means "terrible lizards" and while some were ferocious predators, they ranged from tiny meat-eaters to giant plant-eaters. Most dinosaurs died out 66 million years ago in a mass extinction, although some are still present today in the form of birds.

Dino rivals

Various groups of crocodile relatives were successfulfor millions of years before dinosaurs took over. One of them was *Postosuchus*, a top predator of the Late Triassic, when dinosaurs were small and rare. At 1,500 lb (680 kg), it weighed as much as six adult humans and was 14.5 ft (4.5 m) from head to tail.

Dinosaur features

Dinosaurs were a large and varied group of animals and came in many different shapes and sizes, but they all shared some common physical characteristics, which helped scientists group them together. All dinosaurs had their legs directly under their bodies, and they all had scales, feathers, or both.

Many dinosaurs had scaly skin.

The hip socket is "open," not "closed" as in other reptiles, and the head of the thigh bone fits into it. This open socket is a result of its upright stance.

The tail was held off the ground for balance.

Hinged ankles helped them move fast compared to lizards or crocodiles.

Limbs were held directly under the body.

The first dinosaurs had five fingers, but later dinosaur groups evolved to have different numbers and shapes of fingers.

I don't believe it!

Bee hummingbirds are the smallest dinosaurs. They are around 41 million times lighter than titanosaurs (the heaviest).

Walking tall

Most reptiles have legs that splay out from their bodies, giving them a sprawling stance. Dinosaurs were different from other reptiles because they could stand with their legs straight and walk upright. The stance of dinosaurs meant that they could move faster and hunt more effectively than other reptiles.

Upright stance of a dinosaur

Semisprawling stance of a crocodilian

Sprawling stance of a lizard

Meet the family

Dinosaurs are traditionally split into two main groups: "bird-hipped" ornithischians and "lizard-hipped" saurischians. These can be divided into five subgroups.

Ornithischians had an extra bone at the tip of the lower jaw and leaf-shaped teeth.

Ancestral dinosaurs These were the first dinosaurs, which were small, agile animals that ran on two legs. They later evolved into ornithischians and saurischians.

Saurischians typically had strong thumbs, hollow bones, and long necks.

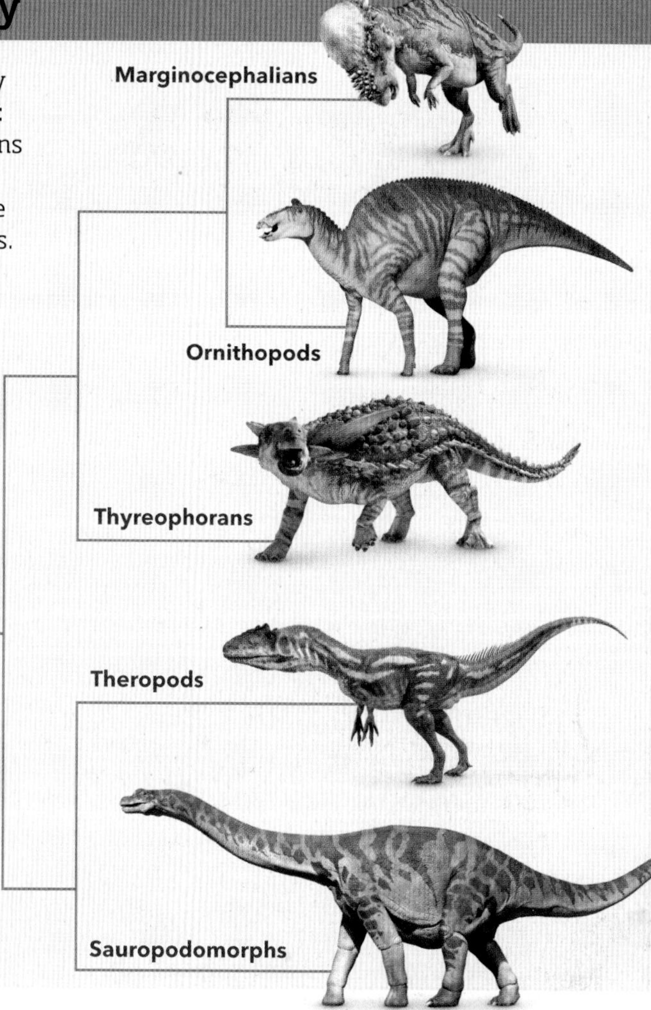

Dinosaurs, like other reptiles, had a joint in the lower jaw.

A large, bony crest on the upper arm bone that muscles attached to was typical of dinosaurs.

What is not a dinosaur?

Alongside dinosaurs on land, several other reptile groups flew in the sky and swam in the seas. These included flying pterosaurs and swimming ichthyosaurs, plesiosaurs, and mosasaurs. Crocodile relatives known as pseudosuchians, which included *Postosuchus* (above left), thrived on land, too. They are all often mistaken for dinosaurs.

Pterosaurs were the first flying reptiles.

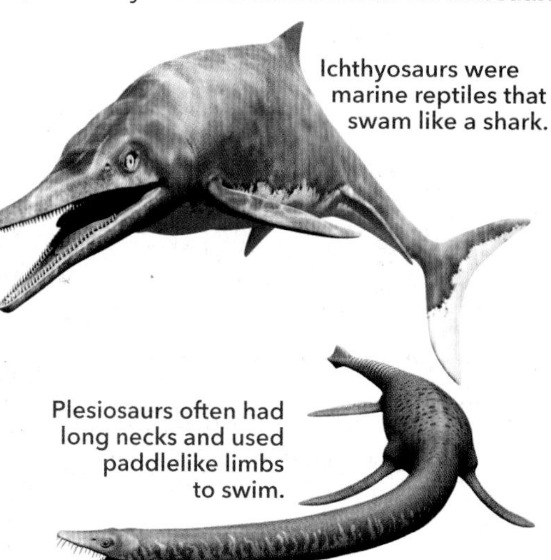

Ichthyosaurs were marine reptiles that swam like a shark.

Plesiosaurs often had long necks and used paddlelike limbs to swim.

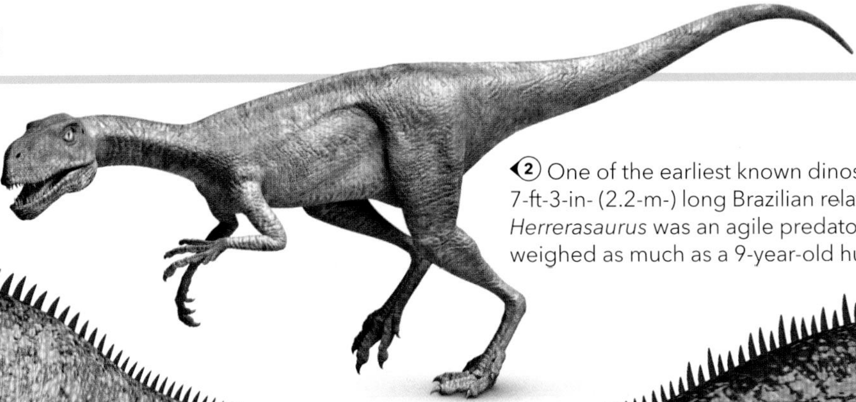

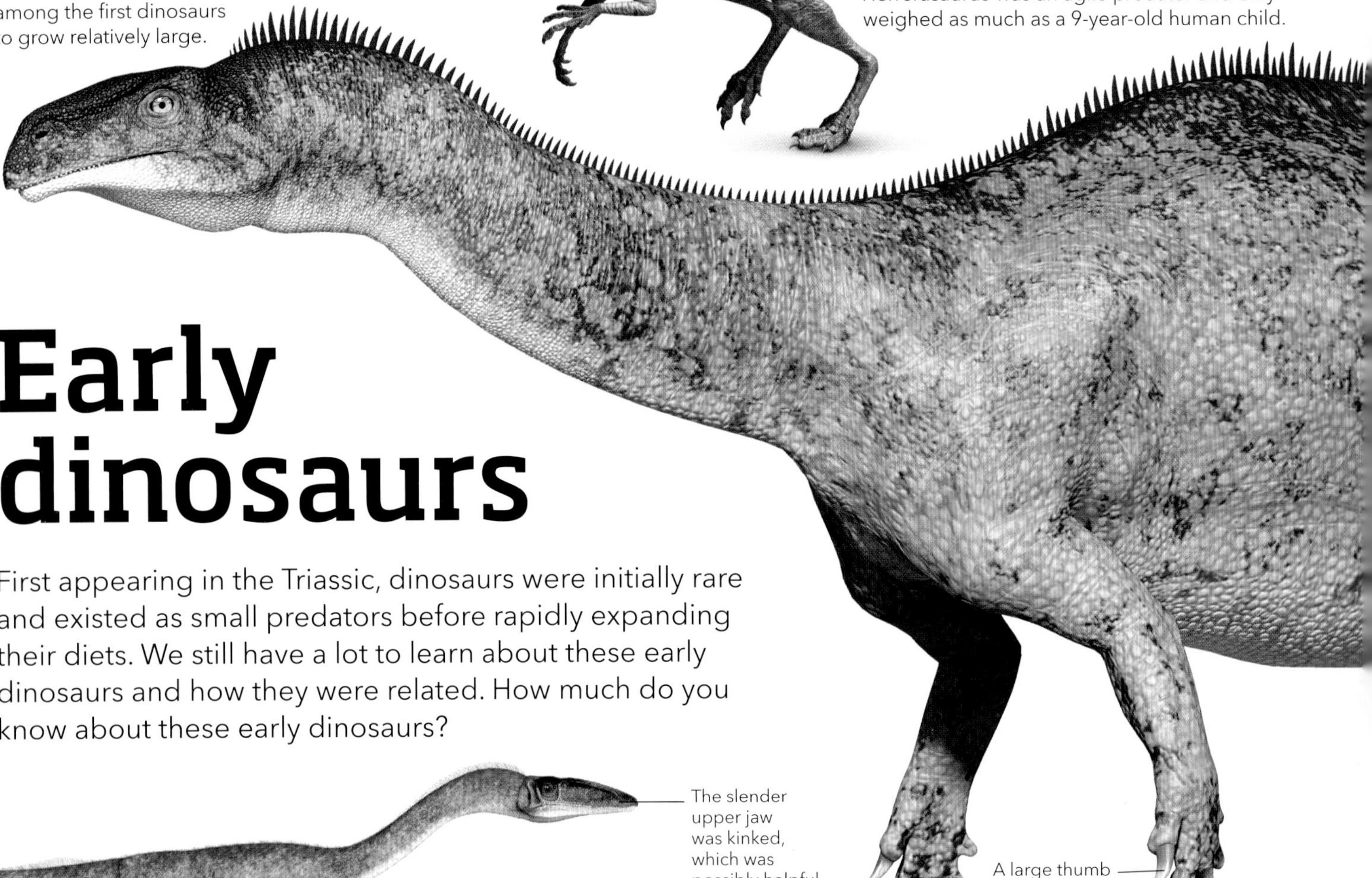

Early dinosaurs

First appearing in the Triassic, dinosaurs were initially rare and existed as small predators before rapidly expanding their diets. We still have a lot to learn about these early dinosaurs and how they were related. How much do you know about these early dinosaurs?

1 This bulky, bipedal sauropodomorph's name means "flat lizard," and it was among the first dinosaurs to grow relatively large.

2 One of the earliest known dinosaurs, this 7-ft-3-in- (2.2-m-) long Brazilian relative of *Herrerasaurus* was an agile predator and only weighed as much as a 9-year-old human child.

A large thumb claw may have been used for fighting.

The slender upper jaw was kinked, which was possibly helpful in trapping prey.

3 Known from hundreds of skeletons found at Ghost Ranch, New Mexico, this little predator had a long, narrow snout that it used for snapping up small reptiles.

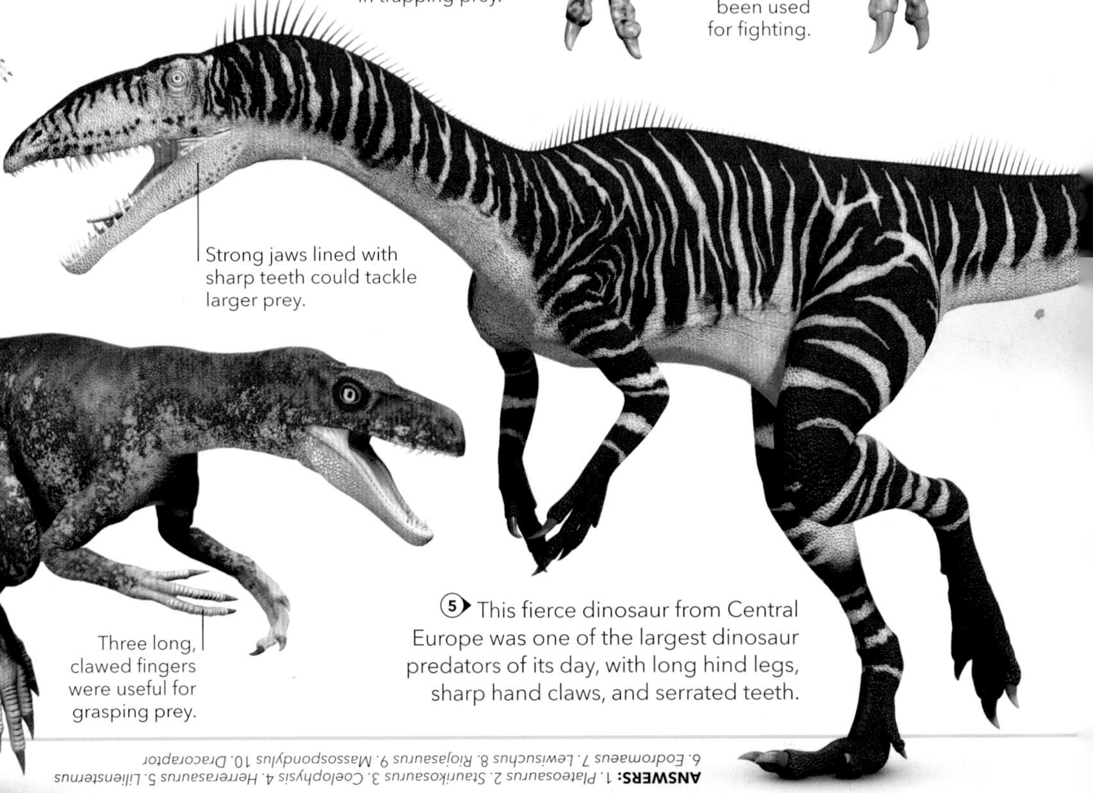

Strong jaws lined with sharp teeth could tackle larger prey.

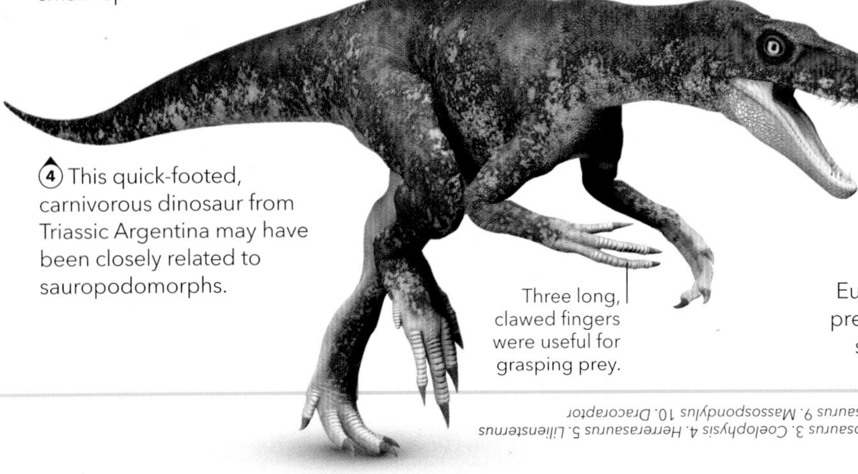

4 This quick-footed, carnivorous dinosaur from Triassic Argentina may have been closely related to sauropodomorphs.

Three long, clawed fingers were useful for grasping prey.

5 This fierce dinosaur from Central Europe was one of the largest dinosaur predators of its day, with long hind legs, sharp hand claws, and serrated teeth.

ANSWERS: 1. *Plateosaurus* 2. *Staurikosaurus* 3. *Coelophysis* 4. *Herrerasaurus* 5. *Liliensternus* 6. *Eodromaeus* 7. *Lewisuchus* 8. *Riojasaurus* 9. *Massospondylus* 10. *Dracoraptor*

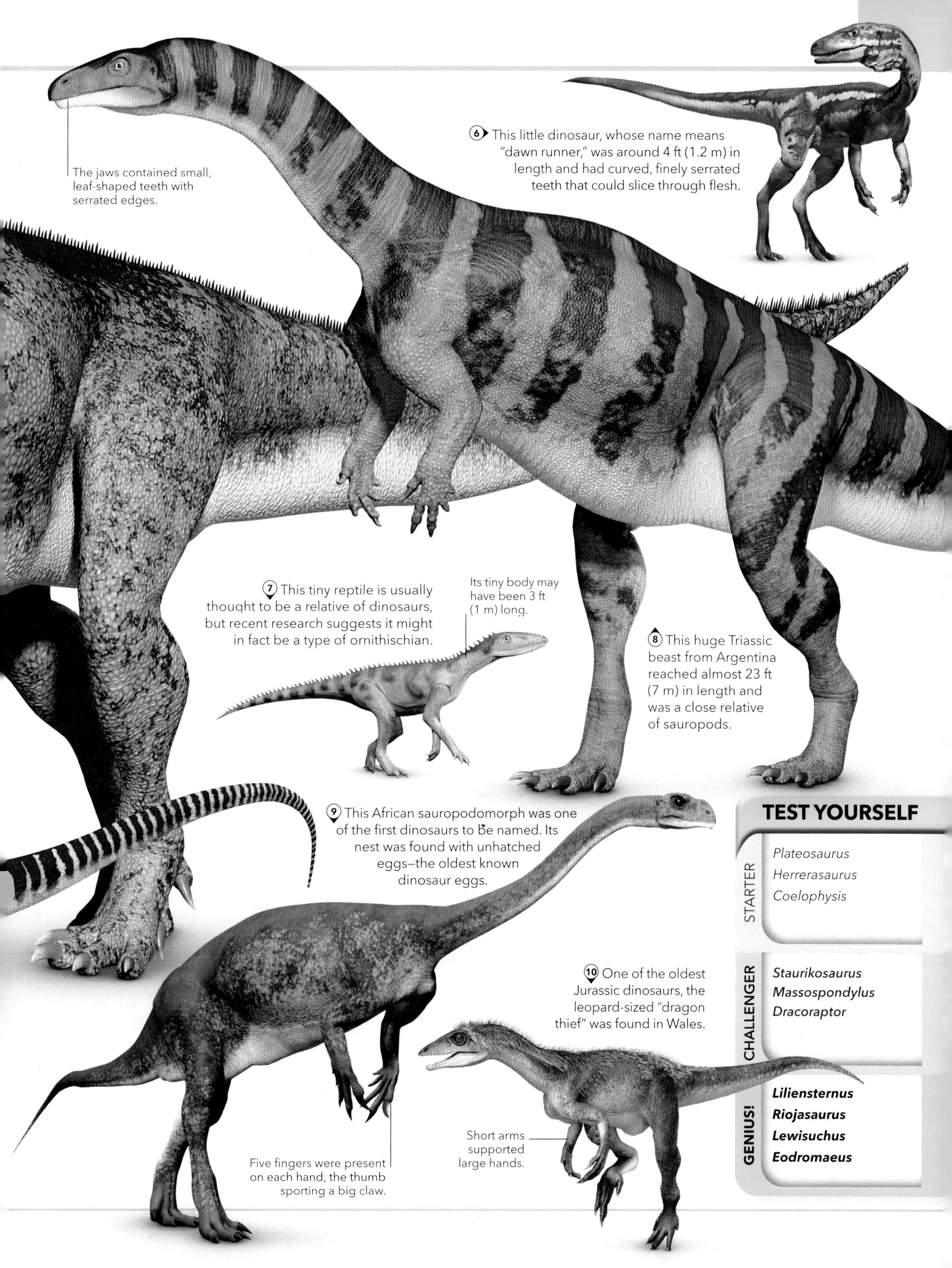

The jaws contained small, leaf-shaped teeth with serrated edges.

6 This little dinosaur, whose name means "dawn runner," was around 4 ft (1.2 m) in length and had curved, finely serrated teeth that could slice through flesh.

7 This tiny reptile is usually thought to be a relative of dinosaurs, but recent research suggests it might in fact be a type of ornithischian.

Its tiny body may have been 3 ft (1 m) long.

8 This huge Triassic beast from Argentina reached almost 23 ft (7 m) in length and was a close relative of sauropods.

9 This African sauropodomorph was one of the first dinosaurs to be named. Its nest was found with unhatched eggs—the oldest known dinosaur eggs.

10 One of the oldest Jurassic dinosaurs, the leopard-sized "dragon thief" was found in Wales.

Short arms supported large hands.

Five fingers were present on each hand, the thumb sporting a big claw.

TEST YOURSELF

STARTER

Plateosaurus
Herrerasaurus
Coelophysis

CHALLENGER

Staurikosaurus
Massospondylus
Dracoraptor

GENIUS!

Liliensternus
Riojasaurus
Lewisuchus
Eodromaeus

Eoraptor

Eoraptor was one of the earliest dinosaurs to evolve in the Late Triassic period and shared similarities with most dinosaurs of this time. In fact, it had so much in common with various different early dinosaurs that scientists were not sure which group it belonged to. Take the quiz on this puzzling dinosaur!

1 Scientists have long been confused about what *Eoraptor* ate because it had teeth of several different shapes. However, new research suggests that it probably ate soft foods. What might they have been?

A. A mix of fruits and meat

B. Tender small animals

C. Fish and shelled aquatic organisms

D. Large herbivorous dinosaurs

Some of its teeth were serrated.

2 How much did *Eoraptor* weigh?

A. Around the same as a 1-year-old human child

B. Around the same as a newborn Asian elephant

C. Around the same as an adult tiger

D. Around the same as an adult cow

3 *Eoraptor* had three long and two short fingers on each hand. How many claws did it have on each hand?

A. Two

B. Three

C. Four

D. Five

The small claws probably helped it handle prey.

4 *Eoraptor* was the size of a fox and measured 3 ft (1 m) from head to tail. How long was its skull?

A. 4.8 in (12.3 cm)

B. 5.9 in (15.3 cm)

C. 7.9 in (20.2 cm)

D. 9.8 in (25.1 cm)

5 *Eoraptor* is believed to have been alive 230 MYA. Its name means "dawn thief." Why was it so named?

A. It was from the earliest era of dinosaurs.

B. It was active only at dawn.

C. It would not eat after dawn.

D. It was the only dinosaur that was active only during daytime.

6 Where was first *Eoraptor* fossil found?

A. Soda Springs, Idaho, USA

B. Valley of the Moon, Argentina

C. Venta de Pantalones, Spain

D. Isle of Wight, England

7 *Eoraptor* ran on its two hind legs. What helped it maintain balance while running at a fast pace?

A. Its light weight

B. Its short height

C. Its long tail

D. Its clawed feet

8 What habitat did *Eoraptor* live in?

A. Snowy mountains

B. Lush flood plains

C. Deserts

D. Rainforests

9 Compared to other dinosaurs, *Eoraptor* had one unique and unusual feature. What was it?

A. It had teeth, which it did not use, on the roof of its mouth.

B. It had an extra pair of arms.

C. It had two stomachs.

D. It had three eyes.

ANSWERS: 1-B, 2-A, 3-B, 4-A, 5-A, 6-B, 7-C, 8-B, 9-A

Meet the family

Theropods evolved into many diverse groups, including one that would become birds.

Coelophysoids These early theropods were light, agile hunters, with some reaching up to 20 ft (6 m) in length.

Ceratosaurs One family of ceratosaurs went on to become the top predators of the southern continents.

Spinosaurids These unusual predators had elongated snouts and conical, ridged teeth that helped them catch fish.

Allosauroids These Jurassic and Cretaceous hunters evolved into some of the largest known land predators.

Tyrannosauroids Early species were generally small and covered in simple feathers, but later evolved into huge predators.

Theropods

This thriving group includes the only dinosaurs to survive the extinction event that ended the Cretaceous period—birds. While they are best known as mighty, meat-eating land predators, some theropods evolved to fly, some became plant-eaters, and some even adapted to live on land and hunt in water.

On the menu

Theropods ate different types of food. While the earliest theropods were carnivores, later theropods became omnivores and even herbivores.

Meat
Many theropods preyed on other dinosaurs, hunting easy victims, such as the young or injured.

Fish
Spinosaurids and some dromaeosaurids ate fish, as well as meat.

Plants
Groups including some ceratosaurs and maniraptorans cropped plants.

Insects
Members of one theropod group, alvarezsaurids, probably also ate insects.

I don't believe it!

Majungasaurus could grow and then replace a tooth in as little as two months.

How to hunt for prey

01. When hungry, be on the lookout for suitable prey. Use your super senses: listen, watch, or sniff the air to detect your next meal.

Therizinosaurs
This unusual theropod group became plant-eaters with large guts to help process plant matter.

Dromaeosaurids
Famous for their "killer claw" on each foot, these feathered hunters evolved into a range of sizes and lifestyles.

Birds
Birds first evolved in the Jurassic, with the ancestor of all living birds appearing during the Cretaceous.

Tale of a tail

In 2015, a small theropod tail was found trapped in amber. The dinosaur's bones, soft tissues, and simple feathers are preserved in the hardened, sticky resin.

Dinosaur ID

- Bladelike teeth with serrated edges
- Bipedal stance, meaning they walked on two legs
- A furcula (wishbone)—the forked bone that helps birds fly

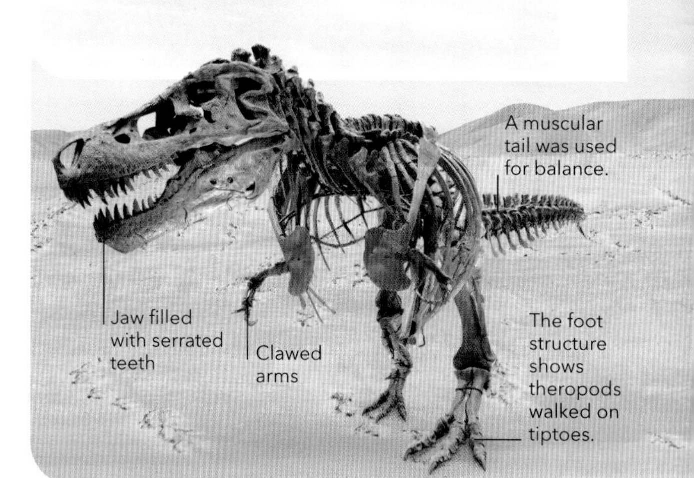

02. Only attack large, healthy dinosaurs if you are desperate for food. Charge at speed, then use your sharp teeth and claws to bring down your prey.

03. Attacks often fail. To save energy, the easiest meal is found by scavenging an already-dead carcass or by stealing the kill of a smaller carnivore.

In numbers

6 oz
(162 g) The mass of a young *Parvicursor*, one of the smallest known theropods

9.8 tons
(8.9 metric tons) The rough mass of the largest known *Tyrannosaurus* specimen

5.7 ft
(1.75 m) The estimated length of a *Spinosaurus* skull

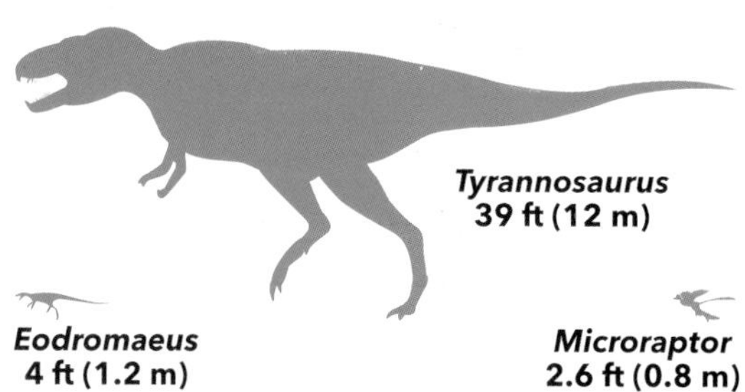

Is bigger better?

Different sizes of theropods evolved in different groups over time. Early theropods, such as *Eodromaeus*, were small. Some later theropods grew as big as *Tyrannosaurus*, while others, such as *Microraptor*, were the size of a crow. Some groups of theropods grew to giant sizes, which helped them tackle larger prey.

1 One of the largest theropod predators of the Mesozoic, it also had the strongest bite force of any land-based animal.

It had one of the largest eyeballs of any dinosaur.

Thickened teeth, serrated like steak knives, could shatter bone.

Strong but light body helped it run fast.

2 A pair of showy head crests gave this Early Jurassic hunter its name. This large carnivore could reach 20 ft (6 m) in height.

3 This Brazilian hunter irritated experts because the snout had been altered by the people who found and sold the fossil specimen.

Many spinosaurids had large hand claws.

Deadly dinos

Many theropods evolved into ferocious predators with a robust skull, powerful jaws, sharp teeth, and sometimes killer claws. They used these built-in weapons, as well as speed, to hunt and kill prey. Which of these terrifying carnivores can you identify?

4 One of the most common predators from North America, this dinosaur tore flesh from prey like a modern-day bird of prey.

Long, bladelike teeth were replaced when worn out.

Well-developed arms may have helped in handling prey.

5 Named after the region of China where it was found, this little tyrannosaurid had a low crest on its snout that was most likely used for display.

Unlike later tyrannosaurs, it had three long fingers.

ANSWERS: 1. *Tyrannosaurus rex* 2. *Dilophosaurus* 3. *Irritator* 4. *Allosaurus* 5. *Guanlong* 6. *Carnotaurus* 7. *Velociraptor* 8. *Ceratosaurus* 9. *Spinosaurus*

⑥ Two short brow horns gave this large, speedy theropod from Argentina its name, which means "meat-eating bull."

⑦ Named after the ability to outrun its victim, this small predator had a killer claw that helped in pinning down prey.

⑧ With long, blade-like teeth, this horned hunter also had bony scutes along its back—a rare feature in theropods.

⑨ This huge, sail-backed hunter stalked the waterways of North Africa in search of prey in both the water and on land.

TEST YOURSELF

STARTER	CHALLENGER	GENIUS!
Tyrannosaurus rex	***Spinosaurus***	***Irritator***
Allosaurus	***Ceratosaurus***	***Dilophosaurus***
Velociraptor	***Carnotaurus***	***Guanlong***

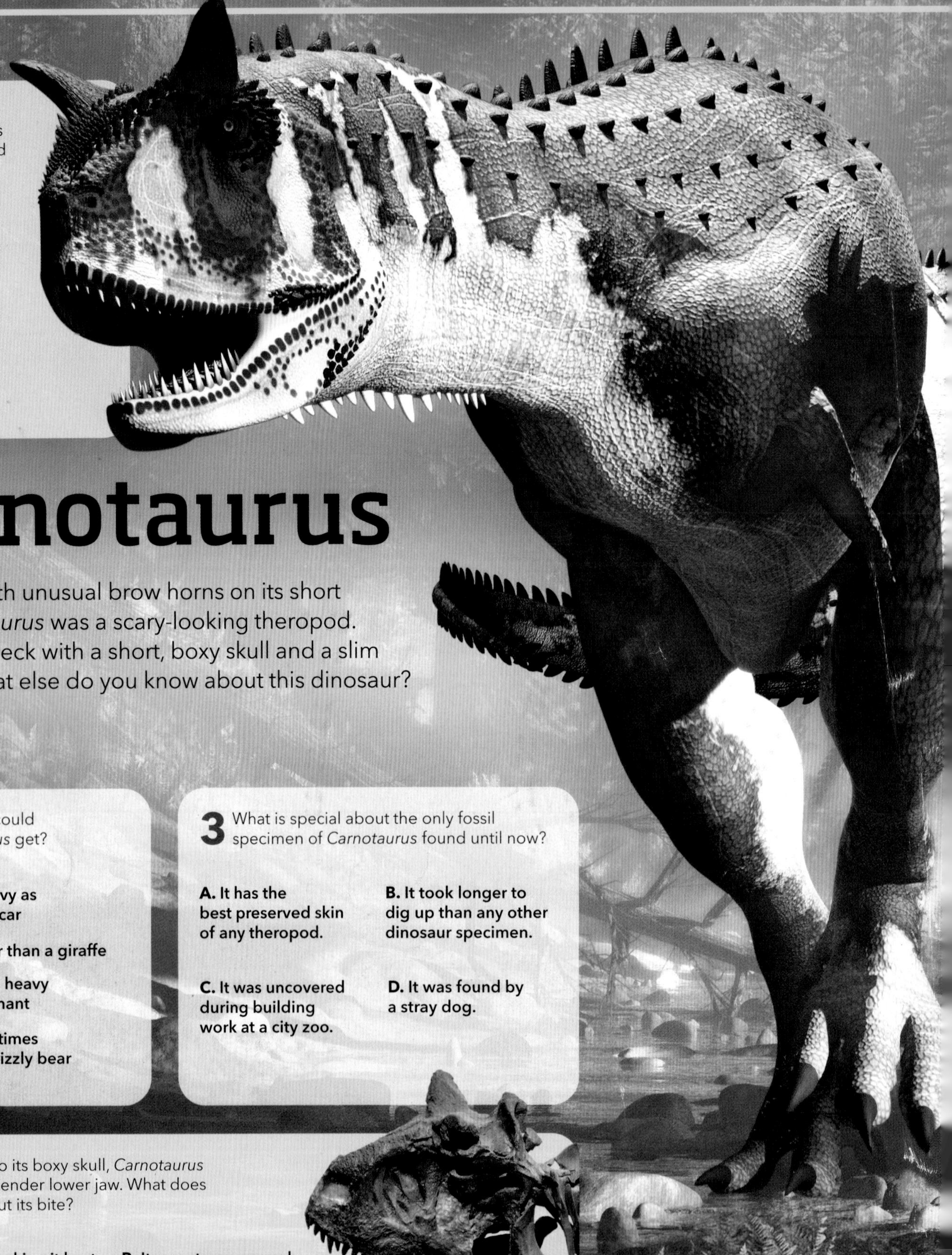

1 The top of *Carnotaurus*'s snout was covered in a gnarly, rough skin. What was it made of?

A. Cartilage (like a human ear)

B. Keratin (like human nails)

C. Fur

D. Bone

Carnotaurus

Muscly and with unusual brow horns on its short snout, *Carnotaurus* was a scary-looking theropod. It had a thick neck with a short, boxy skull and a slim lower jaw. What else do you know about this dinosaur?

2 How heavy could a *Carnotaurus* get?

A. Almost as heavy as a medium-sized car

B. A little heavier than a giraffe

C. Almost half as heavy as an Asian elephant

D. More than 10 times heavier than a grizzly bear

3 What is special about the only fossil specimen of *Carnotaurus* found until now?

A. It has the best preserved skin of any theropod.

B. It took longer to dig up than any other dinosaur specimen.

C. It was uncovered during building work at a city zoo.

D. It was found by a stray dog.

4 Compared to its boxy skull, *Carnotaurus* had a very slender lower jaw. What does this suggest about its bite?

A. It was weak, making it best suited for killing small prey.

B. It was strong enough to break bone.

C. It was slow and weak, so *Carnotaurus* mainly scavenged.

D. It was too slender to be used for hunting.

5 *Carnotaurus's* muscly tail helped it move fast for its size. Despite that, how was its tail a disadvantage at times?

A. The tail was prone to breaking.

B. It could not attract mates using its tail.

C. It may have struggled making tight turns.

D. It was a trip hazard when walking in dense forests.

6 What were the thick horns of *Carnotaurus* used for?

A. Killing prey

B. Sensing the Earth's magnetic field

C. Shoving rivals in fights for resources

D. Recognizing other members of the same species

7 How was *Carnotaurus's* bulky neck unusual for a theropod?

A. It was covered in huge spines.

B. It had no throat bones for the tongue to attach to.

C. It was nearly straight instead of "S" shaped.

D. It had a series of tiny bones that protected the throat.

8 What makes *Carnotaurus's* forelimbs remarkable?

A. They are some of the shortest of any theropod.

B. They were excellent digging tools.

C. They were more muscular than those of any other theropod.

D. Air spaces were present in the bone.

ANSWERS: 1-B, 2-A, 3-A, 4-A, 5-C, 6-C, 7-C, 8-A

TEST YOURSELF

STARTER

Citipati
Utahraptor
Ornithomimus

CHALLENGER

Tianyulong
Sciurumimus
Mononykus

GENIUS!

Caihong
Sinornithosaurus
Yutyrannus
Falcatakely

① The discovery in China of an ornithischian with featherlike "dino-fuzz" confused paleontologists. Usually, feathers are only found on theropods, so it may be that the common dinosaur ancestor had feathers.

② Known from a single fossil skull found in Madagascar, this extinct relative of modern birds was the size of a crow.

③ The iridescent feathers preserved in the fossil of this little theropod—weighing 1 lb (500 g)—earned it the name "rainbow" in Mandarin.

④ Named after one of the states in the US, this huge feathered hunter could weigh more than 660 lb (300 kg) and tackled large prey.

⑤ Stubby arms and a single hand claw, which was probably used for digging, indicate that this small, feathery hunter fed on insects.

Feathered beasts

Feathers of different types, from simple filaments to complex structures. have been found on a range of dinosaurs. Some evidence suggests all dinosaurs may have shared a feathered ancestor, but more research is needed to support this.

Its fossil suggests that it had a bushy tail like that of a squirrel.

⑥ This theropod's name means "squirrel mimic," as its tail resembles that of a squirrel. It is known from a single skeleton of a young one. Patches of a fuzzy coat can be seen with special lights.

⑧ This small dromaeosaur had complex feathers made of many branching filaments and was possibly capable of some sort of flight. Its name means "Chinese bird-lizard."

The long tail helped with balance when running at speed.

⑦ Among the fastest of all dinosaurs, this "bird mimic" could run at 37 mph (60 kph) and had ostrichlike feathers covering its body. Parts of its legs and tail were bare, which may have helped control its temperature.

Its long tail, like the rest of its body, was covered with stiff filaments.

Distinctive crest on its snout

Around 56 sharp teeth lined its jaws.

Bony crest

⑨ Known to have brooded its nest, this dinosaur was covered in complex feathers, some of which may have been used in display.

The tail fan was used to impress others.

⑩ One of the biggest dinosaurs with direct evidence of feathers, this tyrannosaur was covered in a shaggy coat that may have helped keep it warm.

ANSWERS: 1. *Tianyulong* 2. *Falcatakely* 3. *Caihong* 4. *Utahraptor* 5. *Mononykus* 6. *Sciurumimus* 7. *Ornithomimus* 8. *Sinornithosaurus* 9. *Citipati* 10. *Yutyrannus*

1 In which desert was the first fossilized *Velociraptor* discovered?

A. Sahara Desert in Africa

B. Gobi Desert in Asia

C. Atacama Desert in South America

D. Chihuahuan Desert in North America

2 *Velociraptor* was the same length as which present-day animal?

A. Elephant

B. Rhinoceros

C. Lion

D. Wolf

3 In the film *Jurassic Park*, the *Velociraptors* shown are far larger than they were in real life. On which dinosaur was the size of the *Velociraptors* in the film actually based?

A. *Tyrannosaurus*

B. *Rugops*

C. *Deinonychus*

D. *Troodon*

A young *Protoceratops* would have been no match for the sharp fangs and claws of a *Velociraptor*.

Velociraptor

Ferocious for its size, this small, feathered predator was quick and agile and equipped with killer claws. An amazing fossil revealed a *Velociraptor* locked in combat with a *Protoceratops*—both died fighting, buried by a sandstorm. This dinosaur is also a bit of a movie star! But how much do you really know about *Velociraptor*?

4 What is the meaning of the name "*Velociraptor*"?

A. Hunter thief

B. Fearsome thief

C. Cunning thief

D. Swift thief

The bones at the end of the tail overlapped, keeping it rigid.

5 What type of habitat did *Velociraptor* live in?

A. Scrublands and deserts

B. Swamps

C. Tropical forests

D. Mountains

6 *Velociraptor* belonged to a group of dinosaurs called maniraptorans, meaning "hand snatchers." Which present-day group shares a lot of similarities with maniraptorans?

A. Mammals

B. Birds

C. Amphibians

D. Fish

7 *Velociraptor* used the big, curved claw on its second toe to attack its prey. How did it keep the claw sharp at all times?

A. Chewing it

B. Keeping it raised off the ground

C. Rubbing it against tree trunks

D. Getting another *Velociraptor* to clean it

8 According to scientists, how did *Velociraptor* use its "killer claws" on each foot?

A. To pin down small prey

B. To jump onto and grip the backs of the larger dinosaurs

C. To kick at prey or enemies

D. To slice open prey

The killer claw was over 2 in (6 cm) long.

ANSWERS: 1-B, 2-D, 3-C, 4-D, 5-A, 6-B, 7-B, 8-A

Big bite

From serrated, knifelike teeth to toothless beaks, fossil remains have helped scientists understand if prehistoric beasts were rapacious meat-eaters or slow-chewing plant-eaters. Can you recognize these dinosaurs from their bites?

① Rows of stacked teeth in the jaws of this three-horned herbivore helped grind low-lying plants into a pulp.

The beak helped crop plants.

② Having all its teeth located at the very front of the snout enabled this long-necked plant-eater to snip and strip branches with precision.

Soft plants may have been a favourite for this sauropod.

Big eye sockets suggest it had large eyes and relied on its sight.

③ One of the ostrich-mimicking theropods, this dino snipped plants with a beaked, toothless snout.

④ This wetland hunter found in Britain had features for catching fish, such as a long snout and ridged teeth, to help grip onto slippery prey.

As many as 121 teeth lined its jaws.

A wide snout helped it take in large mouthfuls of plants.

⑤ The wide jaws of this plant-eater from Niger were packed with 500 teeth in several rows. The teeth fell out and were replaced every 14 days!

ANSWERS: 1. *Triceratops* 2. *Diplodocus* 3. *Struthiomimus* 4. *Baryonyx* 5. *Nigersaurus* 6. *Dicraeosaurus* 7. *Velociraptor* 8. *Tyrannosaurus rex* 9. *Edmontosaurus* 10. *Allosaurus*

The snout was long and slender and full of razorlike teeth.

The teeth at the front were replaced every 50 days or so.

6 Unlike some other sauropods, this herbivore had a relatively shorter neck, and probably fed on lower-growing plants.

7 This small dromaeosaur had a "killer claw" on each foot to help it subdue its prey.

The large claw helped in pinning down victims.

8 This terrifying "king of lizard tyrants" had thick teeth like knife blades and could deliver a powerful bite capable of puncturing bones.

The rows of teeth were stacked in columns known as dental batteries.

9 With hundreds of teeth, this hadrosaur could chew through tough plants, such as conifers, to extract nutrients.

10 Unlike other allosaurs, this Late Jurassic hunter had thickened teeth, which it could bare by opening its jaws really wide.

Its mouth was filled with 60 serrated teeth, each 12 in (31 cm) long (including the root).

Serrated teeth could slice through muscle and skin.

TEST YOURSELF

STARTER	CHALLENGER	GENIUS!
Diplodocus	***Allosaurus***	***Nigersaurus***
Tyrannosaurus rex	***Baryonyx***	***Edmontosaurus***
Velociraptor	***Triceratops***	***Struthiomimus***
		Dicraeosaurus

Tyrannosaurus

A big-game killer with jaws that could deliver bone-crushing bites, *Tyrannosaurus* was among the largest predators to ever stalk the land. The discovery of many skeletons, some nearly complete, has revealed fascinating facts about this powerful theropod. How many of them do you know?

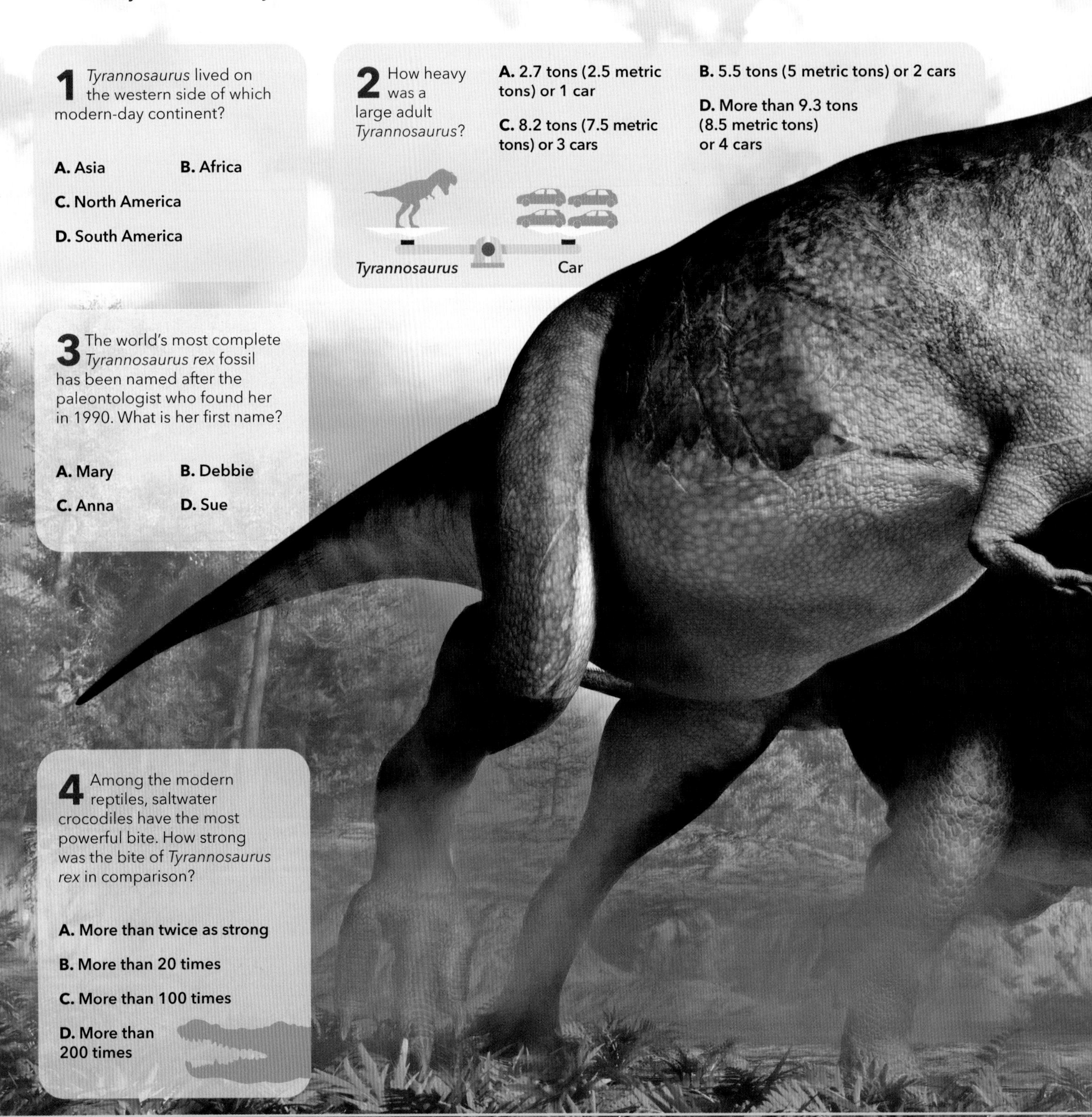

1 *Tyrannosaurus* lived on the western side of which modern-day continent?

A. Asia
B. Africa
C. North America
D. South America

2 How heavy was a large adult *Tyrannosaurus*?

A. 2.7 tons (2.5 metric tons) or 1 car
B. 5.5 tons (5 metric tons) or 2 cars
C. 8.2 tons (7.5 metric tons) or 3 cars
D. More than 9.3 tons (8.5 metric tons) or 4 cars

Tyrannosaurus Car

3 The world's most complete *Tyrannosaurus rex* fossil has been named after the paleontologist who found her in 1990. What is her first name?

A. Mary
B. Debbie
C. Anna
D. Sue

4 Among the modern reptiles, saltwater crocodiles have the most powerful bite. How strong was the bite of *Tyrannosaurus rex* in comparison?

A. More than twice as strong
B. More than 20 times
C. More than 100 times
D. More than 200 times

5 How much weight did a young *Tyrannosaurus* put on in a day during its teenage years?

A. 1.1 lb (500 g)

B. 2.2 lb (1 kg)

C. 4.4 lb (2 kg)

D. 11 lb (5 kg)

6 An adult *Tyrannosaurus* was about 39 ft (12 m) long. How long was its skull?

A. 3 ft (1 m)

B. 4.2 ft (1.3 m)

C. 4.9 ft (1.5 m)

D. 6.5 ft (2 m)

7 What is the name of the rock formation where many *Tyrannosaurus rex* bones have been found?

A. Devil's Pool

B. Hell Creek

C. Death Valley

D. Cape Fear

8 Roughly, how long did a *Tyrannosaurus rex* live?

A. Around 30 years

B. Around 78 years

C. Around 105 years

D. More than 150 years

9 The teeth of *Tyrannosaurus* were thick and shaped like bananas. What was the length of each tooth, including the root (not shown in the picture below)?

A. 7.1 in (18 cm)

B. 7.5 in (19 cm)

C. 7.9 in (20 cm)

D. 11.8 in (30 cm)

10 In what way was *Tyrannosaurus*'s brain different from that of other large-bodied theropods?

A. It had large olfactory bulbs, the part of the brain that is involved in smelling.

B. Its brain was very big.

C. Its brain was very small for the size of its body.

D. It had no brain at all.

ANSWERS: 1-C, 2-D, 3-D, 4-A, 5-C, 6-C, 7-B, 8-A, 9-D, 10-A

Whose claw?

Claws can reveal a lot about an animal's lifestyle and habits. The shape of a dinosaur's claws gives clues about how they were used: from hunting prey to fighting off predators, burrowing, or even supporting body weight. How many of these amazing claws can you identify?

1 This claw belongs to a species of megaraptoran, a group of theropods with huge hand claws. It was named "southern hunter," as its fossils were discovered in Australia.

2 Its "terrible claw" gives this feathered North American predator its name. It was on its second toe and held off the ground.

3 This long-snouted predator ate fish as part of its diet and had a huge claw—12 in (31 cm) long—on its thumb.

4 The hooflike claws of this horned herbivore were small but helped support its huge bulk.

5 The batlike wings attached to the fingers of this theropod from China allowed it to glide, although, unlike many of its feathered cousins, it could not truly fly.

6 The purpose of this bulky European plant-eater's huge thumb spike is not known. Previously, scientists thought this spike was located on its nose.

ANSWERS: 1. *Australovenator* 2. *Deinonychus* 3. *Baryonyx* 4. *Triceratops* 5. *Yi* 6. *Iguanodon* 7. *Diplodocus* 8. *Tyrannotitan* 9. *Mononykus* 10. *Oviraptor* 11. *Velociraptor* 12. *Therizinosaurus*

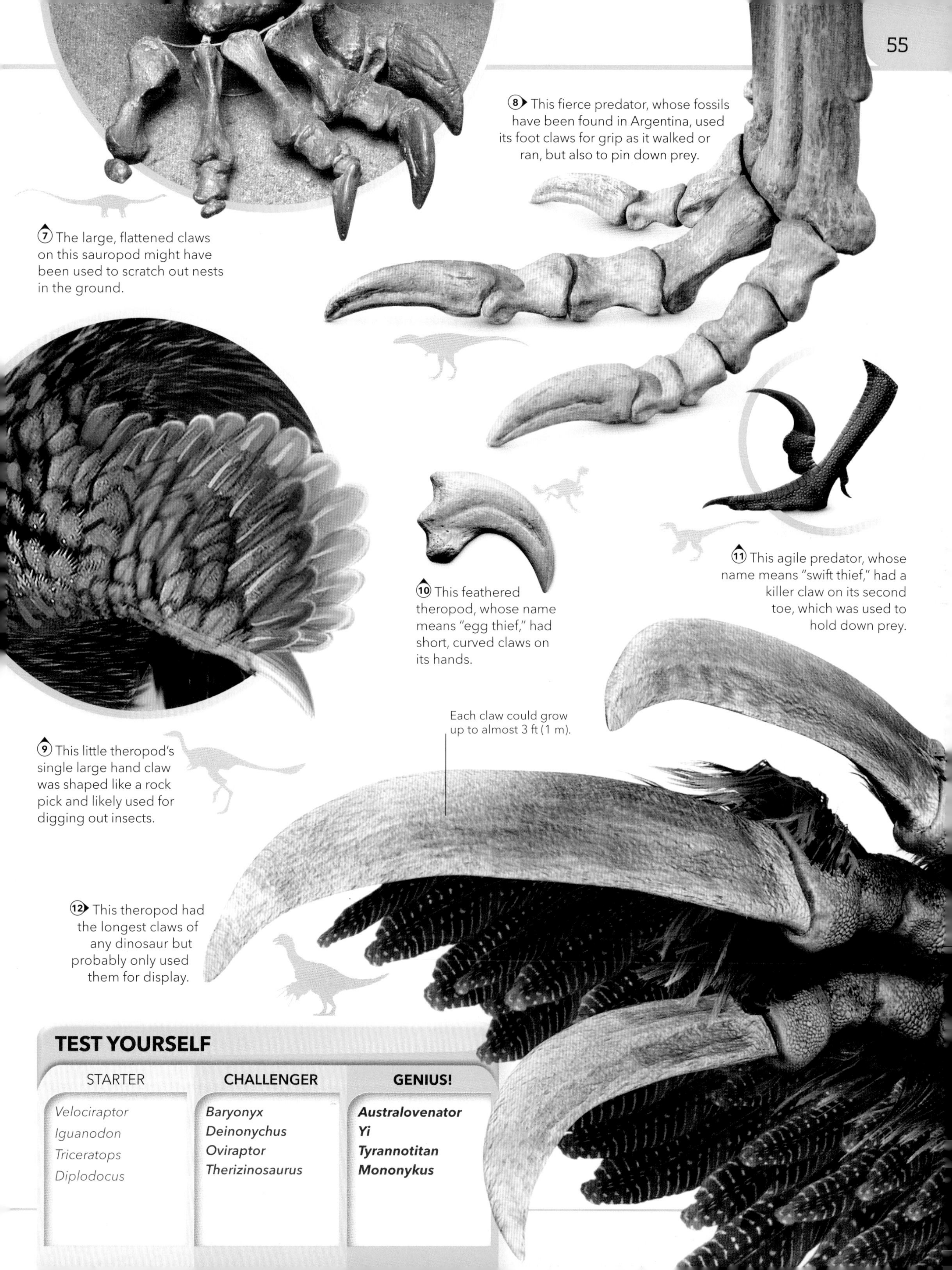

7 The large, flattened claws on this sauropod might have been used to scratch out nests in the ground.

8 This fierce predator, whose fossils have been found in Argentina, used its foot claws for grip as it walked or ran, but also to pin down prey.

9 This little theropod's single large hand claw was shaped like a rock pick and likely used for digging out insects.

10 This feathered theropod, whose name means "egg thief," had short, curved claws on its hands.

11 This agile predator, whose name means "swift thief," had a killer claw on its second toe, which was used to hold down prey.

12 This theropod had the longest claws of any dinosaur but probably only used them for display.

TEST YOURSELF

STARTER	CHALLENGER	GENIUS!
Velociraptor	***Baryonyx***	***Australovenator***
Iguanodon	***Deinonychus***	***Yi***
Triceratops	***Oviraptor***	***Tyrannotitan***
Diplodocus	***Therizinosaurus***	***Mononykus***

Deinocheirus

One of the biggest theropods ever, *Deinocheirus*'s long arms confused paleontologists for decades. It was later identified as a type of ornithomimosaur, a group of dinosaurs that may have looked similar to modern-day ostriches. See if you can work out the answers to these questions about this very odd theropod!

1 *Deinocheirus*'s head was small for its body size. How long was its skull?

A. 11 in (28 cm), same as a wolf

B. 16 in (40 cm), same as a pelican

C. 26 in (66 cm), same as a horse

D. 40 in (102 cm), same as an American bison

Tarbosaurus, a cousin of *Tyrannosaurus rex*, was one of the main predators of *Deinocheirus*.

2 *Deinocheirus*'s beak was similar to that of modern-day ducks, suggesting it may have foraged in water. Its fossil, however, has been found in places that had vegetation then but are deserts today. What was its actual habitat?

A. Deserts

B. Wetlands and riversides

C. Thick forest

D. Grasslands

The skull was toothless.

3 Fossilized animals were found inside the rib cage of one *Deinocheirus* specimen, suggesting it occasionally ate meat. What were the animals?

A. Frogs

B. Fish

C. Insect larvae

D. *Tyrannosaurus* hatchlings

4 *Deinocheirus*'s giant frame helped it eat more food and avoid being targeted by predators. How big could this theropod get?

A. 16 ft (5 m)

B. 23 ft (7 m)

C. 30 ft (9 m)

D. 36 ft (11 m)

The hump on *Deinocheirus*'s back may have been used for display or to scare predators.

Deinocheirus's long, narrow skull had a flattened beak at the tip.

8 The spaces for *Deinocheirus*'s jaw muscles were small compared to the rest of the large skull. What does this imply?

A. **It didn't open its jaws much.**

B. **The fossil specimen had a disease that affected the jaw muscles.**

C. **It needed more space for its large brain.**

D. **It had a weak bite.**

9 What do scientists think *Deinocheirus* used its forelimbs for?

A. **Slashing at predators**

B. **Digging holes**

C. **Pulling plants from the water**

D. **Impressing mates**

5 The first incomplete *Deinocheirus* fossil was found in the Gobi Desert in Mongolia in 1965. When a complete fossil was discovered 50 years later in 2014, what surprising feature did it reveal?

A. **A third eye socket**

B. **A hump on its back**

C. **Tailbone made of cartilage**

D. **Lack of ribcage**

The tip of the tail probably had a small fan of feathers.

6 For a long time, *Deinocheirus* was only known from a single body part. What part was it?

A. **A huge pair of arms**

B. **A skull**

C. **A section of tail**

D. **A single foot**

7 *Deinocheirus* was named "terrible hands" after its giant forelimbs. How long were these?

A. **4 ft (1.6 m)**

B. **5 ft (1.8 m)**

C. **6.5 ft (2 m)**

D. **8 ft (2.4 m)**

ANSWERS: 1-D, 2-B, 3-B, 4-D, 5-B, 6-A, 7-D, 8-D, 9-C

① These are the small, flat scales of a large herbivore. This dinosaur also had large, pointed scales and three horns.

Unlike the scales of many lizards and snakes, these scales do not overlap.

The fringe of stiff feathers on its legs may have helped it glide.

② Feather-like structures seen on this early ornithischian from Kulinda in Russia suggest that theropods were not the only dinosaurs that may have had feathers.

A small, fleshy crest distinguished this dinosaur.

Scales and feathers

All animals have some kind of skin to protect them from their environment. Dinosaurs also evolved additional skin features, such as scales, bony plates, and even feathers for defense, display, warmth, and camouflage.

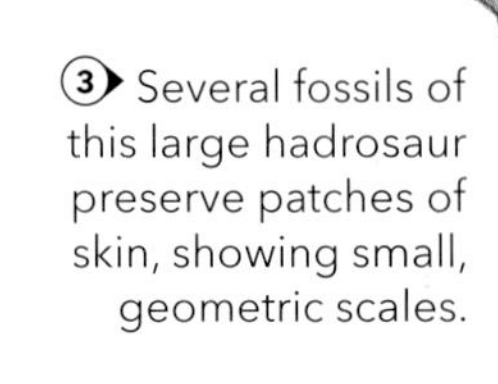

③ Several fossils of this large hadrosaur preserve patches of skin, showing small, geometric scales.

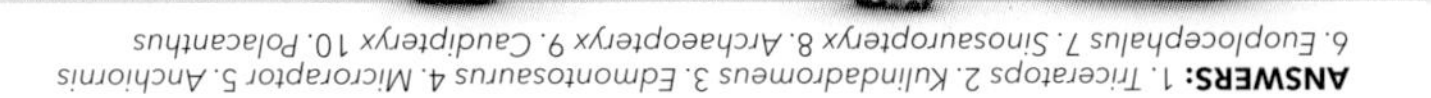

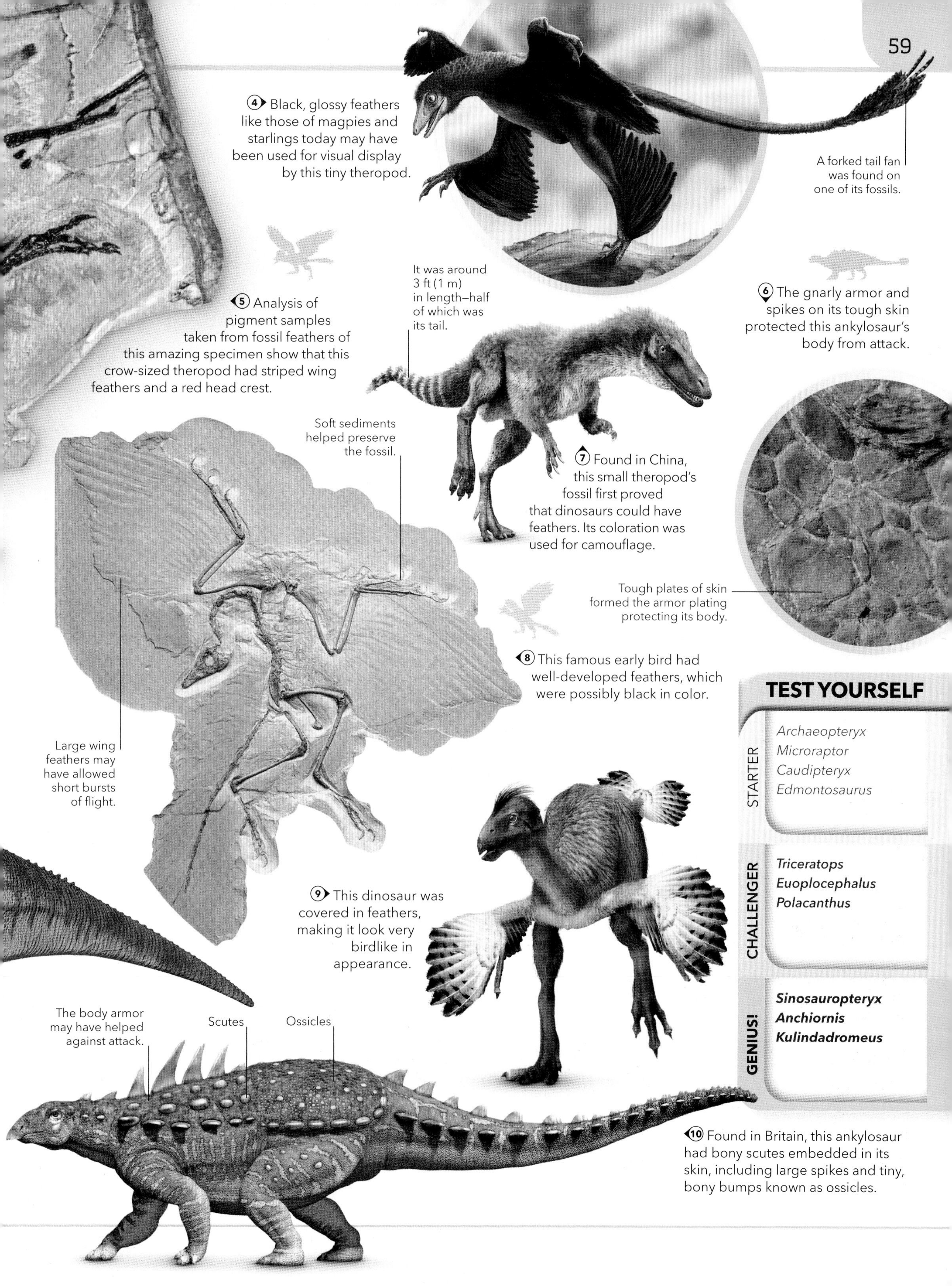

④ Black, glossy feathers like those of magpies and starlings today may have been used for visual display by this tiny theropod.

⑤ Analysis of pigment samples taken from fossil feathers of this amazing specimen show that this crow-sized theropod had striped wing feathers and a red head crest.

⑥ The gnarly armor and spikes on its tough skin protected this ankylosaur's body from attack.

⑦ Found in China, this small theropod's fossil first proved that dinosaurs could have feathers. Its coloration was used for camouflage.

⑧ This famous early bird had well-developed feathers, which were possibly black in color.

⑨ This dinosaur was covered in feathers, making it look very birdlike in appearance.

⑩ Found in Britain, this ankylosaur had bony scutes embedded in its skin, including large spikes and tiny, bony bumps known as ossicles.

TEST YOURSELF

STARTER

Archaeopteryx
Microraptor
Caudipteryx
Edmontosaurus

CHALLENGER

Triceratops
Euoplocephalus
Polacanthus

GENIUS!

Sinosauropteryx
Anchiornis
Kulindadromeus

Sauropodomorphs

A thriving family of dinosaurs, plant-eating sauropodomorphs stomped the Earth for much of the Mesozoic Era. One group, the sauropods, evolved into the largest land animals ever to have lived. Many had long necks and tails, making these humongous herbivores easy to recognize.

Dinosaur ID

- Small heads perched on long necks
- Most walked on four legs, but early species walked on two legs
- Most sauropods evolved to be huge, but early sauropodomorphs were small

How to be giant

A long tail counterbalanced the heavy neck.

1. To grow fast and huge needs a lot of oxygen. Use your great pair of *Patagotitan*-sized lungs to get this from the air.

2. You also need lots of energy to survive and grow. Leave your young to look after themselves—you've got to keep eating!

I don't believe it!

The femur (thigh bone) of *Argentinosaurus* measured 8.2 ft (2.5 m) long.

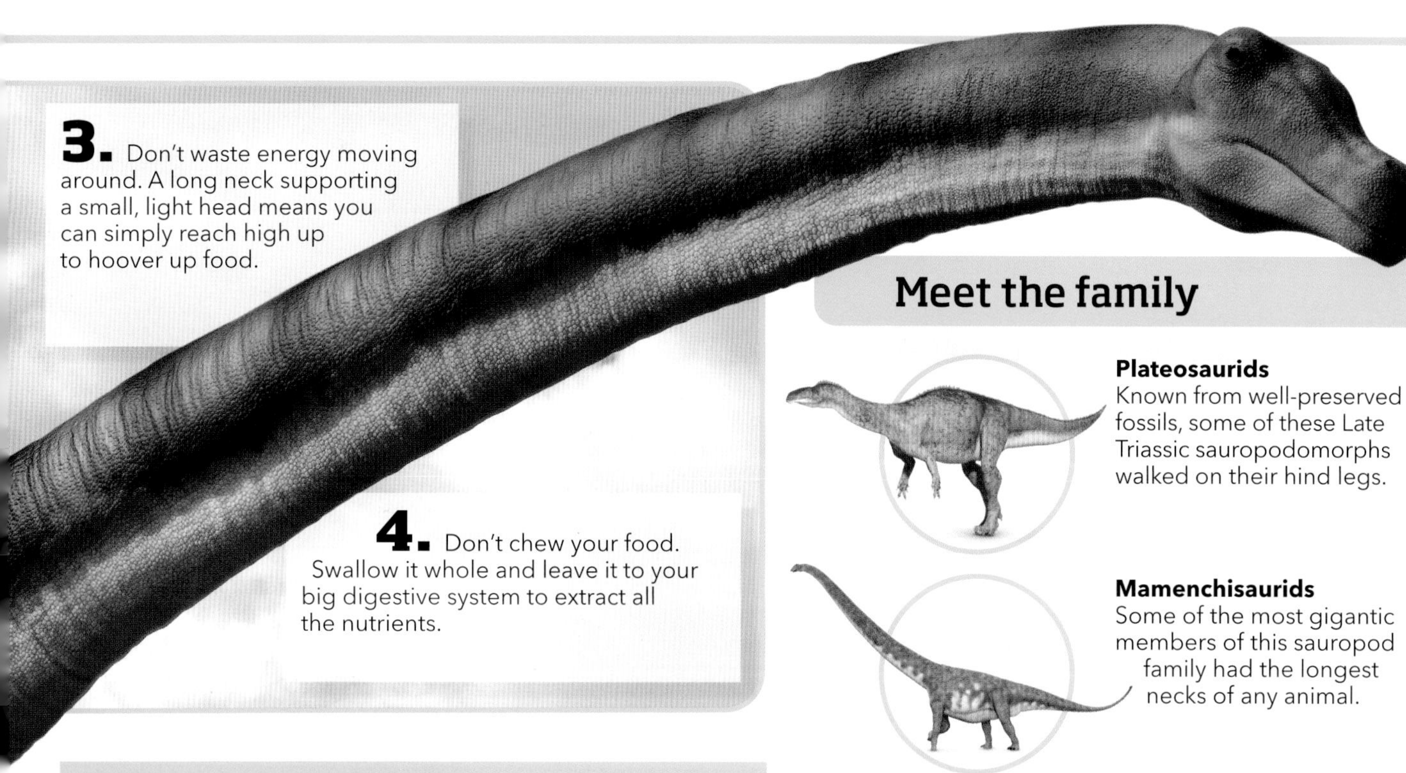

3. Don't waste energy moving around. A long neck supporting a small, light head means you can simply reach high up to hoover up food.

4. Don't chew your food. Swallow it whole and leave it to your big digestive system to extract all the nutrients.

Meet the family

Plateosaurids
Known from well-preserved fossils, some of these Late Triassic sauropodomorphs walked on their hind legs.

Mamenchisaurids
Some of the most gigantic members of this sauropod family had the longest necks of any animal.

Diplodocoids
Long-tailed diplodocoids include *Diplodocus*, one of the most famous dinosaurs ever discovered.

Macronarians
Named after the large openings in their snouts, these include *Camarasaurus*, one of the most commonly found sauropods.

Titanosaurs
Common during the Cretaceous, this sauropod group included some of the biggest ever land animals.

Home, sweet home

Sauropods spread across the globe but never reached the poles. Unlike other dinosaurs, sauropods seem to have preferred the warm climate nearer the equator. Experts are not sure why this is, but it may have been linked to how sauropods controlled their body temperature.

In numbers

300
The number of sauropodomorph species currently known

22 lb
(10 kg) Maximum weight of the earliest sauropodomorphs, which were small omnivores

49 ft
(15 m) The length of *Mamenchisaurus*'s neck—the longest neck of any sauropod

Different menus

Where several species of sauropods lived together, they may have eaten different plants to avoid competing for food. While *Camarasaurus* could rip off tough leaves, its neighbor *Diplodocus* (shown here) probably preferred softer foods.

1 *Diplodocus* had a very long tail made up of around 80 bones. What did this dinosaur **not** use its tail for?

A. Counterbalance

B. Striking potential attackers

C. Making whiplike sounds to scare away enemies

D. Using it as a "third leg" when standing on its hind legs

2 *Diplodocus* weighed 11 tons (10 metric tonnes) but ate less than an African elephant around half its size. If an elephant eats 331 lb (150 kg) of plants per day, how much do you think *Diplodocus* ate?

A. 51 lb (23 kg)

B. 73 lb (33 kg)

C. 95 lb (43 kg)

D. 117 lb (53 kg)

3 Despite its enormous length, *Diplodocus* did not weigh as much as you might expect. What physical trait helped keep its weight relatively low?

A. A short torso

B. Light muscles

C. Air spaces in the backbones

D. Skeleton mostly made of cartilage instead of bones

4 *Diplodocus* had a small skull relative to its size. Which living animal's head matches the size of *Diplodocus*'s head?

A. Horse

B. Cat

C. Sheep

D. Goat

5 Which of the following dinosaurs was *Diplodocus's* closest relative and known for having an even longer neck?

A. *Brachiosaurus*

B. *Allosaurus*

C. *Barosaurus*

D. *Brontosaurus*

A long tail helped this relative of *Diplodocus* to balance its long neck.

Its weight was supported by four strong, pillarlike legs.

6 *Diplodocus* continually replaced its teeth, meaning they never wore out. How long would each tooth last before it was replaced by a new one?

A. 35 days

B. 55 days

C. 75 days

D. 110 days

Diplodocus

One of the best-known dinosaurs, *Diplodocus* has captivated museumgoers for over a hundred years. Famous for its super-long neck, it could reach the top of trees and rake off leaves from branches with its peglike teeth. How well do you know this fascinating plant-eater?

7 Evidence suggests that the longest *Diplodocus* was much longer than an average school bus, which is 36 ft (11 m) long. How long was it?

A. 108 ft (33 m)

B. 180 ft (55 m)

C. 217 ft (66 m)

D. 253 ft (77 m)

8 American philanthropist Andrew Carnegie donated a cast of a *Diplodocus* skeleton to the Natural History Museum in London, UK, in 1905. What is it called?

A. Carrie

B. Dippy

C. Drew

D. Anna

ANSWERS: 1-C, 2-B, 3-C, 4-A, 5-C, 6-A, 7-A, 8-B

Long necks

Sauropodomorphs are famous for their long necks, some of which were six times longer than a giraffe's! A combination of features—small heads, distinctive neck-bone shapes, and air spaces in their bones—enabled their necks to evolve so long. How many of these dinosaurs can you identify?

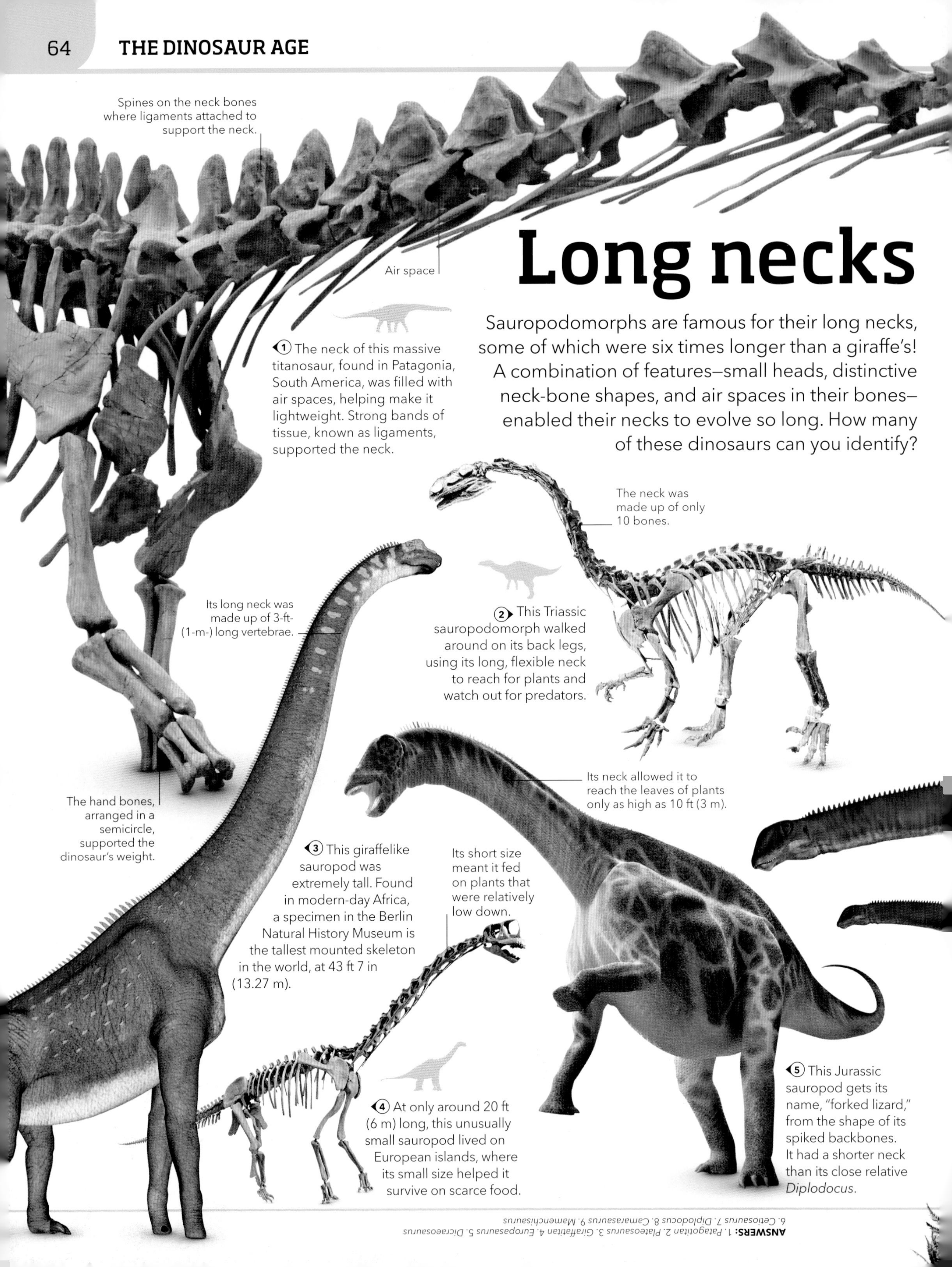

1. The neck of this massive titanosaur, found in Patagonia, South America, was filled with air spaces, helping make it lightweight. Strong bands of tissue, known as ligaments, supported the neck.

2. This Triassic sauropodomorph walked around on its back legs, using its long, flexible neck to reach for plants and watch out for predators.

3. This giraffelike sauropod was extremely tall. Found in modern-day Africa, a specimen in the Berlin Natural History Museum is the tallest mounted skeleton in the world, at 43 ft 7 in (13.27 m).

4. At only around 20 ft (6 m) long, this unusually small sauropod lived on European islands, where its small size helped it survive on scarce food.

5. This Jurassic sauropod gets its name, "forked lizard," from the shape of its spiked backbones. It had a shorter neck than its close relative *Diplodocus*.

ANSWERS: 1. *Patagotitan* 2. *Plateosaurus* 3. *Giraffatitan* 4. *Europasaurus* 5. *Dicraeosaurus* 6. *Cetiosaurus* 7. *Diplodocus* 8. *Camarasaurus* 9. *Mamenchisaurus*

TEST YOURSELF

STARTER
Diplodocus
Plateosaurus
Patagotitan

CHALLENGER
Giraffatitan
Camarasaurus
Mamenchisaurus

GENIUS!
Europasaurus
Dicraeosaurus
Cetiosaurus

1 In which country was the first *Argentinosaurus* fossil found?

A. Brazil
B. Chile
C. Argentina
D. Bolivia

2 The largest land animal alive today, the African elephant, eats around 331 lb (150 kg) of plants each day. How much food is *Argentinosaurus* believed to have eaten in a day?

A. 375 lb (170 kg)
B. 508 lb (230 kg)
C. 882 lb (400 kg)
D. 1,764 lb (800 kg)

Its long neck helped it browse over a large area.

3 Which physical feature helped reduce the weight of the massive neck of *Argentinosaurus*?

A. Strong neck muscles
B. Fewer neck bones
C. Air sacs in the neck bones
D. Relatively slim neck

4 While *Argentinosaurus* probably roamed what is now South America in search of food, they have not been found in today's North America. Why is that?

A. North America did not exist at that time.
B. Predators made North America unsafe for *Argentinosaurus*.
C. North and South America were not connected.
D. Their food did not grow in North America.

5 While an adult *Argentinosaurus* reached around 115 ft (35 m) in length, the hatchlings were surprisingly small in comparison. How long were they at birth?

A. 3.9 in (10 cm)
B. 19.6 in (50 cm)
C. 3 ft (1 m)
D. 6.5 ft (2 m)

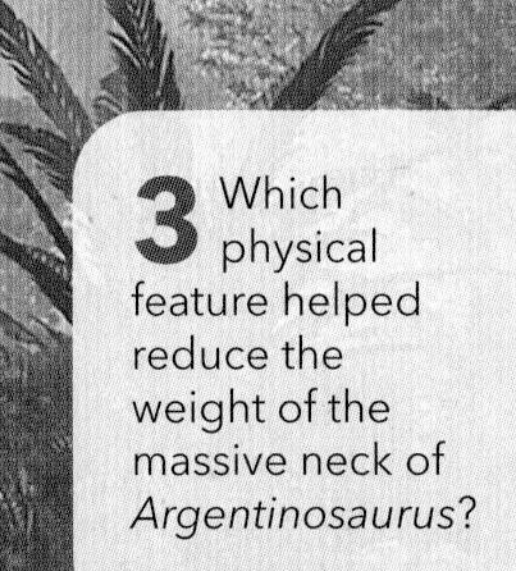

Argentinosaurus

One of the biggest animals ever to have walked the Earth, this South American sauropod was so imposing that only the most desperate predator would dare to attack it. The giant body of an *Argentinosaurus* was fueled by swallowing huge amounts of plants, which were processed in its massive stomach. Take this quiz to challenge the dino genius in you.

6 What did the finder of the original *Argentinosaurus* bones mistakenly think he had discovered?

A. *Diplodocus* fossils

B. Logs turned into rocks

C. A giant crocodile's bones

D. A blue whale skeleton

7 The most complete fossil from *Argentinosaurus* is a shin bone, which formed part of its leg below the knee. How long is this bone?

A. 3 ft (1 m)

B. 5 ft (1.5 m)

C. 6.5 ft (2 m)

D. 10 ft (3 m)

8 How fast do scientists believe *Argentinosaurus* could run?

A. 1 mph (2 kph)

B. 5 mph (8 kph)

C. 6 mph (10 kph)

D. 14 mph (22 kph)

9 *Argentinosaurus* is possibly the heaviest land animal of all time. According to scientists, what was its estimated weight?

A. 91 tons (83 metric tons)

B. 165 tons (150 metric tons)

C. 220 tons (200 metric tons)

D. 551 tons (500 metric tons)

ANSWERS: 1-C, 2-B, 3-C, 4-C, 5-C, 6-B, 7-B, 8-B, 9-A

Footprints

It can be hard to identify the dinosaurs that left footprints, but tracks and trackways can provide important clues about their behavior. For example, they can tell us whether the dinosaur that made them moved on two or four legs, was running or walking, and if it traveled on its own or in a herd.

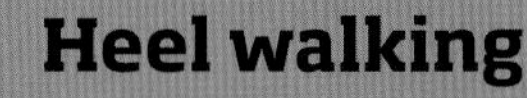

Heel walking

As this footprint shows, pterosaurs walked on their back foot, with the heel touching the ground, like humans do.

In numbers

34 in
(86 cm) The length of a *Tyrannosaurus* footprint

0.39 in
(10 mm) The size of the smallest known dinosaur footprint, which was left by a dromaeosaur

508 ft
(155 m) The length of the longest sauropod trackway

5.6 ft
(1.7 m) The longest known dinosaur footprint, which belongs to a sauropod

Herds on the move

Trackways, which are trails of tracks, have been found showing large numbers of dinosaurs moving together in herds. Some show a mix of adults and young traveling together.

I don't believe it!

Some footprints reveal dinosaur injuries. One theropod print preserved the impression of a dislocated toe!

Footprint forensics

The distance between the prints helps scientists guess the speed at which the dinosaurs walked.

The long trail of sauropod footprints may have belonged to a titanosaur.

This limestone cliff at Cal Orcko in Bolivia is crisscrossed with dinosaur tracks. The 465 trackways exposed are 0.74 mile (1.2 km) in length and include 12,092 individual footprints. They were created 68 MYA, when several dinosaur species trampled a lakeshore. The tracks fossilized and the hardened rock was pushed into a vertical position over time.

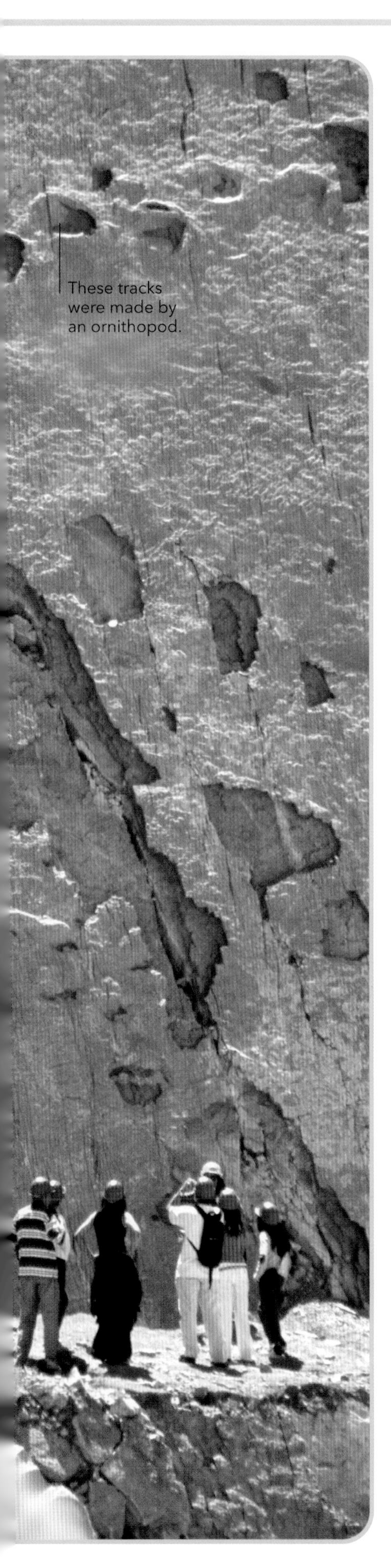

How fossil tracks are made

Footprint fossils are made in wet sediments, such as mud or wet sand, when the conditions are just right–the ground must be neither too hard nor too soft. They are most often found on prehistoric mudflats or shorelines.

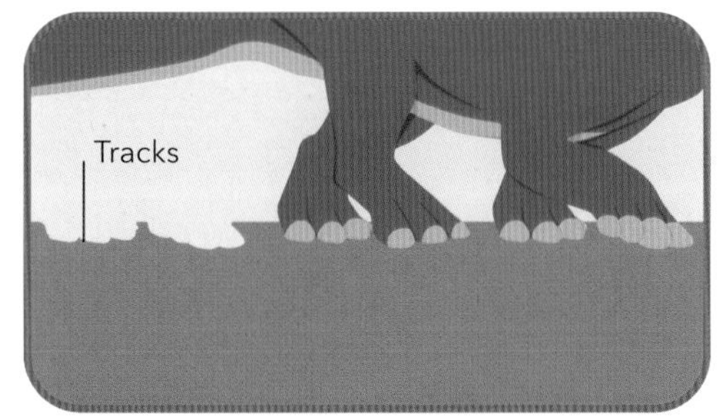

01. A dinosaur walks over mud or wet sand, leaving impressions of single footprints, known as tracks.

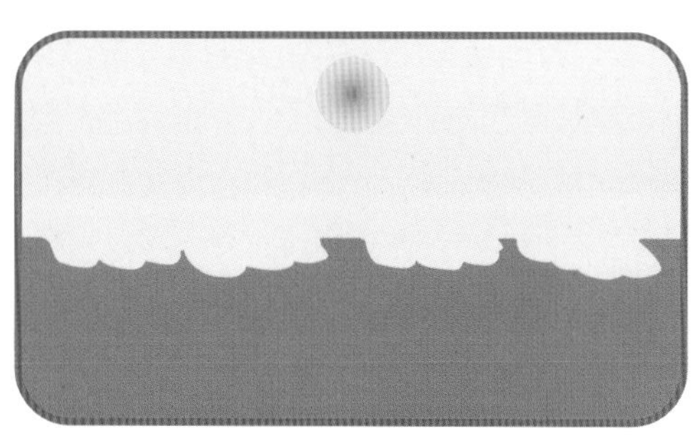

02. The tracks are baked hard by the Sun over days or months, making them less likely to get eroded or washed away.

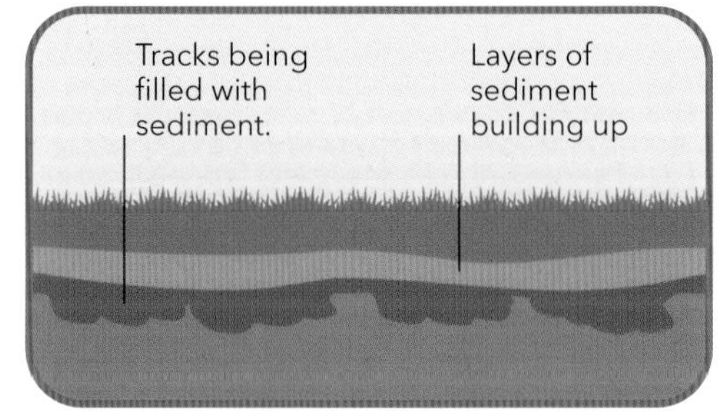

03. The tracks fill with sand, pebbles, or ash and are covered with more sediment layers, eventually hardening into rock.

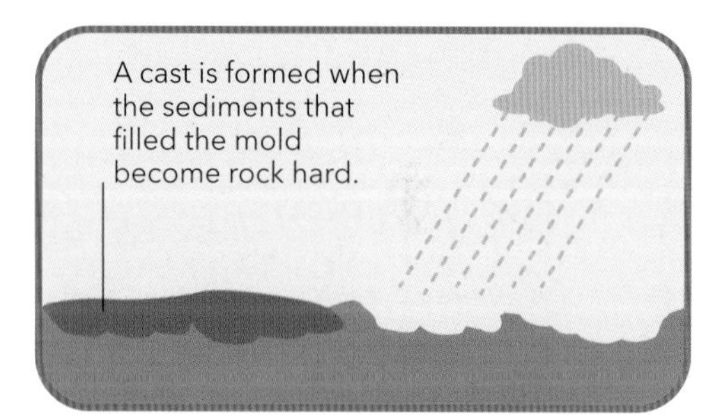

04. The tracks may become exposed later on as molds. Some may have filled with sediments that have hardened to form casts.

Interpreting footprints

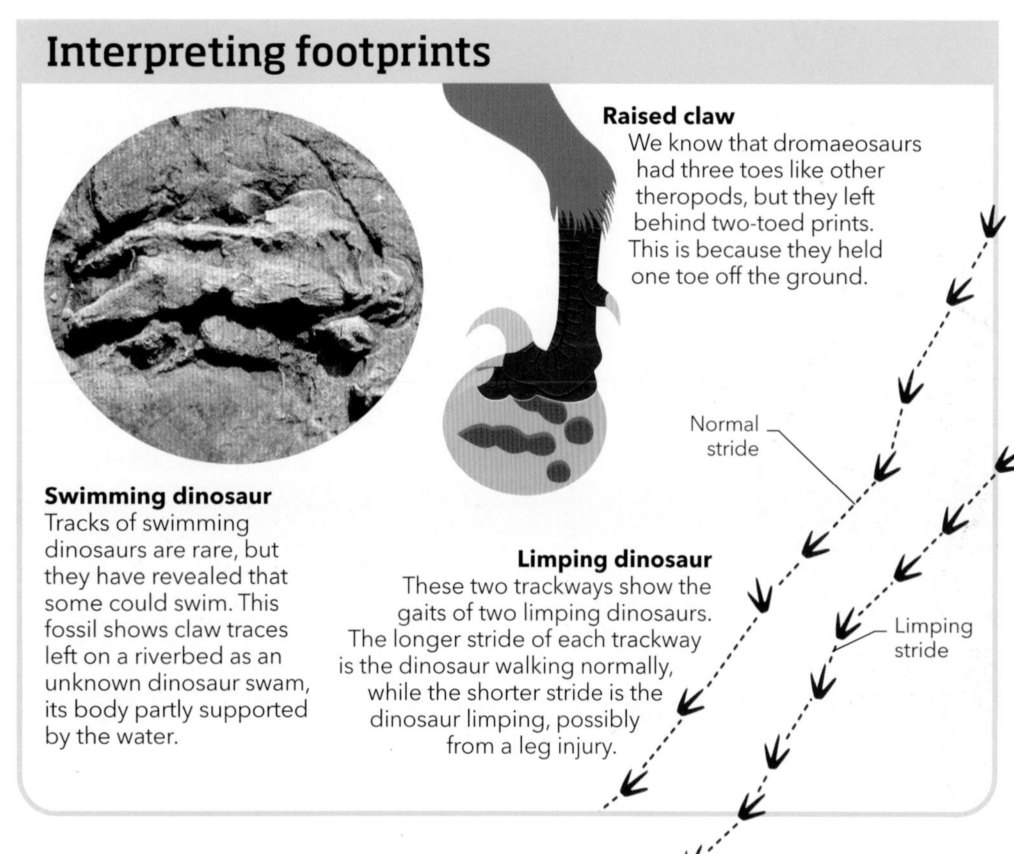

Raised claw
We know that dromaeosaurs had three toes like other theropods, but they left behind two-toed prints. This is because they held one toe off the ground.

Swimming dinosaur
Tracks of swimming dinosaurs are rare, but they have revealed that some could swim. This fossil shows claw traces left on a riverbed as an unknown dinosaur swam, its body partly supported by the water.

Limping dinosaur
These two trackways show the gaits of two limping dinosaurs. The longer stride of each trackway is the dinosaur walking normally, while the shorter stride is the dinosaur limping, possibly from a leg injury.

Thyreophorans

These tough dinosaurs, whose name means "shield bearers," are famous for their incredible body armor. Almost all thyreophorans, including ankylosaurs and stegosaurs, were slow-moving plant-eaters who walked on four legs. They were widespread from the Early Jurassic until the mass extinction that ended the dinosaur age.

The plates of *Stegosaurus* could grow to over 19.5 in (50 cm) long.

Triangular plates lined the neck, back, and tail of *Stegosaurus*.

Feasting on plants

Thyreophorans were plant-eaters. Stegosaurs used a relatively strong bite to tackle a range of plants, while some ankylosaurs were unfussy feeders of low-lying vegetation.

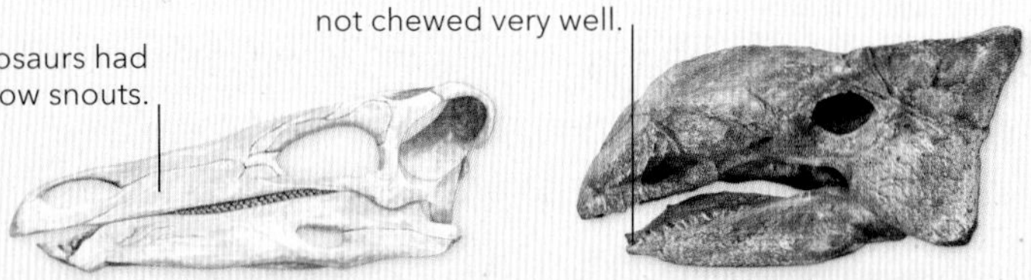

Stegosaurs had narrow snouts.

Small teeth meant food was not chewed very well.

Stegosaurus

Ankylosaurus

How to fight like a thyreophoran

01. If you sense a predator nearby, keep very still and hope your camouflage hides you.

02. If that does not work and you find yourself face to face with a predatory theropod, look big and scary and rattle your spine plates. You are not going to outrun your enemy!

Meet the family

First thyreophorans
The earliest thyreophorans were smaller in size and had less elaborate armor than their later relatives.

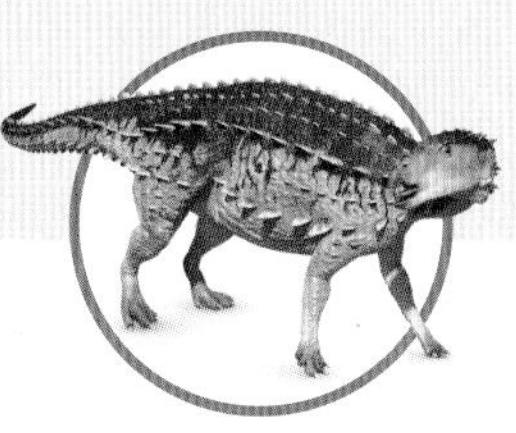

Ankylosaurs
Divided into two main groups—nodosaurids and ankylosaurids—these tanklike herbivores could weigh up to 6.6 tons (6 metric tons).

Stegosaurs
The plated and spiked stegosaurs mostly thrived during the Late Jurassic in various parts of the world.

In numbers

3 ft
(1 m) The length of the tail spike of a *Stegosaurus*

26 ft
(8 m) The maximum length of an *Ankylosaurus*

22 in
(57 cm) The width of an *Anodontosaurus* tail club

I don't believe it!

Spicomellus, an ankylosaur from Morocco, had spikes coming out of its ribs.

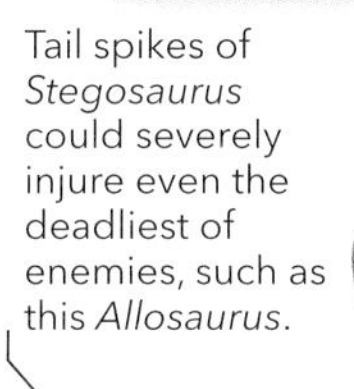

Tail spikes of *Stegosaurus* could severely injure even the deadliest of enemies, such as this *Allosaurus*.

Bones called osteoderms were embedded in the skin of thyreophorans.

Some of the bony osteoderms evolved into weapons, such as tail clubs.

Euoplocephalus

Battle ready

The body armor of thyreophorans provided defense against predators. However, the tail weapons of some stegosaurs and ankylosaurs could be used in attack, against either predators or rivals of their own kind. Certain ankylosaurs even had armored eyelids.

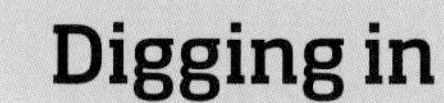

03. If your enemy is still there, spin quickly around and slash with your flexible tail. The spikes on it could land a deadly blow.

Digging in

Ankylosaurs had bulky upper arm bones with massive muscle attachments, which suggest they were good diggers. They may have dug to find food or water or for protection.

Stegosaurs and ankylosaurs

These dinosaurs made up for their lack of speed by evolving armor and weapons on their bodies. These might have been used in fights against predators, and in some cases, members of their own kind. Some used their spikes for display, too.

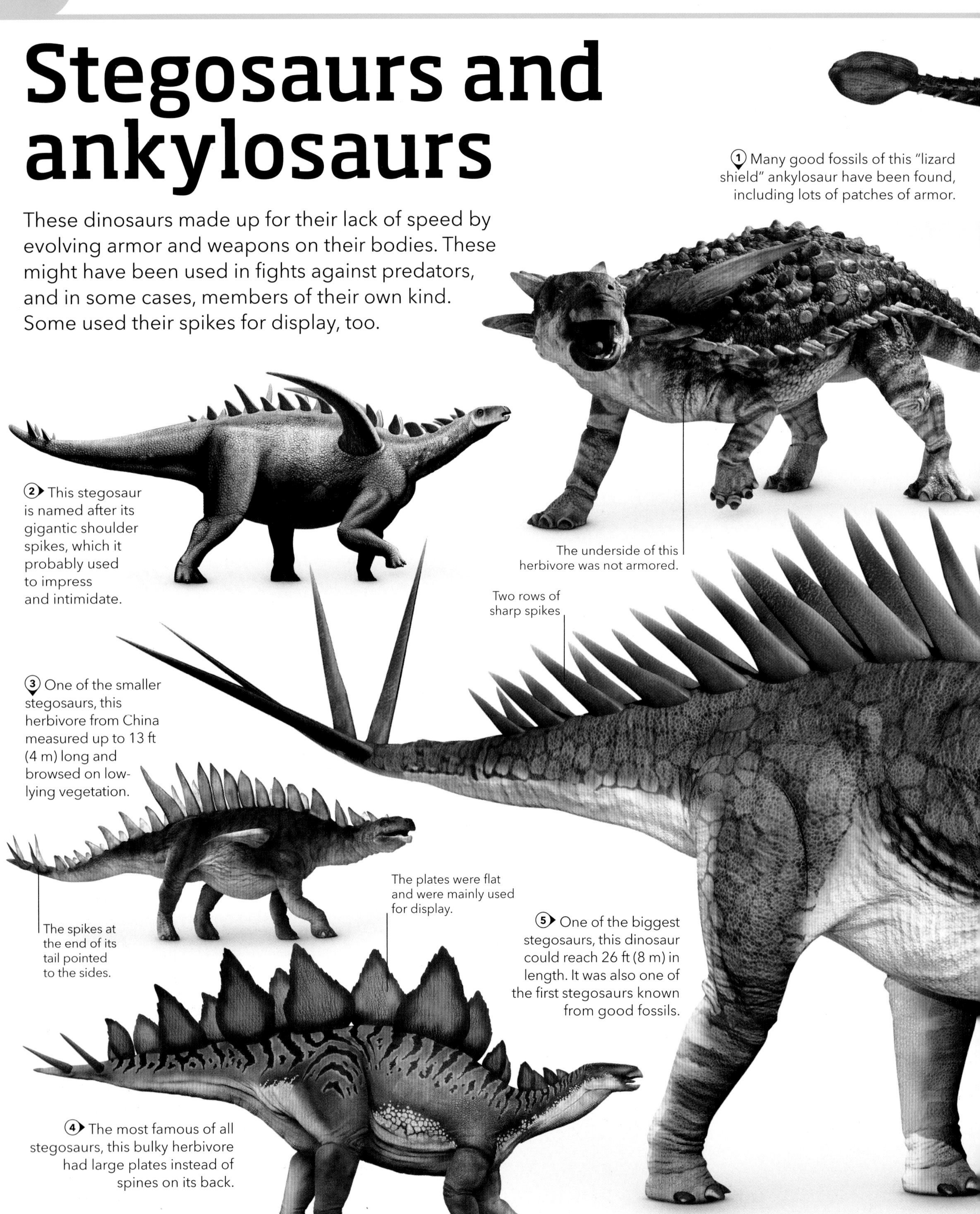

6 This North American dinosaur is famous for its massive, bone-shattering club. It was one of the biggest ankylosaurs.

Rings of bony plates protected the neck.

This shoulder spine was lighter than the others, perhaps making it stand out.

Bony spikes on its body deterred predators.

7 This dinosaur's spikes were some of the earliest stegosaur fossils ever found. It was named after the Chinese river where they were discovered.

At only 6.5 ft (2 m) long fully grown, it was very small for an ankylosaur.

8 This ankylosaur is known from a beautifully preserved specimen found at a mine in Canada. Scientists have even been able to reconstruct its coloration.

9 First described in 2021, this ankylosaur had bladelike plates jutting out of its very unusual tail.

10 Found in China and named after the river Tuo, this relatively large species is one of the best-known stegosaurs from Asia.

TEST YOURSELF

STARTER

Stegosaurus
Ankylosaurus
Sauropelta
Gigantspinosaurus

CHALLENGER

Huayangosaurus
Borealopelta
Stegouros

GENIUS!

Dacentrurus
Chialingosaurus
Tuojiangosaurus

ANSWERS: 1. *Sauropelta* 2. *Gigantspinosaurus* 3. *Huayangosaurus* 4. *Stegosaurus* 5. *Dacentrurus* 6. *Ankylosaurus* 7. *Chialingosaurus* 8. *Borealopelta* 9. *Stegouros* 10. *Tuojiangosaurus*

1 *Stegosaurus* had a stronger bite than other dinosaurs with similar-shaped skulls. What did this bite force allow it to do?

A. Eat a wider range of plants

B. Make louder noises

C. Defend against predators

D. Grind its teeth for display

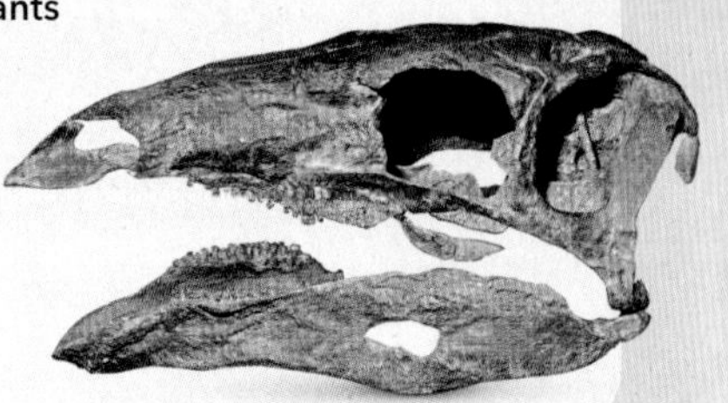

2 A potential prey for carnivorous dinosaurs, why was *Stegosaurus* never hunted by *Tyrannosaurus rex*?

A. It was too big for *Tyrannosaurus rex* to hunt.

B. The two species were not found on the same continent.

C. *Tyrannosaurus rex* was wary of the tail spike of *Stegosaurus*.

D. *Stegosaurus* went extinct before *Tyrannosaurus rex* lived.

3 Fossils believed to belong to *Stegosaurus* have been found in North America and in Portugal in Europe. What does this indicate?

A. It was an expert swimmer.

B. The eggs of this dinosaur floated across the ocean.

C. North America and Europe were once joined by a land bridge.

D. The same species evolved in two different locations.

4 On average, how long were *Stegosaurus*'s tail spikes?

A. 3 ft (1 m)

B. 16 ft (5 m)

C. 33 ft (10 m)

D. 49 ft (15 m)

5 What did *Stegosaurus* use to defend itself against carnivorous dinosaurs?

A. Its horns

B. Its claws

C. Loud roars

D. Spikes at the end of its muscular tail

6 *Stegosaurus* was one of the largest members of the stegosaur family. How much did an adult *Stegosaurus* weigh?

A. 2.7 tons (2.4 metric tons) or as much as a white rhinoceros

B. 4.4 tons (4 metric tons) or as much as an Asian elephants

C. 6.6 tons (6 metric tons) or as much as an African bush elephant

D. 30 tons (27 metric tons) or as much as a gray whale

Stegosaurus

The spiked and plated *Stegosaurus* is one of the largest and best-studied of the stegosaurs. Although slow, this large herbivore had a potentially lethal weapon, which helped it fend off the many big predators. How well do you know this spiky dinosaur?

Its plates may have helped *Stegosaurus* seem bigger and more intimidating to dinosaurs who were looking for a fight.

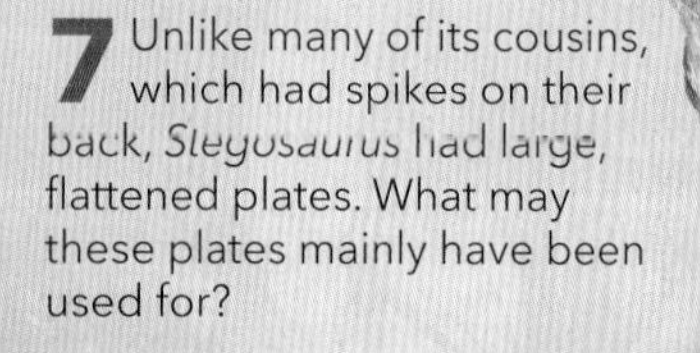

7 Unlike many of its cousins, which had spikes on their back, *Stegosaurus* had large, flattened plates. What may these plates mainly have been used for?

A. Rattling to scare off enemies

B. Radiating heat away from the body

C. Looking impressive

D. Detaching and throwing at enemies

8 How many plates did *Stegosaurus* have on its back?

A. 9 **B.** 11

C. 17 **D.** 23

9 What were the plates on the back of *Stegosaurus* attached to?

A. Its spine **B.** Its ribcage

C. Its skin **D.** Its shoulder blade

10 Fossils of a carnivorous dinosaur have been found with injury holes in its bones, probably made by a *Stegosaurus*'s tail spikes. Which dinosaur was it?

A. *Allosaurus*

B. *Carnotaurus*

C. *Giganotosaurus*

D. *Utahraptor*

ANSWERS: 1-A, 2-D, 3-C, 4-A, 5-D, 6-C, 7-C, 8-C, 9-C, 10-A

1 *Ankylosaurus* had a complex nose with mazelike inner workings, but its sense of smell was poor. Other than breathing, what was its main role?

A. Searching for food
B. Sniffing out predators
C. Controlling body temperature
D. Reducing the weight of its head

2 Despite being almost twice the length of an Indian rhinoceros, *Ankylosaurus* had a similar-sized head. How long was its head?

A. 14 in (36 cm)
B. 20 in (50 cm)
C. 25 in (66 cm)
D. 3 ft (1 m)

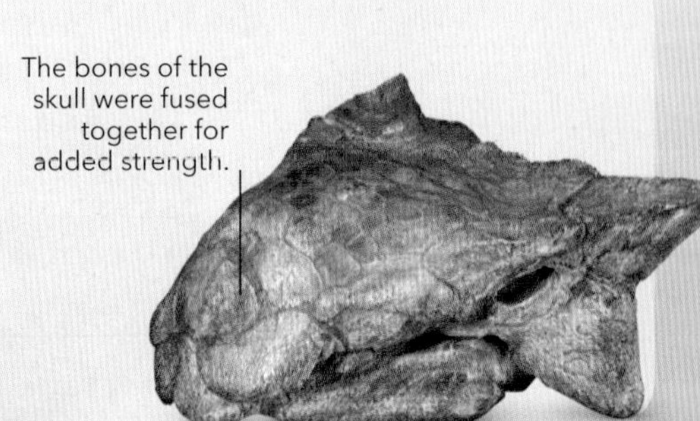
The bones of the skull were fused together for added strength.

3 *Ankylosaurus* had teeth that could chew small fruits but could not grind down hard plants. What did the shape of the teeth resemble?

A. Spikes
B. Cones
C. Leaves
D. Plant bulb

4 *Ankylosaurus* walked on four feet. How many toes did it have on each of its two front feet?

A. Two
B. Three
C. Four
D. Five

5 The entire body of *Ankylosaurus* was protected by bony armor except for one part. Which part of it was unprotected?

A. Eyelids
B. Base of tail
C. Forelimb
D. Belly

ANSWERS: 1-C, 2-C, 3-C, 4-D, 5-D, 6-C, 7-D, 8-A

Ankylosaurus

Even a predator as deadly as *Tyrannosaurus* would have thought twice about attacking massive *Ankylosaurus*, with its impressive body armor and bone-crushing clubbed tail. However, these body defenses probably needed a lot of energy, so it spent most of its time browsing low-growing plants. How well do you know this armored dinosaur?

6 *Ankylosaurus* fossils have been found on only one continent. It shared this habitat with *Tyrannosaurus rex*. On which continent did they both live?

A. Asia

B. Europe

C. North America

D. Australia

The club may have been used against predators and rivals of its own species.

Small horns projected from the back of the head.

7 Approximately how much was the heaviest *Ankylosaurus* believed to have weighed?

A. 1.6 tons (1.5 metric tons) or as much as a hippopotamus

B. 2.7 tons (2.4 metric tons) or as much as a white rhinoceros

C. 4.4 tons (4 metric tons) or as much as an Asian elephant

D. 6.6 tons (6 metric tons) or as much as an African bush elephant

8 What was *Ankylosaurus*'s tail club made of?

A. The same bony plates as its armor

B. Solid bone

C. Solid muscle

D. Tough cartilage

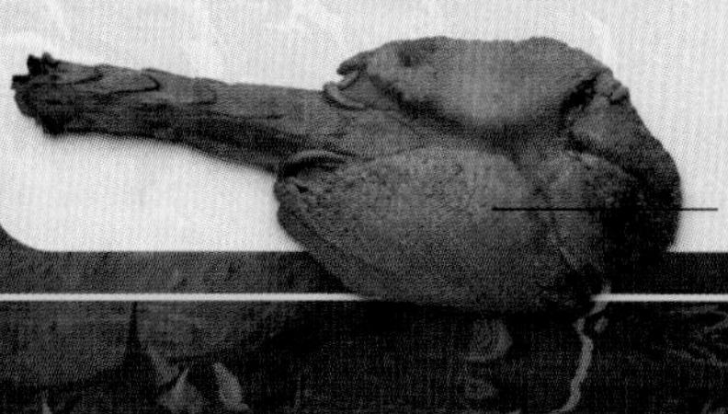

The tail club was powerful enough to shatter bones with one blow.

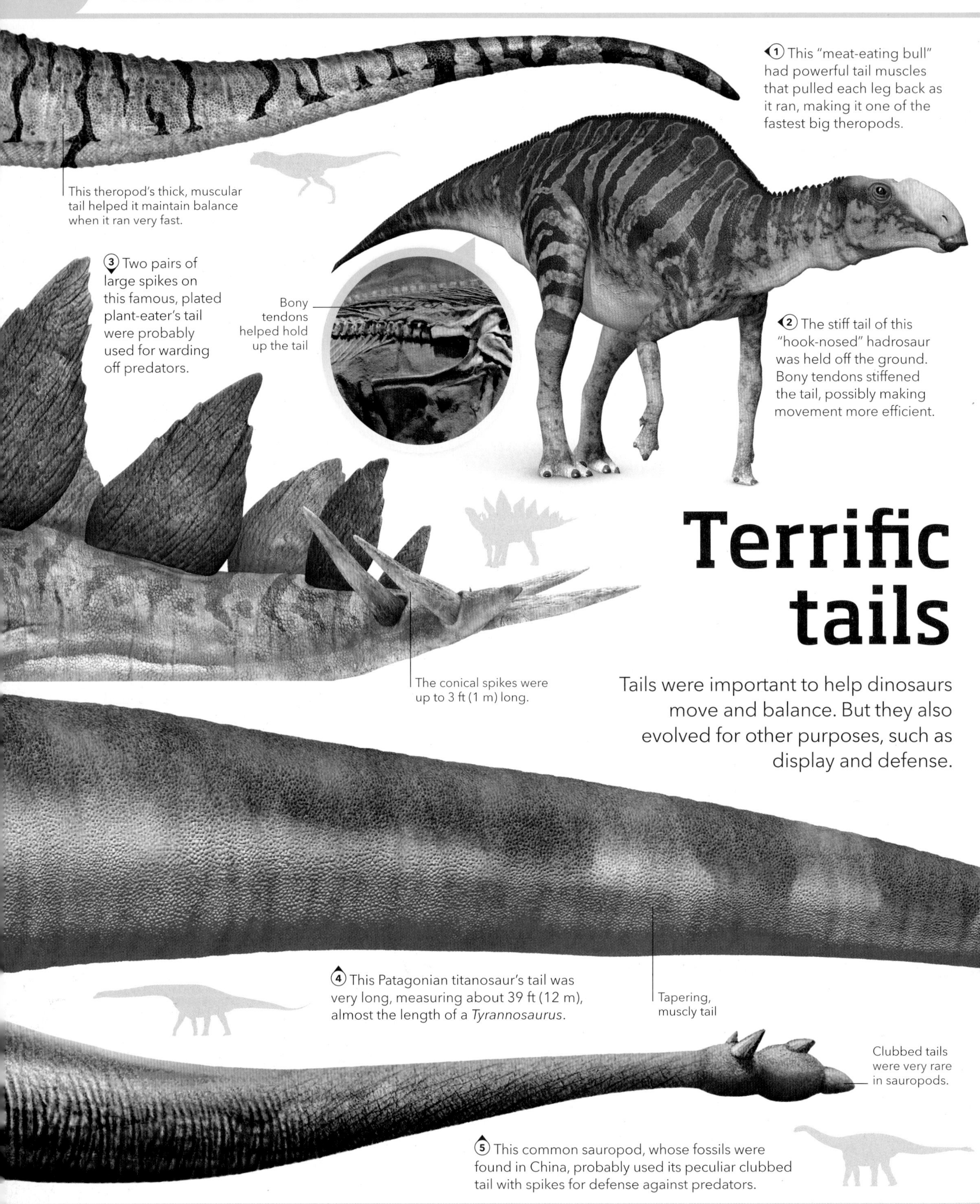

Terrific tails

Tails were important to help dinosaurs move and balance. But they also evolved for other purposes, such as display and defense.

ANSWERS: 1. *Carnotaurus* 2. *Gryposaurus* 3. *Stegosaurus* 4. *Patagotitan* 5. *Shunosaurus* 6. *Spinosaurus* 7. *Sinosauropteryx* 8. *Euoplocephalus* 9. *Stegouros* 10. *Caudipteryx* 11. *Kentrosaurus*

6 This sail-backed theropod had an unusually deep tail, which it probably used for display.

Long, deep tail

The tail was made up of 64 bones—one of the highest numbers for any theropod.

7 The traces of color found in the fossils of this fuzzy little theropod shows it had a banded tail.

The club was used for fighting other species, as well as its own kind.

8 The bulky club at the end of this ankylosaur's tail needed a lot of support to keep it off the ground.

10 This little theropod had a short, stiff tail tipped with a distinctive fan of feathers.

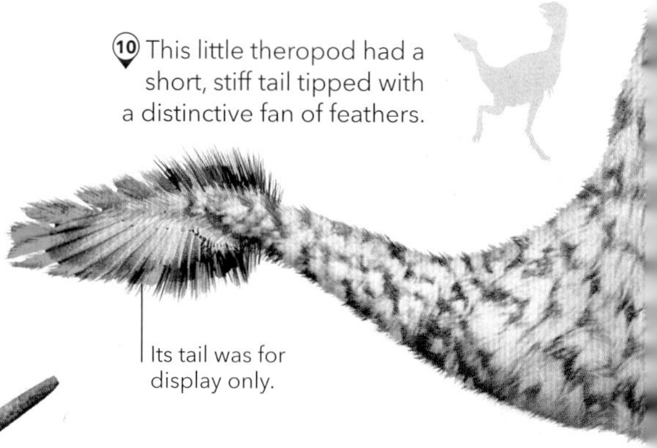

The tail had seven pairs of flattened osteoderms (bony plates).

Its tail was for display only.

9 The tail of this ankylosaur has been compared to a *macuahuitl*, a wooden Aztec war club with obsidian blades.

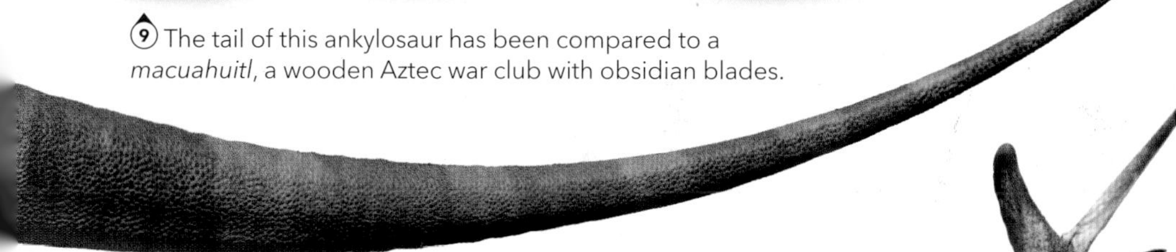

11 The long, spearlike spikes of this stegosaur found in Africa were used to slash at attackers, inflicting deep cuts.

TEST YOURSELF

STARTER	CHALLENGER	GENIUS!
Patagotitan	***Carnotaurus***	***Stegouros***
Spinosaurus	***Kentrosaurus***	***Sinosauropteryx***
Stegosaurus	***Shunosaurus***	***Caudipteryx***
	Euoplocephalus	***Gryposaurus***

Marginocephalians

The group of dinosaurs known as marginocephalians had extravagant features on their heads, including spikes, horns, frills, and domed skulls. Many used their prominent skulls for display, and some even fought with them. There are two major groups of marginocephalians: the horned and frilled ceratopsians and the dome-headed pachycephalosaurs.

How to defend your territory

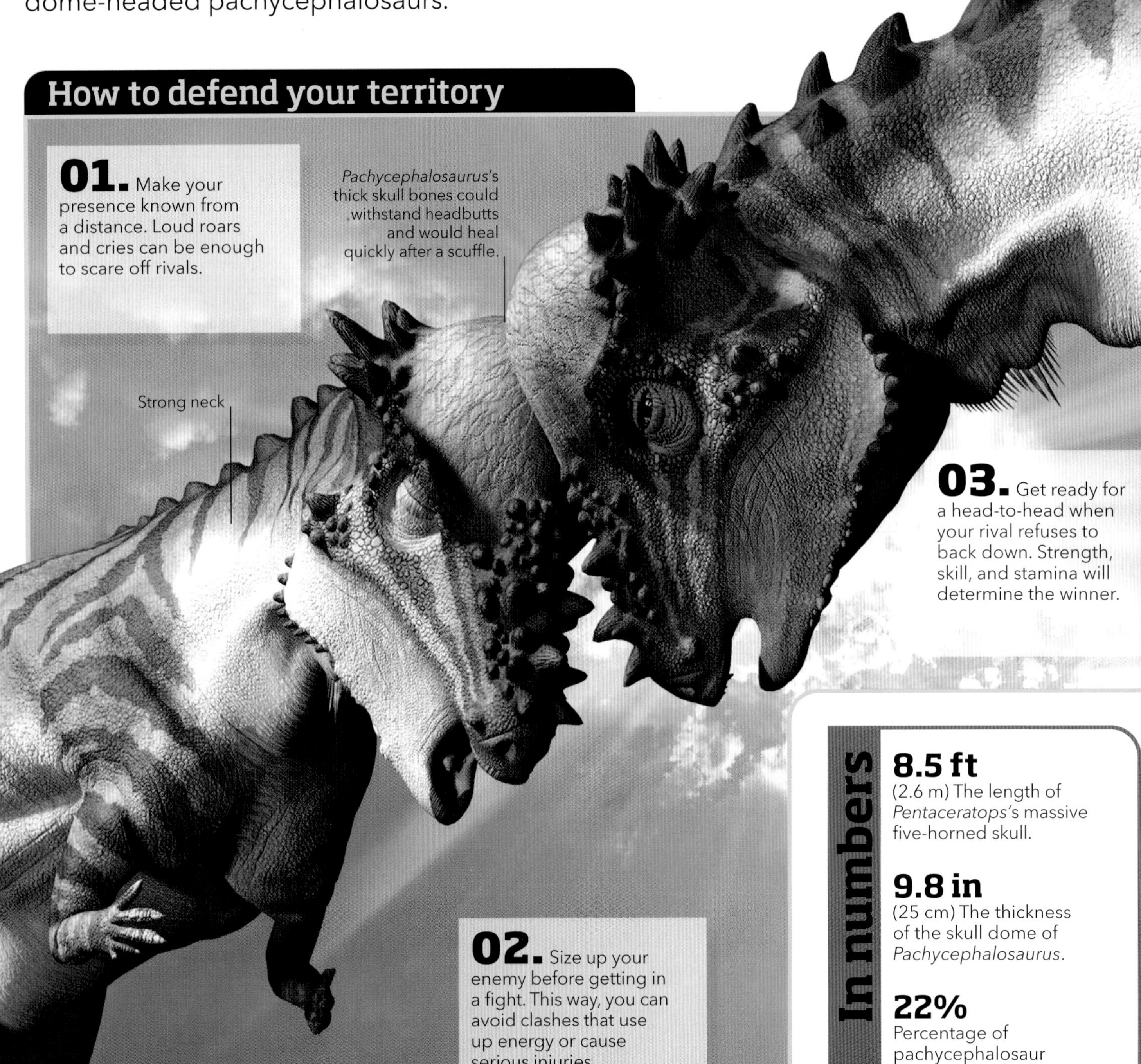

01. Make your presence known from a distance. Loud roars and cries can be enough to scare off rivals.

02. Size up your enemy before getting in a fight. This way, you can avoid clashes that use up energy or cause serious injuries.

03. Get ready for a head-to-head when your rival refuses to back down. Strength, skill, and stamina will determine the winner.

In numbers

8.5 ft
(2.6 m) The length of *Pentaceratops*'s massive five-horned skull.

9.8 in
(25 cm) The thickness of the skull dome of *Pachycephalosaurus*.

22%
Percentage of pachycephalosaur domes with signs of infection from battle wounds.

I don't believe it!

The first few neck bones in big, horned ceratopsids were fused to support their heavy heads.

Combat ready

The prominent skull features, such as domes and horns, found in various marginocephalians may have evolved to impress and fight members of their own species. These may have also played some role in defense.

Triceratops frills often show healed injuries.

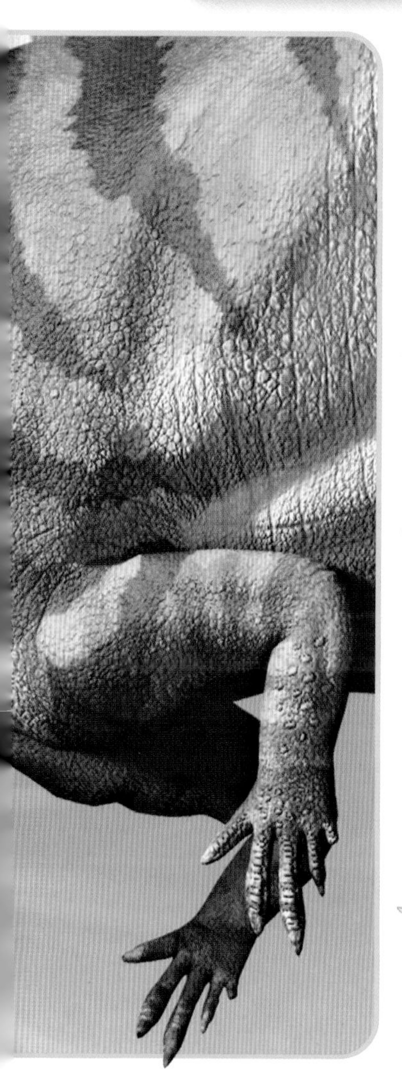

Getting around

Pachycephalosaurs and ceratopsians looked quite different from one another and moved in different ways, too. Pachycephalosaurs were bipedal, meaning they walked on two legs. Early ceratopsians were also bipedal, but later some evolved and became bulky quadrupeds, meaning they walked on four legs.

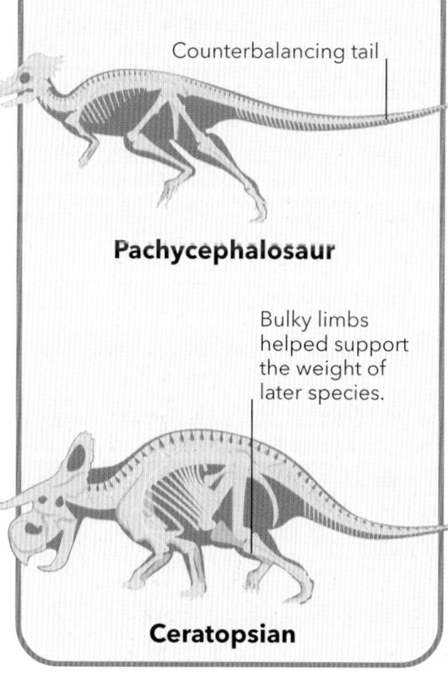

Meet the family

Pachycephalosaurs
Notable for their domed heads, these odd dinosaurs are known from only a few fossils.

Ceratopsians
The dinosaurs in this group had a parrotlike beak that was supported by a special bone at the tip of its upper jaw.

Chaoyangsaurids
Among some of the earliest ceratopsians, these dinosaurs had small skulls and low frills.

Leptoceratopsids
These small ceratopsians walked on four legs and had bulky lower jaws with large teeth.

Ceratopsids
The most diverse subgroup of ceratopsians, these horned herbivores could grow as big as elephants.

Feeder jaws

While some small ceratopsians preferred soft plants, ceratopsids went on to evolve complex teeth to chew tougher plants. These were arranged in sets known as batteries. The diet of pachycephalosaurs is less certain, but they may have eaten meat as well as plants.

Weak jaws suggest some early ceratopsians ate soft plants.

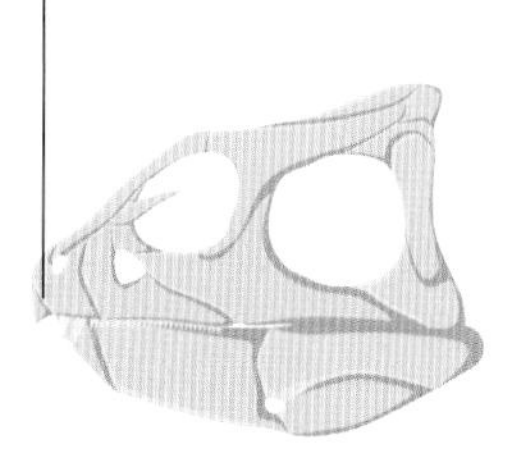

This leptoceratopsid had efficient jaws capable of chewing a wide range of plants.

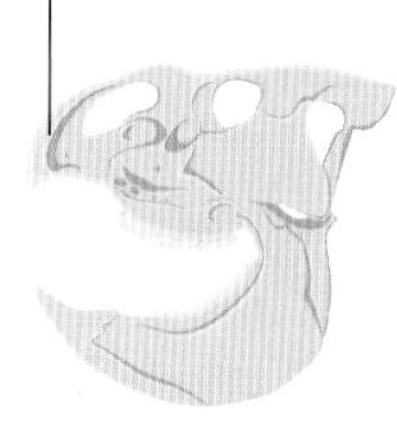

A mix of broad, leaf-shaped teeth and sharp, bladelike teeth suggest pachycephalosaurs may have been omnivores.

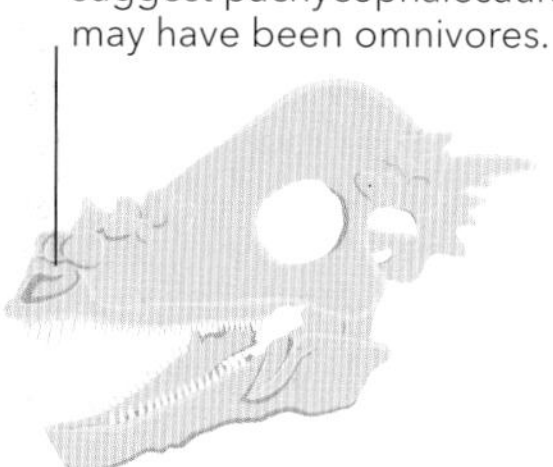

Triceratops

Triceratops was spectacularly built, like a massive rhinoceros, and had one of the largest skulls of any land animal. While the neck frill was likely for defense and display, its three horns may have helped in fighting off predators or rivals. Challenge yourself to learn more!

1 Scars have been found on the frills of several *Triceratops* individuals. What was the cause of these injuries?

A. Horn marks made by fighting rivals

B. Falling off cliffs

C. Walking into trees

D. Parasite burrows

2 How heavy could a *Triceratops* get?

A. 1.6 tons (1.5 metric tons) or as much as a hippopotamus

B. 2.7 tons (2.4 metric tons) or as much as a white rhinoceros

C. 4.4 tons (4 metric tons) or as much as an Asian elephant

D. 7.7 tons (7 metric tons) or more than an African elephant

3 *Triceratops* used the teeth at the back of its jaw, as well as its beak, to tear off and chew the low-growing plants it fed off. How many teeth did *Triceratops* have on average?

A. 50

B. 100

C. 800

D. 2,000

4 The skull of a full-grown *Triceratops* is 8 ft (2.5 m) long. But how small is the skull of the youngest known *Triceratops*?

A. 6 in (15 cm)

B. 7 in (22 cm)

C. 15 in (38 cm)

D. 20 in (38 cm)

5 *Triceratops* bones have been found bearing the marks of injuries caused by the teeth of a carnivorous dinosaur. Which dinosaur caused the injuries?

A. *Tyrannosaurus rex*

B. *Allosaurus*

C. *Carnotaurus*

D. *Spinosaurus*

6 *Triceratops* bones were first found in 1887. However, the horns of *Triceratops* were first mistaken for those of a different animal. Which animal was that?

A. Elephant

B. Bison

C. Deer

D. Goat

7 *Triceratops*'s sharp-tipped horns could reach impressive lengths. How long are the longest estimated *Triceratops* horns?

A. 24 in (60 cm)

B. 39 in (100 cm)

C. 45 in (115 cm)

D. 51 in (130 cm)

ANSWERS: 1-A, 2-D, 3-C, 4-C, 5-A, 6-B, 7-C

Super skulls

One of the most recognizable dinosaur groups, marginocephalians evolved a range of impressive skull shapes. They used their horns, frills, and domes to impress mates and intimidate rivals.

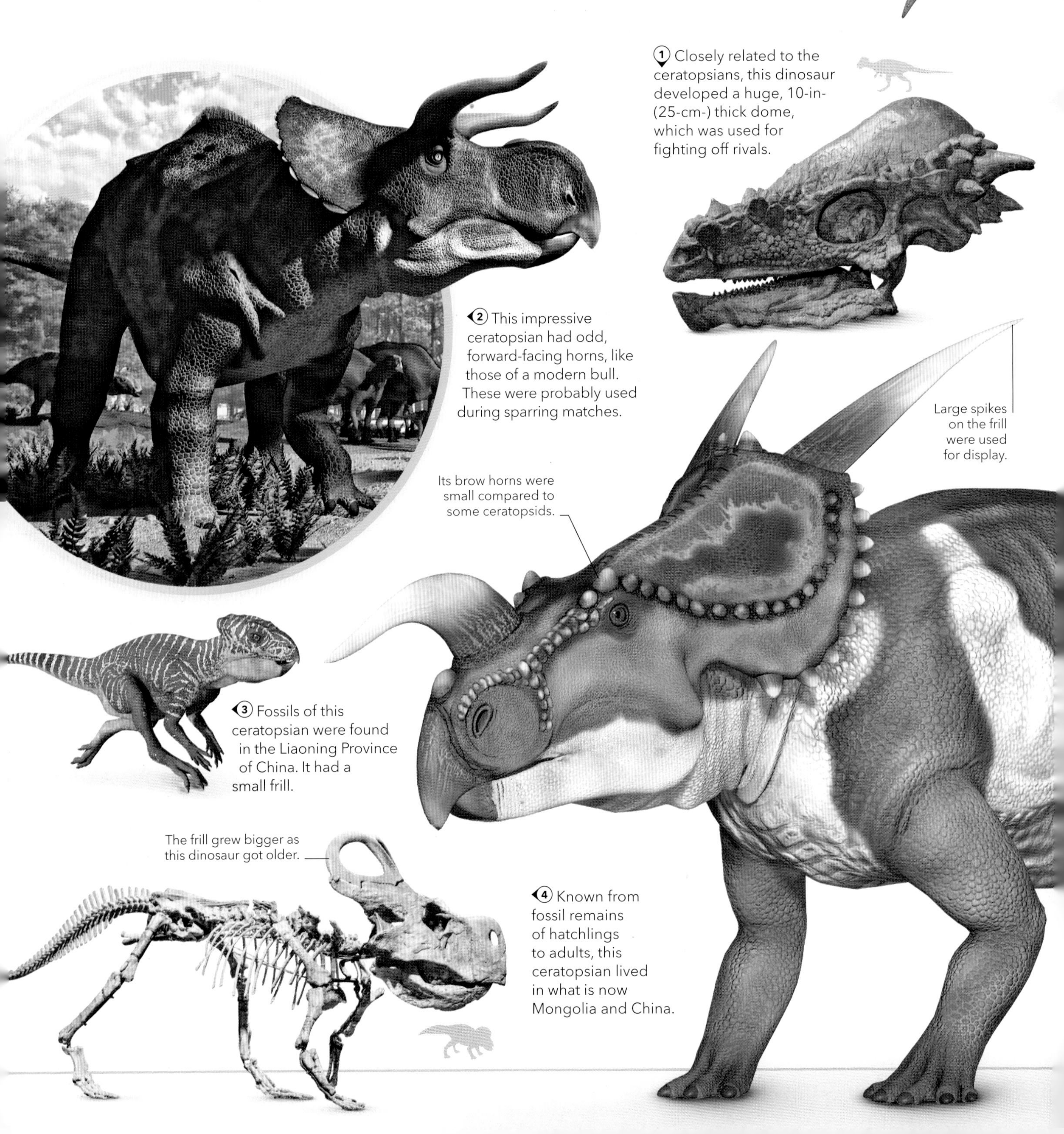

1 Closely related to the ceratopsians, this dinosaur developed a huge, 10-in- (25-cm-) thick dome, which was used for fighting off rivals.

2 This impressive ceratopsian had odd, forward-facing horns, like those of a modern bull. These were probably used during sparring matches.

3 Fossils of this ceratopsian were found in the Liaoning Province of China. It had a small frill.

4 Known from fossil remains of hatchlings to adults, this ceratopsian lived in what is now Mongolia and China.

5 This dinosaur, named after the place where it was found, had a deep lower jaw, suggesting a strong bite.

6 Discovered in Alberta, Canada, this ceratopsid is known from a single well-preserved skull.

7 Discovered in South Korea, only the back half of this little ceratopsian has been found. It had a deep tail, but we do not yet know how it was used.

8 This ceratopsian was named after the tall but lightweight "devil horns" on its frill.

9 This Cretaceous dinosaur from North America was the size of a rhino and had an unusual, forward-curving horn on the tip of its skull.

10 Known from some superbly preserved fossils that include soft tissues, this little ceratopsian had a parrotlike face, from which it gets its name.

TEST YOURSELF

STARTER

Pachycephalosaurus
Protoceratops
Psittacosaurus

CHALLENGER

Albertaceratops
Diabloceratops
Nasutoceratops

GENIUS!

Liaoceratops
Koreaceratops
Einiosaurus
Udanoceratops

ANSWERS: 1. *Pachycephalosaurus* 2. *Nasutoceratops* 3. *Liaoceratops* 4. *Protoceratops* 5. *Udanoceratops* 6. *Albertaceratops* 7. *Koreaceratops* 8. *Diabloceratops* 9. *Einiosaurus* 10. *Psittacosaurus*

Crests, frills, and horns

Many dinosaurs evolved showy structures on their skulls, mostly for impressive mating displays or to scare off competitors. However, some of these unusual facial features could have been used to make sounds, and some were also used as weapons during fights!

1 The bull-like horns of this frilled ceratopsian may have helped shove and wrestle opponents during fights.

2 This "thick-nosed" ceratopsian had a large bump on its snout, which grew as the dinosaur got older.

Horns lined the frill.

3 Named for the double crests on its snout, this Early Jurassic predator had one of the most unusual theropod skulls.

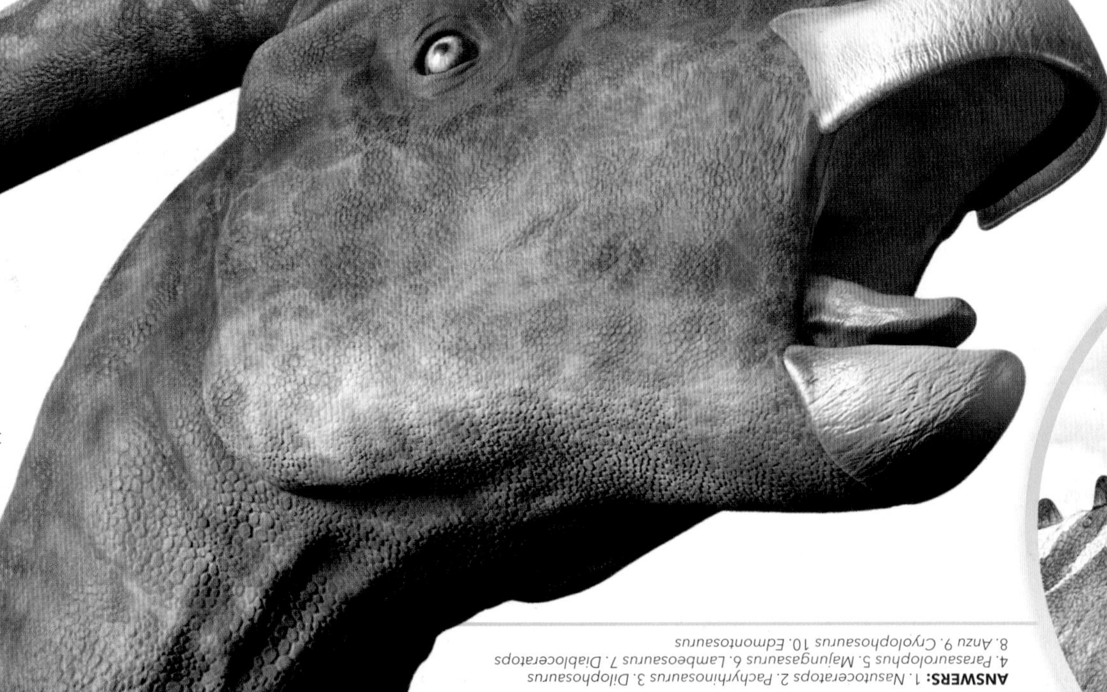

4 This dinosaur's crest grew early in its life, giving it time to grow as long as its head—the largest crest of any ornithopod.

ANSWERS: 1. *Nasutoceratops* 2. *Pachyrhinosaurus* 3. *Dilophosaurus* 4. *Parasaurolophus* 5. *Majungasaurus* 6. *Lambeosaurus* 7. *Diabloceratops* 8. *Anzu* 9. *Cryolophosaurus* 10. *Edmontosaurus*

⑤ This Madagascan predator had a single hollow horn low on its head, probably used for display.

⑥ The elegant crest of this hadrosaur may have been used for show, as well as making sounds to communicate with others of its kind.

⑦ This ceratopsian's heavy, "devilish" horns were probably mainly for show. Two large holes in the bony frill helped lighten the weight.

⑧ This theropod had a head crest, unlike most of its group, which had feathers for display. It is named after a birdlike ancient demon.

⑨ The strange, flared shape of its bony crest made this Antarctic predator distinct from other theropods.

⑩ A small, fleshy crest sat on the head of this bulky hadrosaur. The crest was similar to the wattles of some modern birds.

TEST YOURSELF

STARTER	CHALLENGER	GENIUS!
Dilophosaurus	***Nasutoceratops***	***Pachyrhinosaurus***
Parasaurolophus	***Lambeosaurus***	***Majungasaurus***
Cryolophosaurus	***Diabloceratops***	***Anzu***
	Edmontosaurus	

Psittacosaurus

This little ceratopsian has been studied from hundreds of well-preserved fossils, including some specimens where soft tissues have been found preserved. It used its birdlike beak to feed on plants. While it is not clear how many species of *Psittacosaurus* existed, there are a lot of fun facts about this dinosaur to challenge your brain!

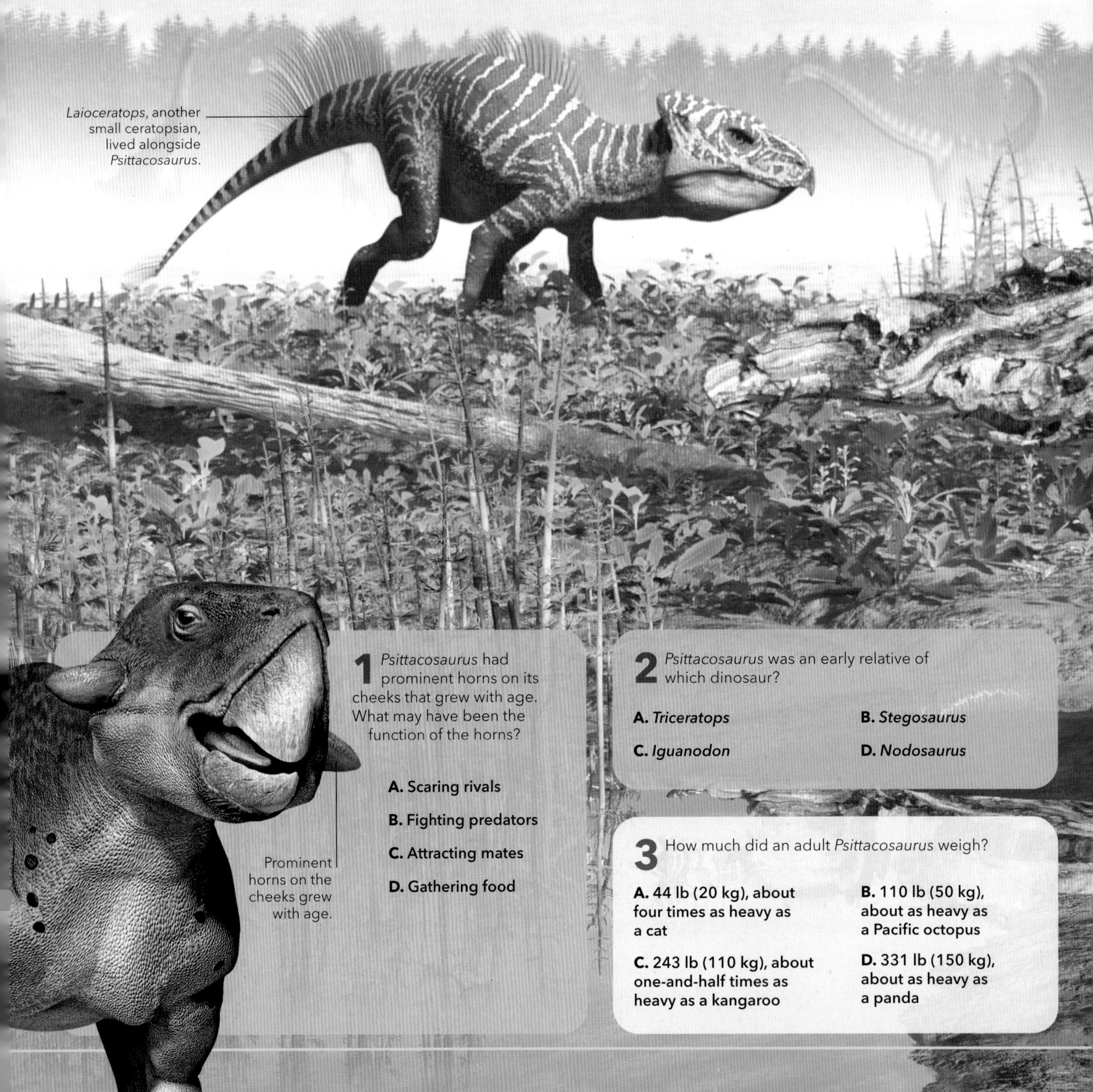

Laioceratops, another small ceratopsian, lived alongside *Psittacosaurus*.

Prominent horns on the cheeks grew with age.

1 *Psittacosaurus* had prominent horns on its cheeks that grew with age. What may have been the function of the horns?

A. Scaring rivals

B. Fighting predators

C. Attracting mates

D. Gathering food

2 *Psittacosaurus* was an early relative of which dinosaur?

A. *Triceratops*

B. *Stegosaurus*

C. *Iguanodon*

D. *Nodosaurus*

3 How much did an adult *Psittacosaurus* weigh?

A. 44 lb (20 kg), about four times as heavy as a cat

B. 110 lb (50 kg), about as heavy as a Pacific octopus

C. 243 lb (110 kg), about one-and-half times as heavy as a kangaroo

D. 331 lb (150 kg), about as heavy as a panda

4 What did *Psittacosaurus* mostly eat?

A. Small dinosaurs **B.** Fish

C. Early mammals **D.** Plants and seeds

5 *Psittacosaurus* gets its name from its beak, which is similar to that of a type of modern bird. Which bird is it?

A. Hawk **B.** Owl

C. Woodpecker **D.** Parrot

6 How many fingers did *Psittacosaurus* have on each hand?

A. 1 **B.** 2

C. 3 **D.** 4

7 *Psittacosaurus* is the first known dinosaur fossil to show a particular physical feature. What is that feature?

A. Horns **B.** Eyelids

C. Belly button **D.** Clawed fingers

8 How long were *Psittacosaurus* hatchlings?

A. 9 in (23 cm) **B.** 31 in (80 cm)

C. 3 ft (1 m) **D.** 16 ft (5 m)

ANSWERS: 1-C, 2-A, 3-A, 4-D, 5-D, 6-D, 7-C, 8-A

Ornithopods

With their distinctive beaks, ornithopods are easy to identify. They were plant-eaters and thrived on every continent. These dinosaurs walked on two feet at first, but later species began to support their weight on all fours. Later ornithopods evolved highly specialized teeth as well as beaks. Some of them had showy crests, which were probably for display.

Polar young
Some ornithopods adapted to live near the poles. The polar regions were not as cold as they are today, but winters were still chilly.

Meet the family

Early ornithopods
Not much is known about the earliest ornithopods, but they were probably small and agile.

Elasmarians
These small to midsized ornithopods, found in the Southern Hemisphere, all walked on two feet and were fast runners.

Iguanodontians
This large, diverse ornithopod group was widespread and includes *Iguanodon*, one of the best-known dinosaurs.

Rhabdodontomorphs
Evolving late in the dinosaur age, these were a subgroup of iguanodontians. One species had a showy crest.

Hadrosaurids
Hadrosaurids had tough, grinding teeth and often sported elaborate head crests.

How to survive in a herd

Fossil evidence, such as trackways that show the footprints of many dinosaurs walking together, suggests that many ornithopods traveled in groups. This *Edmontosaurus* herd includes adults and young, sticking together for safety.

01. Gather together as a large group—the bigger the group, the more eyes there will be to look out for predators and the fewer the chances of being attacked.

I don't believe it!
Some hadrosaurs had more than 1,000 teeth.

Toothy tale

The teeth of early ornithopods were small and limited in number. But later hadrosaurids evolved hundreds of small teeth, packed into columns to grind plants down. They chewed conifer needles, twigs, and bark with the many teeth that lined their jaws.

***Edmontosaurus* jaw bone and teeth**

Crested calls

One group of ornithopods–the hadrosaurids–evolved a variety of fancy head crests. Most were probably used for display–to impress and attract a mate. However, some species used the hollow crests to make their cries louder.

Edmontosaurus had a small, fleshy crest like a cockerel's comb that was used to attract mates.

Parasaurolophus had a 3-ft- (1-m-) long hollow crest and could make sounds with it.

Corythosaurus made low sounds with its hollow crest.

In numbers

17.6 tons
(16 metric tons)
The weight of *Shantungosaurus*, the largest-known ornithopod

6.5 ft
(2 m) The length of a *Parasaurolophus*'s skull

40%
Percentage of all known ornithopod species that are hadrosaurids

02. Less time looking out for danger means more time eating, helping you get bigger quicker. This gives young a better chance of survival.

03. Watch out for sick herd members! One disadvantage of group living is disease, as parasites can quickly spread from one body to another.

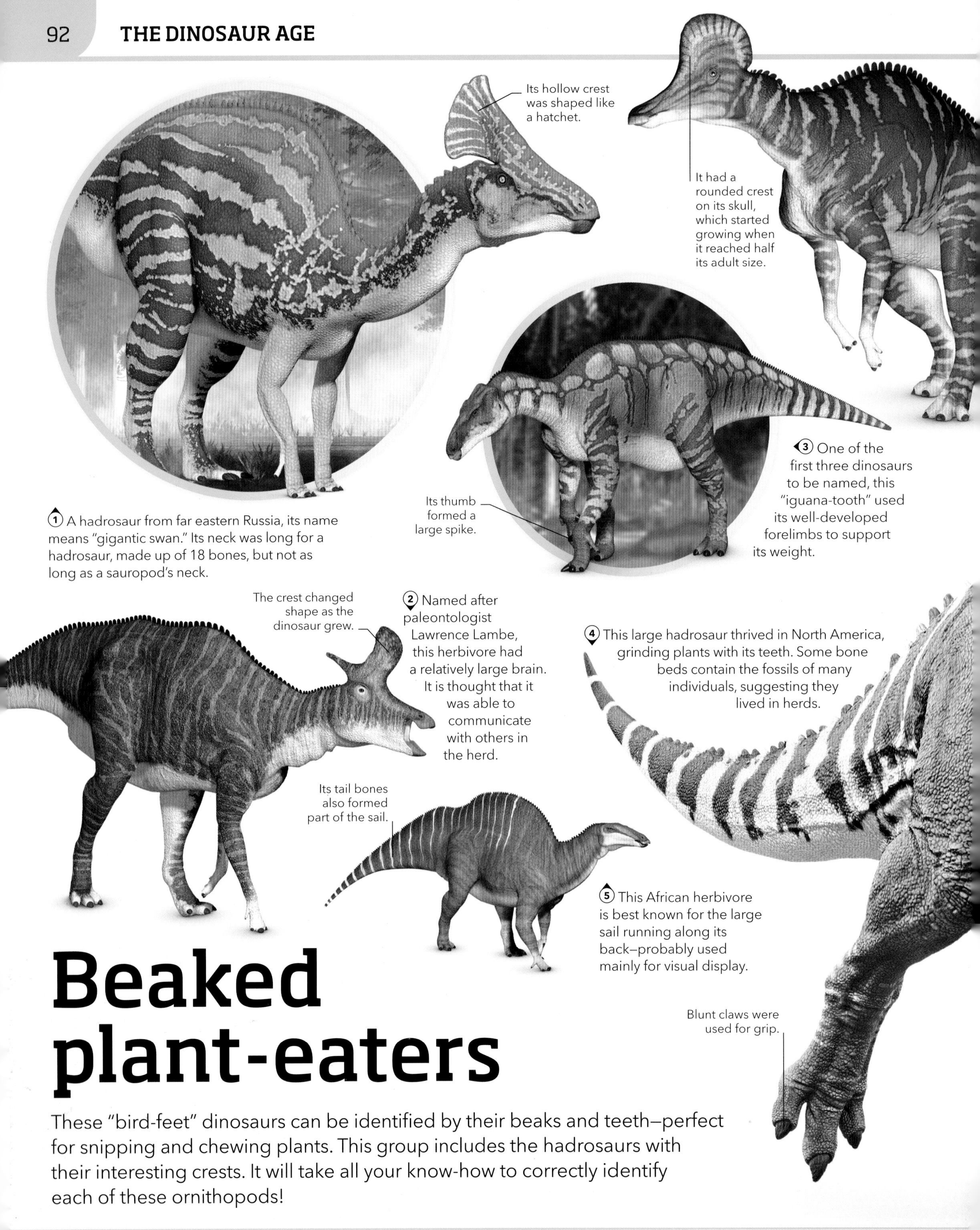

1. A hadrosaur from far eastern Russia, its name means "gigantic swan." Its neck was long for a hadrosaur, made up of 18 bones, but not as long as a sauropod's neck.

2. Named after paleontologist Lawrence Lambe, this herbivore had a relatively large brain. It is thought that it was able to communicate with others in the herd.

3. One of the first three dinosaurs to be named, this "iguana-tooth" used its well-developed forelimbs to support its weight.

4. This large hadrosaur thrived in North America, grinding plants with its teeth. Some bone beds contain the fossils of many individuals, suggesting they lived in herds.

5. This African herbivore is best known for the large sail running along its back—probably used mainly for visual display.

Beaked plant-eaters

These "bird-feet" dinosaurs can be identified by their beaks and teeth—perfect for snipping and chewing plants. This group includes the hadrosaurs with their interesting crests. It will take all your know-how to correctly identify each of these ornithopods!

ANSWERS: 1. *Olorotitan* 2. *Lambeosaurus* 3. *Iguanodon* 4. *Edmontosaurus* 5. *Ouranosaurus* 6. *Corythosaurus* 7. *Camptosaurus* 8. *Magnapaulia* 9. *Iguanacolossus* 10. *Parasaurolophus*

6 This dinosaur is known from several well-preserved skeletons. Although it walked on all fours, it could probably move around on two legs from time to time.

7 This *Iguanodon* relative from the Late Jurassic lived in North America and possibly Europe. It moved mainly on its hind legs but could get around on all fours.

8 This giant Mexican herbivore with an extremely deep tail is one of the largest known hadrosaurs. Adults reached 41 ft (12.5 m) in length.

9 A North American cousin of *Iguanodon*, this "colossal iguana" is named after its large, bulky body, which could grow to 30 ft (9 m).

10 This hadrosaur had a huge, distinctive head crest that pointed backward beyond the skull.

TEST YOURSELF

STARTER	CHALLENGER	GENIUS!
Iguanodon	***Iguanacolossus***	***Magnapaulia***
Corythosaurus	***Camptosaurus***	***Lambeosaurus***
Edmontosaurus	***Parasaurolophus***	***Olorotitan***
		Ouranosaurus

1 Unlike earlier ornithopods, *Iguanodon* had huge forelimbs and bulky hand bones. What were these mainly used for?

A. For doing press-ups

B. For display

C. To dig up roots

D. To support its body when it walked on four legs

2 Which modern animal weighs as much as *Iguanodon*?

A. Polar bear, 1,764 lb (800 kg)

B. Giraffe, 1.3 tons (1.2 metric tonnes)

C. Hippopotamus, 1.6 tons (1.5 metric tonnes)

D. Asian elephant, 4.4 tons (4 metric tonnes)

3 *Iguanodon* had a large beak made of the same material as a bird's beak. What is the material?

A. Chitin

B. Bone

C. Keratin

D. Cartilage

4 *Iguanodon* means "iguana teeth" because its giant teeth look like a modern iguana's, but how big are they?

A. 10 times bigger

B. 20 times bigger

C. 50 times bigger

D. 100 times bigger

Iguanodon

When the fossils of *Iguanodon* were found in the early 1800s, the term "dinosaur" had not been coined yet. Early scientists thought they came from a large lizard or some sort of rhino. But in 1842, British biologist Richard Owen realized the fossils formed part of a new group of reptiles—dinosaurs! Quiz yourself on this historically important ornithopod.

5 Which other beaked dinosaurs were *Iguanodon*'s closest relatives?

A. Hadrosaurs

B. *Corythoraptor*

C. Marginocephalians

D. *Dilophosaurus*

6 What was in *Iguanodon*'s long, stiff, and heavy tail?

A. Bony tendons for support

B. Scent glands that gave it a distinctive smell

C. Large pores to remove excess salt in the body

D. Air spaces in bones for lightness

Large sauropods also lived at this time, and were able to feed on taller vegetation.

Iguanodons probably lived in herds much of the time.

"Metacarpals" or bones of the palm of the hand

Thumb spike

Fused wrist bones

7 What was the length of *Iguanodon*'s thumb spike?

A. 4 in (10 cm) **B.** 5 in (12 cm)

C. 6 in (14 cm) **D.** 7 in (16 cm)

8 Where did scientists first think *Iguanodon* had a spike?

A. On its thumb

B. On its tail

C. On its back

D. On its nose

ANSWERS: 1-D, 2-C, 3-C, 4-B, 5-A, 6-A, 7-C, 8-D

Nests and eggs

All dinosaurs reproduced by laying eggs, from which their young hatched. Eggs protected the developing embryo, and the calcium in the shell helped build the embryo's bones. Like crocodiles and birds today, which also lay eggs, some dinosaurs took care of their hatchlings. Others, however, left their young to fend for themselves.

Keeping them warm

Various dinosaurs, including oviraptorosaurs and troodontids, probably sat on their nests. Keeping the eggs warm helped the embryos to develop, just as it does for modern birds. Larger species, such as *Heyuannia*, created a central space in the nest where they could sit without crushing their brood.

In numbers

27 in
(60 cm) The length of the longest dinosaur egg, which was laid by an oviraptorosaur

0.08 in
(2 mm) The average thickness of a titanosaur eggshell

0.34 oz
(9.9 g) The weight of the smallest known egg, which was laid by a theropod, *Himeoolithus murakamii*

How to raise a family

Sauropods did not care for their young, leaving hatchlings to forage for food and survive alone. But other dinosaur groups, including some theropods and the ornithopod *Maiasaura*, cared for their eggs and hatchlings.

01. *Maiasaura*, meaning "good mother lizard," nested in colonies. These ornithopods made simple nests covered in leaves and branches to lay their eggs in.

Extraordinary eggs

With the discovery of lots of fossilized eggs and nests, we now know that dinosaur eggs came in a variety of shapes and sizes—from small, circular ones to very large ones.

Sauropod egg Gigantic sauropods hatched from round eggs that were not much bigger than a soccer ball.

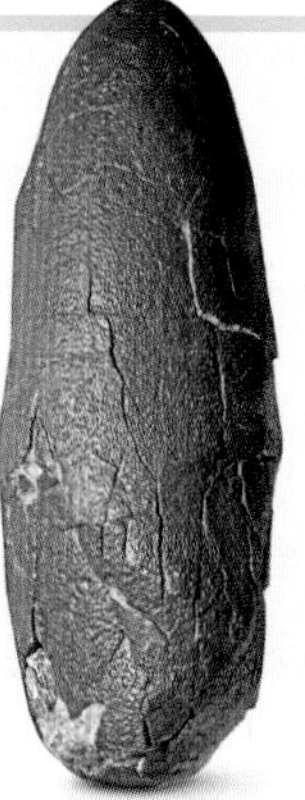

Oviraptorosaur egg Some oviraptorosaurs had blue-green oval eggs. This helped them hide the eggs from predators.

Chicken egg Modern birds such as chickens lay eggs, just as the early dinosaurs did.

I don't believe it!

Some sauropods kept their eggs warm using geothermal energy, which is heat generated deep under the Earth's surface.

02. Once the eggs hatched, *Maiasaura* parents brought food—such as leaves—back to the hatchlings. They needed time to develop before leaving the nest.

03. Life was tough for young *Maiasaura*. Almost 90 percent of hatchlings did not survive their first year. Many were eaten by predators or succumbed to disease.

Inside an egg

This illustration of a *Stenonychosaurus* egg is based on fossil finds of eggs with dinosaur embryos inside. *Stenonychosaurus* was a feathered theropod dinosaur.

The embryo would have tucked its head between its legs before hatching. This is seen in modern birds, too.

Evidence suggests baby dinosaurs wiggled their legs in the egg.

Dinosaur incubation took 3–6 months, depending on the species.

Eggshells thin over time, making hatching easier.

Growing up

Growing years were dangerous for baby dinosaurs. They were easy prey for predators and were commonly hunted. To boost their chances of survival, the young of some species, such as *Psittacosaurus*, were probably raised in a herd. These ceratopsians formed groups consisting of dinosaurs of different ages.

1 A fully grown *Citipati* was around 10 ft (3 m) long, but how large were *Citipati* eggs?

A. 6 in (15 cm)

B. 7 in (18 cm)

C. 8 in (22 cm)

D. 9 in (24 cm)

2 Emu eggs hatch in around 50 days. How long did it take *Citipati* eggs to hatch?

A. 44

B. 57

C. 75

D. 90

3 *Citipati* was related to a fierce dinosaur predator. The fossils of both dinosaurs have even been found in the same rocks. Which predator was it?

A. ***Velociraptor***

B. ***Patagotitan***

C. ***Carnotaurus***

D. ***Allosaurus***

Citipati

Citipati belonged to a group of feathered theropods called oviraptorosaurs. We know a lot about its behavior from several fossils of parents brooding their nest. They were attentive parents who covered their eggs with their outstretched wings, protecting them from the elements and predators.

4 *Citipati* was roughly the size of which modern bird?

A. Ostrich

B. Emu

C. Emperor penguin

D. Flamingo

5 Several *Citipati* fossils have been found in Mongolia. What type of habitat did *Citipati* live in?

A. Woodland

B. Desert

C. Forest

D. Mountain

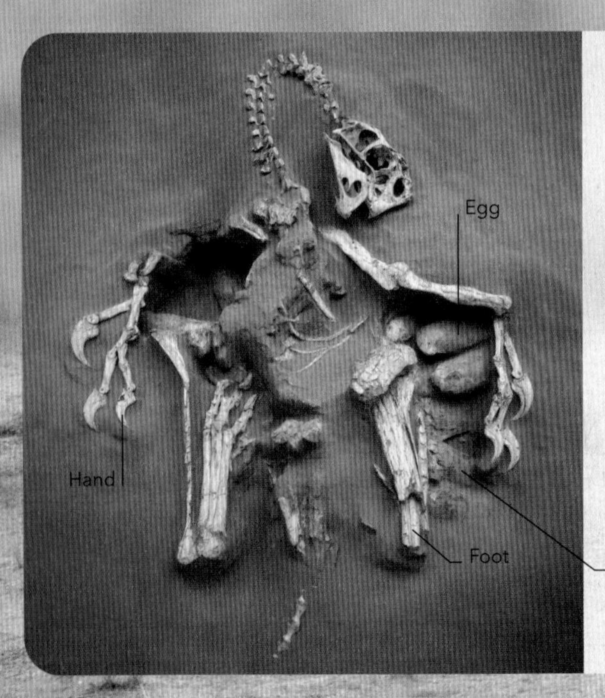

The *Citipati* in this fossil was probably protecting the eggs from a sandstorm.

6 *Citipati* weighed around 176 lb (80 kg) but sat on its nest to protect the eggs from the weather and danger. How did it not break its eggs?

A. It laid its eggs in a ring with a space in the middle.

B. It buried its eggs in sand and rocks before sitting on them.

C. The eggs had abnormally thick shells.

D. The eggs were too small to crush.

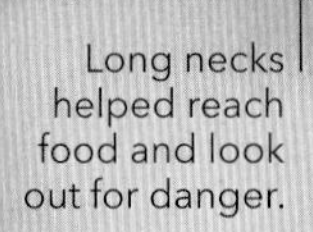

Long necks helped reach food and look out for danger.

ANSWERS: 1-B, 2-D, 3-A, 4-B, 5-B, 6-A, 7-B, 8-B, 9-B, 10-C

Like many oviraptorosaurs, *Citipati* had a toothless beak.

7 The tail of *Citipati* was relatively short and flexible and is likely to have ended in a fan of feathers. What was this tail probably used for?

A. Fanning itself to stay cool

B. Impressing mates with a display

C. Confusing predators

D. Shading its eyes while sleeping

8 *Citipati* had long arms and powerful, grasping hands. It and other oviraptorosaurs were part of a group of theropods whose name means "hand snatchers." What was the name of this group?

A. Therizinosaurs

B. Maniraptorans

C. Ceratosaurs

D. Dromaeosaurids

9 Approximately how many eggs did *Citipati* lay in its nest?

A. 14 **B.** 22

C. 30 **D.** 50

10 *Citipati* had a relatively strong bite. What did it eat?

A. Eggs **B.** Insects

C. Plants **D.** Meat

Senses and brains

Brains and nerves are soft tissues that do not preserve well. However, the bony structures that house them can help paleontologists understand how the brain and senses of many dinosaurs worked. We now know about the brains and senses of many different dinosaurs.

I don't believe it!

Mazelike air spaces behind ankylosaur's nose may have helped cool its brains.

How a dinosaur brain works

A dinosaur's brain controlled the rest of its body, including its temperature. Twelve nerves were connected to the brain and gathered information from all around the body, such as from the dinosaur's face, eyes, and heart.

The purple area is a 3D model of this *Baryonyx*'s brain, based on the shape of its brain cavity—the space inside the skull where the brain sits.

The front of the brain contained the olfactory bulbs, the parts that helped dinosaurs interpret smells.

Inside the ear, two tiny parts helped stabilize the dinosaur's gaze, as well as being essential for its hearing.

Arteries supplied blood to the brain.

The silver area is the braincase, which protected the brain.

The snout had nerves that helped the dinosaur feel pressure on the skin and teeth.

Modeling dinosaur brains

Natural casts
Sometimes, skull fossils are naturally worn away to reveal the rocky cast that fills the brain cavity.

Man-made casts
To see the shape of the brain, the brain cavity can be filled with rubber or resin to make a cast. But this damages the fossil.

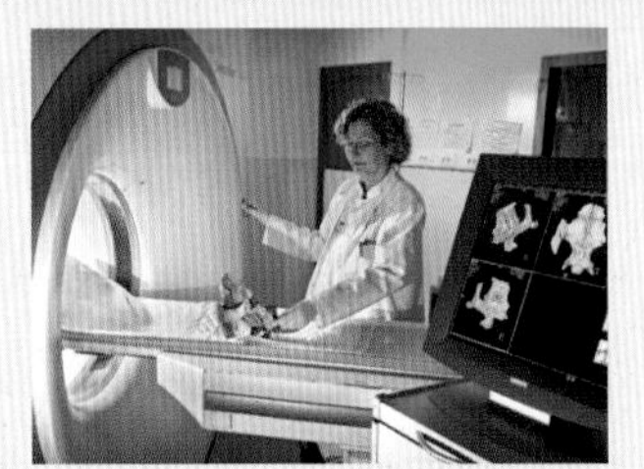

Digital models
CT or MRI scanners can look inside a dinosaur skull without damaging it. The scan is then used to create 3D digital models of the brain.

In numbers

1871
The year when the first dinosaur brain cavity was studied

1.6 in
(4 cm) Size of *Troodon*'s brain—the biggest dinosaur brain relative to its body size

50%
The amount of space inside a dinosaur's brain cavity taken up by its brain

Brain power

To get an idea of how complex a dinosaur's range of behaviors were, scientists measure the size of their brains compared to their body weight. The biggest brains relative to body size were in the small theropods. At the other end of the scale, armored thyreophorans, such as ankylosaurs and stegosaurs, had small brains for their bulk.

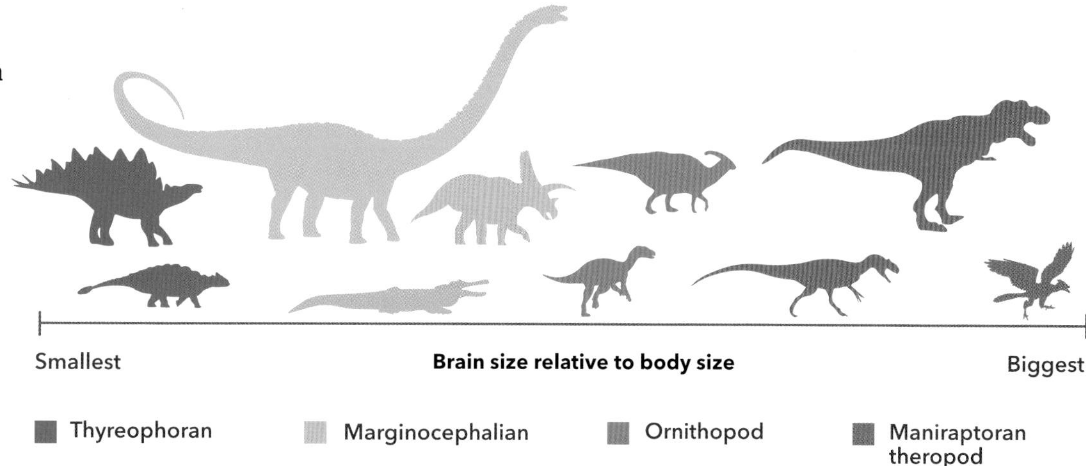

- Thyreophoran
- Sauropod
- Marginocephalian
- Crocodylomorph
- Ornithopod
- Theropod
- Maniraptoran theropod

Bird brains

Early birds and their close cousins the dromaeosaurs (small but ferocious dinosaurs with bladelike teeth and hooked claws) had similar brain sizes. After the Cretaceous extinction, many birds evolved smaller bodies. Relative to their body size, their brains were now bigger than they had been before.

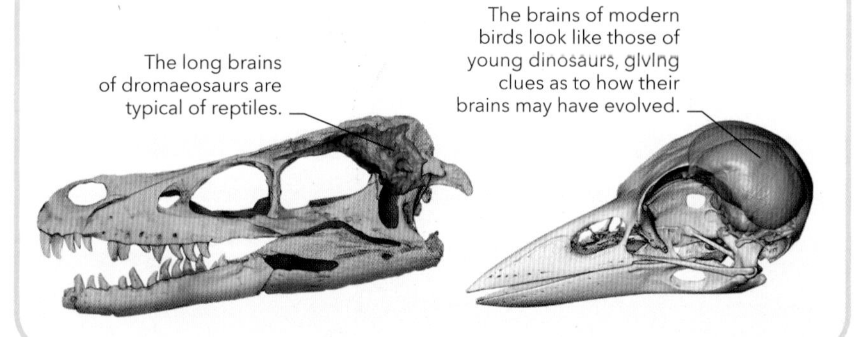

Making friends

The relatively large brains of hadrosaurs suggest that these plant-eaters may have been capable of more complex social behaviors. Fossils show that they lived in herds, using their bigger brains to communicate and live together effectively.

Super senses

New technologies have helped scientists understand the senses of many different dinosaurs. By comparing them to modern animals, experts can help explain how these reptiles may have used their senses.

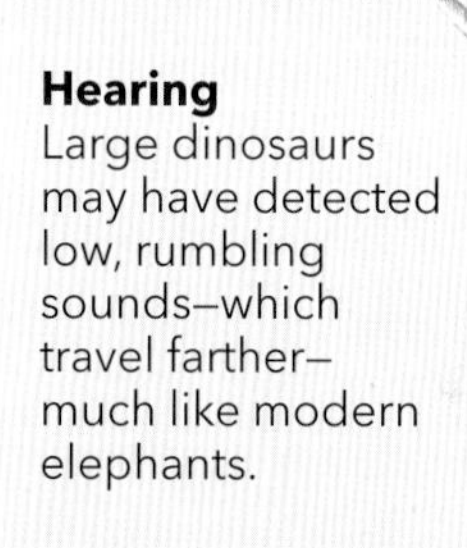

Hearing
Large dinosaurs may have detected low, rumbling sounds—which travel farther—much like modern elephants.

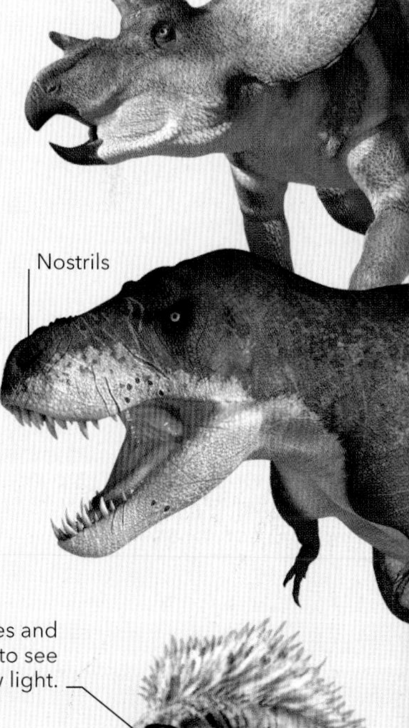

Smell
Tyrannosaurids and dromaeosaurs had a relatively good sense of smell compared to other theropods.

Sight
Some dinosaurs, such as the small theropod *Shuvuuvia*, probably had excellent night vision, which it combined with owl-like sharp hearing.

3 REPTILES OF SEA AND SKY

Marine life

While dinosaurs roamed the land, life flourished in the seas and skies, too. Many reptiles evolved to live in the oceans, pterosaurs flew through the air, and the first mammals appeared, too, among ancient forests. Some of the most impressive and strangest creatures evolved during this time.

Reptiles of the deep

Ichthyosaurs
Many resembled fast-swimming sharks. Fossils of *Stenopterygius* indicate that they gave birth to live young at sea.

Hupehsuchians
An early group of marine reptiles, they existed briefly in the Triassic. *Hupesuchus* relatives evolved armored bodies.

Placodonts
These turtlelike reptiles lived in the shallow seas. *Placodus* used its typically flat teeth to crush hard shells.

Plesiosaurs
This group included both long-necked predators, such as *Elasmosaurus*, and the typically short-necked pliosaurs.

Crocodylomorphs
Some crocodile relatives evolved to live at sea. *Dakosaurus* used its daggerlike teeth to hunt large prey along the coasts.

Sea turtles
Turtles entered marine habitats many times during the Mesozoic, but only one group adapted to life in deep water.

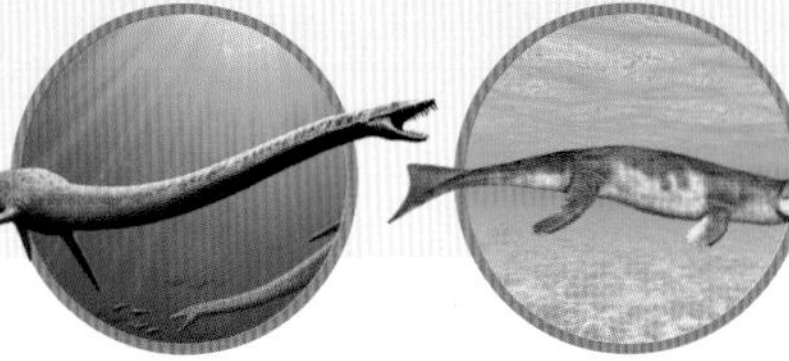

In numbers

70 ft
(21 m) The size to which the biggest ichthyosaur *Shastasaurus sikanniensis* could grow

70
The number of teeth the mosasaur *Tylosaurus* had, including 20 on the roof of its mouth to grip prey

Mesozoic marine life

Marine reptiles were specially adapted for life in the oceans. They used their streamlined bodies, flipper-shaped limbs, and tails to swim rapidly through the water, preying on other sea creatures.

The front (pectoral) flippers helped ichthyosaurs, such as *Temnodontosaurus*, steer.

Small fish form "bait balls" to make it harder for predators to catch individual fish.

Marine reptiles had to return to the surface to breathe. Many had nostrils located on top of their snouts instead of on the side.

The fins and flippers of marine reptiles evolved from the arms and legs of their land-dwelling ancestors. The bones of these flippers are similar to the bones of your arms and legs!

I don't believe it!

The first ichthyosaurs were only 2 ft (0.6 m) long, but within 8 million years, some had evolved to grow more than 49 ft (15 m) long.

Mosasaurs
Mosasaurs were relatives of today's lizards and snakes. *Mosasaurus* was one of the last and largest.

Hammerheaded herbivore

Living around 245 MYA, *Atopodentatus* was the earliest known plant-eating marine reptile. This strange, hammerheaded herbivore used its broad mouth of tiny teeth to scrape plant food from rocks in the shallows.

Marine reptiles

While dinosaurs roamed the land, other reptiles moved into the oceans, adapting to life in the water. Some stuck close to the shores, while others lived entirely at sea. These diverse reptiles found many ways to thrive.

Large eyes allowed it to see 1,640 ft (500 m) below the water's surface.

Eye lizards

With eyes measuring 9 in (23 cm) across, *Ophthalmosaurus* had some of the largest eyes of any known animal. Paleontologists think big eyes would have helped these ichthyosaurs see in dark waters, deep down where sunlight does not penetrate.

Early ichthyosaurs moved in a snakelike motion, but later species kept the front of their body still while using their fishlike bodies and crescent tails to swim fast in the open ocean.

A streamlined body shape helped ichthyosaurs swim very fast.

Plesiosaurs, such as *Rhomaleosaurus*, could "fly" through the water by alternating beats of their flippers.

Two sets of flippers propelled plesiosaurs through the water.

Neck or tail?

When *Elasmosaurus* fossils were first found, scientists mistook its neck for its tail because it was so long. Its neck had 72 bones and was longer than a giraffe is tall.

1 One of the last placodonts—marine reptiles with armored backs—this species crushed shellfish prey with large, rounded teeth.

The pebblelike skin of this placodont gives it its name.

A sharklike tail fin helped it to swim.

2 This crocodylomorph's serrated teeth and ability to bite down with extreme force gave it its name, which means "biter lizard." It mainly ate the flesh of large prey.

3 The largest sea turtle of all time, it could grow to over 3 tons (2.7 metric tons). A skeleton of this reptile was found with a missing flipper, possibly bitten off by a predator.

It had a short and toothless snout.

4 This large, toothless ichthyosaur's fossils were found in China. It caught prey by suction. When it opened its mouth, the motion created a vacuum, pulling squid and fish right in.

This ichthyosaur could grow to be more than 26 ft (8 m) long.

Reptiles of the sea

Marine reptiles were the top predators of the oceans during the Mesozoic Era. While dinosaurs flourished on land, they swam in the seas. Some of them were giants, while others were so small you could hold them in your hands.

ANSWERS: 1. Psephoderma 2. Dakosaurus 3. Archelon 4. Guanlingsaurus 5. Globidens 6. Mosasaurus 7. Nothosaurus 8. Albertonectes 9. Stenopterygius

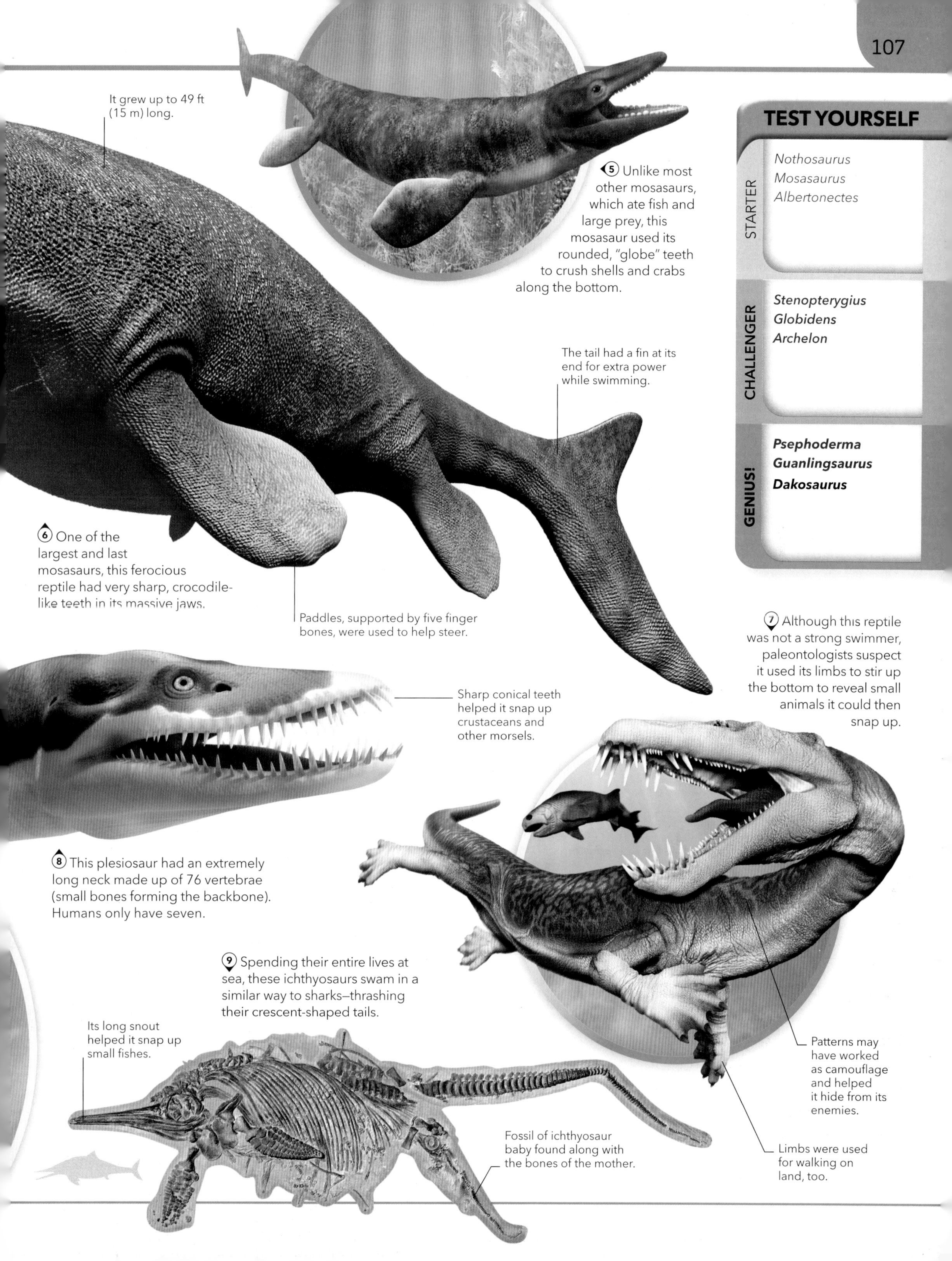
It grew up to 49 ft (15 m) long.
(5) Unlike most other mosasaurs, which ate fish and large prey, this mosasaur used its rounded, "globe" teeth to crush shells and crabs along the bottom.
TEST YOURSELF
STARTER
Nothosaurus
Mosasaurus
Albertonectes
CHALLENGER
Stenopterygius
Globidens
Archelon
GENIUS!
Psephoderma
Guanlingsaurus
Dakosaurus
The tail had a fin at its end for extra power while swimming.
(6) One of the largest and last mosasaurs, this ferocious reptile had very sharp, crocodile-like teeth in its massive jaws.
Paddles, supported by five finger bones, were used to help steer.
(7) Although this reptile was not a strong swimmer, paleontologists suspect it used its limbs to stir up the bottom to reveal small animals it could then snap up.
Sharp conical teeth helped it snap up crustaceans and other morsels.
(8) This plesiosaur had an extremely long neck made up of 76 vertebrae (small bones forming the backbone). Humans only have seven.
(9) Spending their entire lives at sea, these ichthyosaurs swam in a similar way to sharks—thrashing their crescent-shaped tails.
Its long snout helped it snap up small fishes.
Patterns may have worked as camouflage and helped it hide from its enemies.
Fossil of ichthyosaur baby found along with the bones of the mother.
Limbs were used for walking on land, too.

Pliosaurus

Mesozoic seas were teeming with marine reptiles, and few were more fearsome than the plesiosaur *Pliosaurus*. As the top predator of the Jurassic seas, these short-necked plesiosaurs chased after ichthyosaurs; fish; or even other, smaller plesiosaurs.

A wide gape allowed *Pliosaurus* to swallow large chunks of its prey.

Powerful flippers propelled *Pliosaurus* through the water.

1 What made the huge front teeth of *Pliosaurus* interesting?

A. They were never replaced.

B. They were replaced more slowly than the back teeth.

C. They were weaker than the teeth at the back.

D. They were not covered in enamel.

2 How long was the biggest *Pliosaurus*'s skull ever found?

A. 1.6 ft (0.5 m) **B.** 3 ft (1 m)

C. 5 ft (1.5 m) **D.** 6.5 ft (2 m)

3 How strong was the bite of *Pliosaurus* compared to that of *Tyrannosaurus rex*?

A. Half as strong **B.** Equally strong

C. Four times as strong **D.** Eight times as strong

4 *Pliosaurus* needed to eat a lot to sustain itself. What did it eat?

A. Small herbivorous dinosaurs

B. Large marine plants

C. Large fish and marine reptiles

D. Giant clams and squids

5 The first fossil of *Pliosaurus funkei*, found in 2006 on the island of Svalbard in Norway, was named after paleontologist couple Bjørn Funke and May-Liss Knudsen Funke. However, a media company gave it a more catchy name. What was it?

A. Killer Z

B. Aqua Y

C. Hunter Q

D. Predator X

6 How many flippers did *Pliosaurus* have?

A. Two

B. Four

C. Six

D. Eight

Its paddles had five fingers with many finger bones to make them extra long.

Bitten bones suggest ichthyosaurs were common prey for *Pliosaurus*.

7 When the fragments of a *Pliosaurus* skull were found in Dorset, England, how long did it take to collect all of the pieces from the seashore?

A. Almost six months

B. Almost two years

C. Almost four years

D. Almost eight years

The skull of the Dorset *Pliosaurus* is the most complete found yet.

ANSWERS: 1-B, 2-D, 3-B, 4-C, 5-D, 6-B, 7-D

Meet the family

Rauisuchids
Some of these Triassic pseudosuchians were at the top of the food chain. The biggest reached 20 ft (6 m) in length. *Postosuchus* may have walked on its back legs.

Aetosaurs
These "armadillodiles" of the Triassic were omnivores and herbivores with armored backs. *Desmatosuchus* had huge spikes on its shoulders.

Crocodylomorphs
This group includes modern crocodilians and their prehistoric relatives. Some lived in swamps and at sea; others, such as *Hesperosuchus*, lived on land.

Notosuchians
This diverse crocodylomorph group evolved into many forms, including herbivores such as *Simosuchus* from Cretaceous Madagascar.

Pseudosuchians

Dinosaurs were not the only reptiles to flourish in the Mesozoic Era. The prehistoric relatives of today's crocodiles and alligators were abundant, too. While a few were plant-eaters, most were predatory meat-eaters. These lurked in swamps waiting to ambush prey, sometimes chasing their victims on land.

I don't believe it!
Sarcosuchus had 132 teeth at a time, which could be replaced if any of them fell out.

Toothy eaters

Pseudosuchians evolved a variety of different tooth shapes for slicing, piercing, or grinding. This gives us an idea of these crocodile relatives' diet.

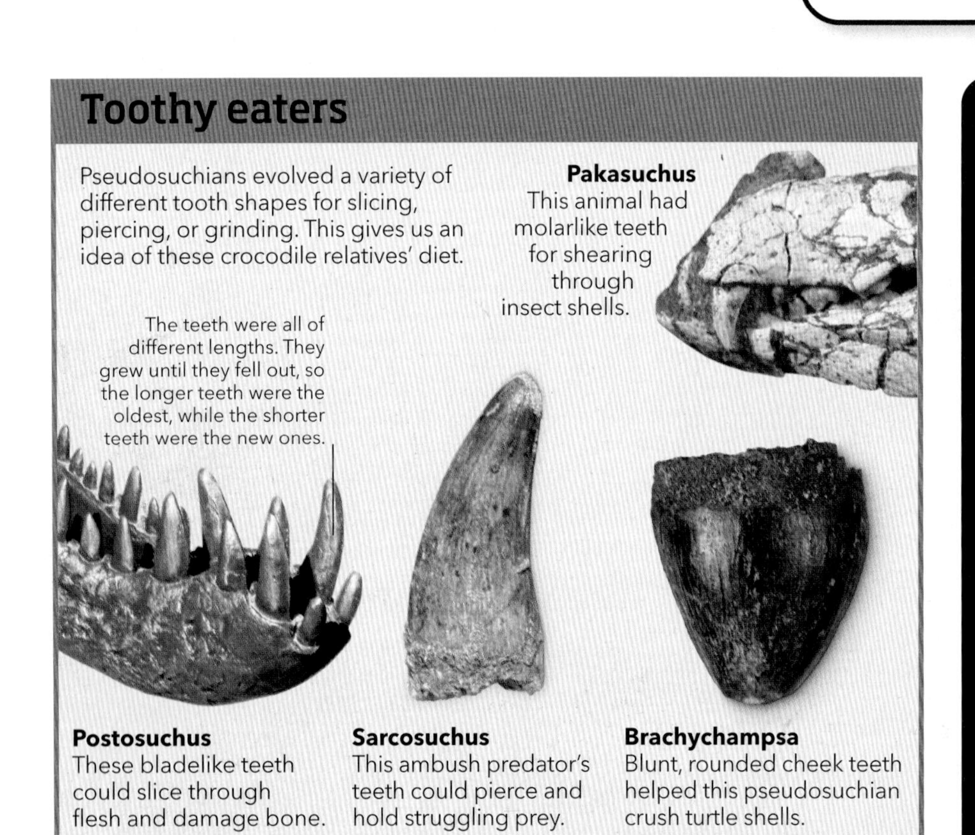

Pakasuchus
This animal had molarlike teeth for shearing through insect shells.

The teeth were all of different lengths. They grew until they fell out, so the longer teeth were the oldest, while the shorter teeth were the new ones.

Postosuchus
These bladelike teeth could slice through flesh and damage bone.

Sarcosuchus
This ambush predator's teeth could pierce and hold struggling prey.

Brachychampsa
Blunt, rounded cheek teeth helped this pseudosuchian crush turtle shells.

How to ambush your prey

01. Lurk in the waters of a swamp in a spot popular with prey. Make sure your body is hidden under the water, with only your eyes and nose visible.

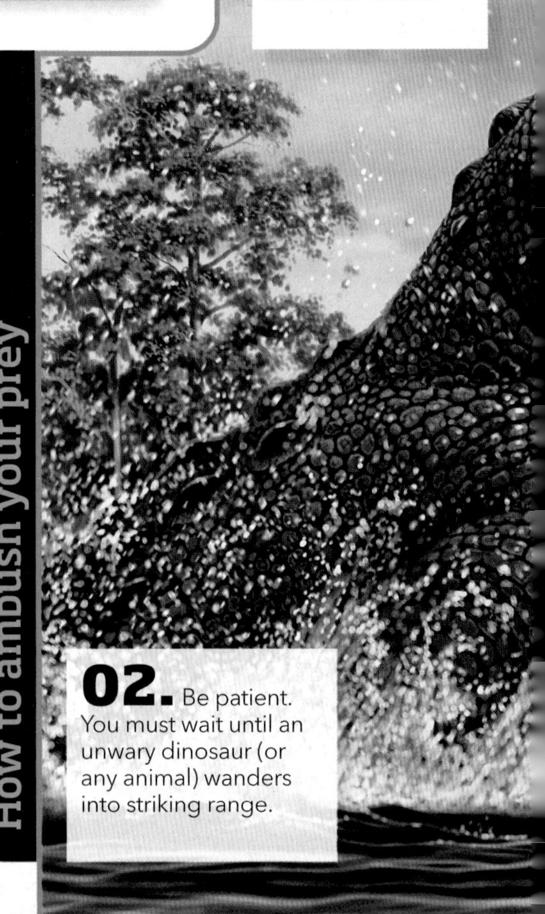

02. Be patient. You must wait until an unwary dinosaur (or any animal) wanders into striking range.

Nature's armor

Like most modern relatives, early crocs had scutes. These were spongy-looking bones, known as osteoderms, that grew in the skin and offered protection.

In numbers

60
The number of times stronger the bite of *Deinosuchus* was than that of a human

31 in
(79 cm) The size of an adult *Trilophosuchus*, one of the smallest crocodilians

247 MYA
When the oldest pseudosuchians appeared

03. As soon as your victim is close enough, use your powerful tail to propel your body forward to grip your prey. Getting a firm first bite is critical.

04. Clamp your jaws together hard, driving your piercing teeth into your prey. Using all your strength, drag your victim into the water and drown it.

1 The snorkel-like snout formed a large part of the *Kaprosuchus* skull. What could it have been used for?

A. Maintaining body temperature

B. Attracting mates

C. Catching prey

D. Breathing while lurking underwater

2 *Kaprosuchus* fossils have been found only in Africa, but do you know where?

A. Nile Delta, Egypt

B. Kalahari Desert, Namibia

C. Sahara Desert, Niger

D. Mount Kilimanjaro, Tanzania

Kaprosuchus

Crocodile relatives, such as *Kaprosuchus*, filled the Mesozoic world alongside the dinosaurs and other reptiles. A *Kaprosuchus* on the hunt was a scary sight, with its menacing, fanglike teeth. Paleontologists are just getting to know this Cretaceous predator, which was only named in 2009. Find out how many questions you can answer!

Protective body armor was probably formed of flat plates called scutes embedded in the skin.

3 *Kaprosuchus* got its name from its unusually large, fanglike teeth. What does its name mean?

A. Giant crocodile

B. Boar crocodile

C. Dragon crocodile

D. Horned crocodile

4 *Kaprosuchus* ate small dinosaurs, among other things. How did it hunt?

A. Attacked the prey head-on

B. Ambushed the prey

C. Waited for the prey to be attacked by another predator

D. Attacked sleeping prey

5 *Kaprosuchus* was a large-sized crocodile relative, but only a 20-in- (51-cm-) long skull has been found so far. What was the maximum length experts think it could reach?

A. 20 ft (6 m)

B. 26 ft (8 m)

C. 32 ft (10 m)

D. 39 ft (12 m)

ANSWERS: 1-D, 2-C, 3-B, 4-B, 5-A, 6-D, 7-A, 8-C

6 *Kaprosuchus*'s teeth looked like tusks. How long was its biggest tooth?

A. 0.7 in (2 cm)

B. 1.5 in (4 cm)

C. 2 in (5 cm)

D. 2.6 in (6.5 cm)

7 What was the natural habitat of *Kaprosuchus*?

A. Floodplains

B. Tundra

C. Deserts

D. Tropical forests

8 *Kaprosuchus* lived toward the end of the Mesozoic Era. During which period did it roam the world?

A. Triassic

B. Jurassic

C. Cretaceous

D. Paleogene

Tails, flippers, and fins

Life evolved into a wide variety of different forms in the oceans that covered most of Earth in the Mesozoic Era. Giant fish, including sharks, as well as all kinds of marine reptiles swam through the waves using their tails, flippers, and fins. Find out which of these you can identify!

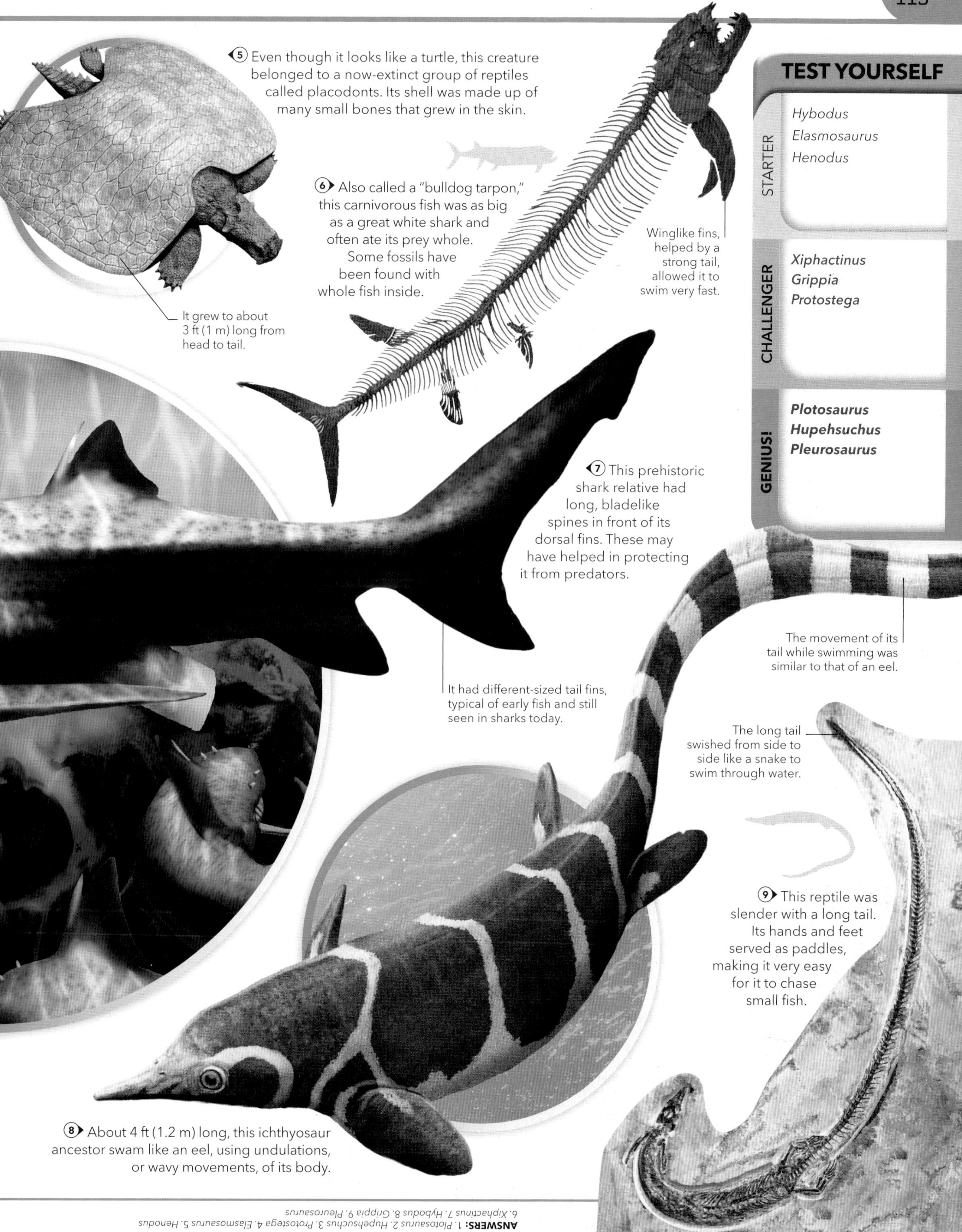

5 Even though it looks like a turtle, this creature belonged to a now-extinct group of reptiles called placodonts. Its shell was made up of many small bones that grew in the skin.

It grew to about 3 ft (1 m) long from head to tail.

6 Also called a "bulldog tarpon," this carnivorous fish was as big as a great white shark and often ate its prey whole. Some fossils have been found with whole fish inside.

Winglike fins, helped by a strong tail, allowed it to swim very fast.

TEST YOURSELF

STARTER

Hybodus
Elasmosaurus
Henodus

CHALLENGER

Xiphactinus
Grippia
Protostega

GENIUS!

Plotosaurus
Hupehsuchus
Pleurosaurus

7 This prehistoric shark relative had long, bladelike spines in front of its dorsal fins. These may have helped in protecting it from predators.

It had different-sized tail fins, typical of early fish and still seen in sharks today.

The movement of its tail while swimming was similar to that of an eel.

The long tail swished from side to side like a snake to swim through water.

9 This reptile was slender with a long tail. Its hands and feet served as paddles, making it very easy for it to chase small fish.

8 About 4 ft (1.2 m) long, this ichthyosaur ancestor swam like an eel, using undulations, or wavy movements, of its body.

ANSWERS: 1. *Plotosaurus* 2. *Hupehsuchus* 3. *Protostega* 4. *Elasmosaurus* 5. *Henodus* 6. *Xiphactinus* 7. *Hybodus* 8. *Grippia* 9. *Pleurosaurus*

Pterosaurs

Pterosaurs filled the Mesozoic skies. They were the first vertebrates to evolve powered flight—flapping their wings to generate lift and travel through the air. Evolving into a range of sizes, some were as small as sparrows, while others were giraffe-sized giants.

Show-offs

Many pterosaur species evolved elaborate, flashy crests. These probably helped pterosaurs look impressive while courting mates.

Tapejara Fossils show that *Tapejara* had a tall crest jutting from its snout all the way to the back of the skull.

Dsungaripterus Its crest was covered in keratin, which rarely fossilizes, so it was probably bigger in life than its fossils show.

Ludodactylus Some large pterosaurs, such as *Ludodactylus*, had pointed crests jutting from the back of their skulls.

Pointed, sharp teeth helped it snatch slippery prey, such as fish.

Tupandactylus Bright feather colors found on one fossil hint that its crest may also have been strikingly colored.

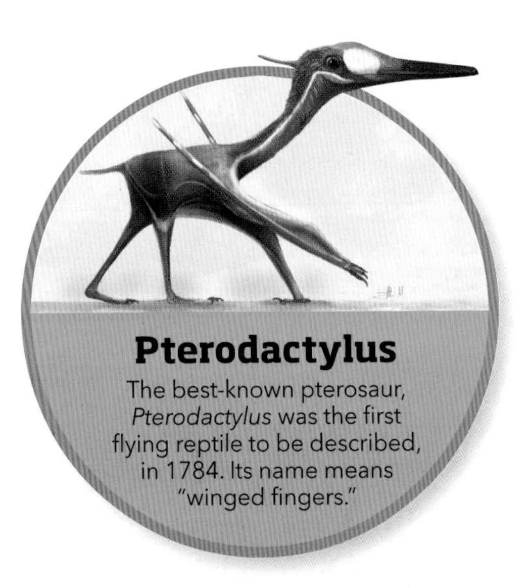

Pterodactylus

The best-known pterosaur, *Pterodactylus* was the first flying reptile to be described, in 1784. Its name means "winged fingers."

In numbers

10 in
(25 cm) Wingspan of the smallest pterosaur, *Nemicolopterus*

220 MYA
When pterosaurs first appeared, during the late Triassic

1,000
The number of teeth of *Pterodaustro*

How to fly like a pterosaur

01. If you are a *Quetzalcoatlus*, walk on all fours while on the ground. Fold your wings at the elbow and wrist to allow your hands to reach the ground, acting like front legs.

Meet the family

Dimorphodon
Dimorphodon belonged to a group of pterosaurs with large heads and prominent teeth. They hunted lizards and small vertebrates.

Jeholopterus
Jeholopterus was a small flier that chased insects in the air. Some fossils have well-preserved, fuzzy feathers around the bones.

Rhamphorhynchus
Rhamphorhynchus belonged to a group of fish-eating pterosaurs. They used their sharp teeth to snatch small prey from the water.

Tapejara
Tapejara was a crested pterosaur. Its crest was probably larger in life than in the fossils and covered in keratin, similar to what our fingernails are made of.

Quetzalcoatlus
Quetzalcoatlus was one of the largest fliers of all time. With a toothless beak and short tail, it was the last pterosaur to thrive before the Cretaceous mass extinction.

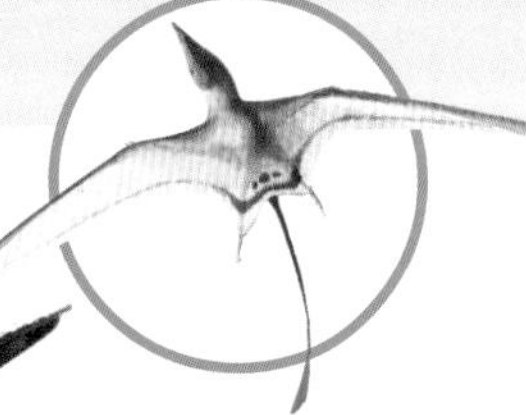

02. To prepare for take-off, flex your folded wings and rock your body forward. Paleontologists call this method "quad launching."

I don't believe it!

The largest pterosaurs might have been able to fly 10,000 miles (16,000 km) nonstop and visited different continents.

Quetzalcoatlus could fly at speeds up to 80 miles (129 km) per hour.

03. Then jump, using your limbs to push yourself into the air. Use enough force to get your whole body off the ground with time for your folded wings to pivot into a flight stroke.

04. Once off the ground, fling open your wings and begin flapping to stay in the air. The quad launch technique will allow you to take off almost vertically.

Flying reptiles

For more than 150 million years, pterosaurs soared in the skies. These reptiles were the first vertebrates to evolve the ability to fly. Fuzzy feathers covered their bodies, but they flapped their way skyward with leathery wings. How many of these pterosaurs do you know?

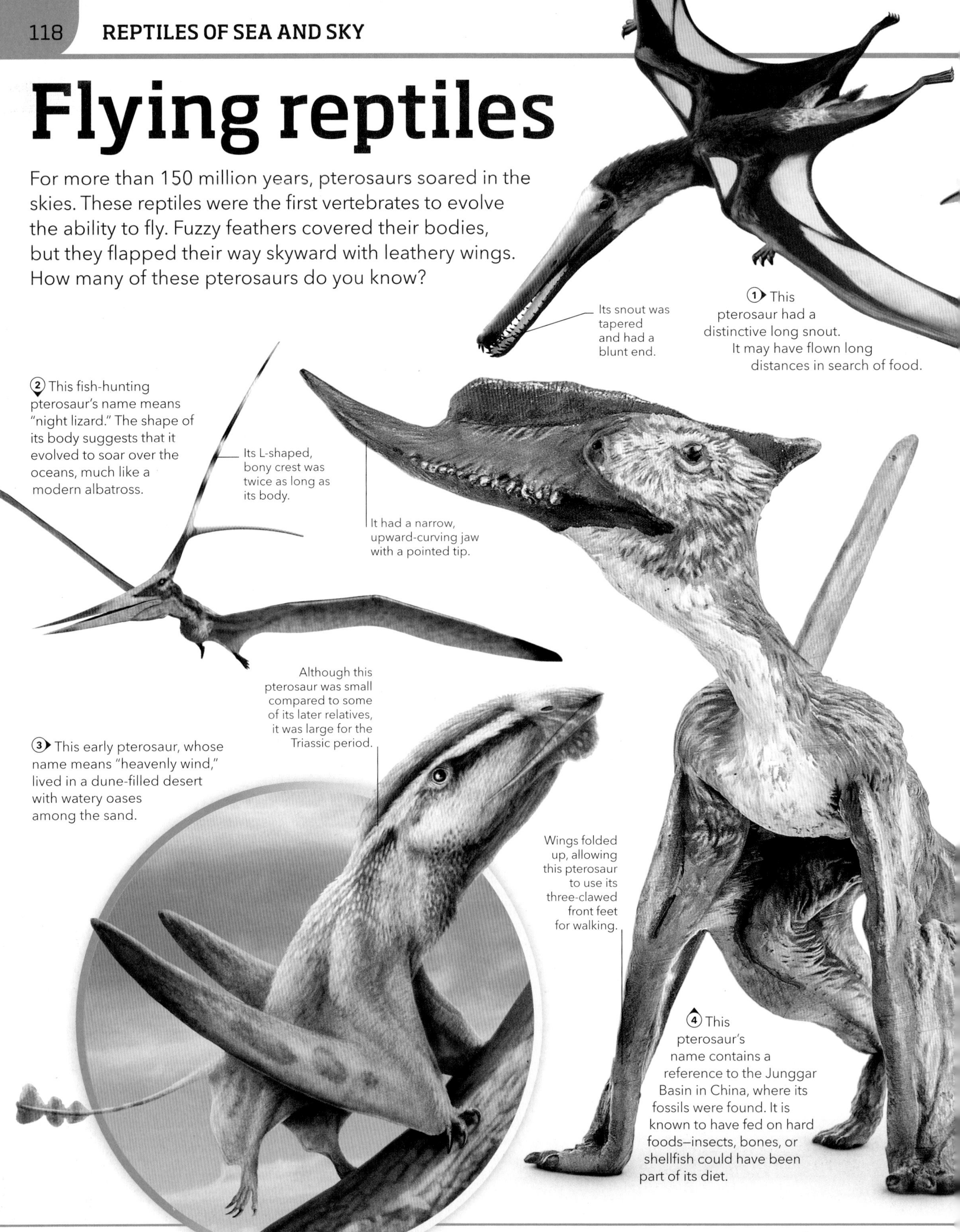

Its snout was tapered and had a blunt end.

① This pterosaur had a distinctive long snout. It may have flown long distances in search of food.

② This fish-hunting pterosaur's name means "night lizard." The shape of its body suggests that it evolved to soar over the oceans, much like a modern albatross.

Its L-shaped, bony crest was twice as long as its body.

It had a narrow, upward-curving jaw with a pointed tip.

Although this pterosaur was small compared to some of its later relatives, it was large for the Triassic period.

③ This early pterosaur, whose name means "heavenly wind," lived in a dune-filled desert with watery oases among the sand.

Wings folded up, allowing this pterosaur to use its three-clawed front feet for walking.

④ This pterosaur's name contains a reference to the Junggar Basin in China, where its fossils were found. It is known to have fed on hard foods—insects, bones, or shellfish could have been part of its diet.

ANSWERS: 1. Camposipterus 2. Nyctosaurus 3. Caelestiventus 4. Dsungaripterus 5. Pteranodon 6. Pterodactylus 7. Pterodausto 8. Thalassodromeus

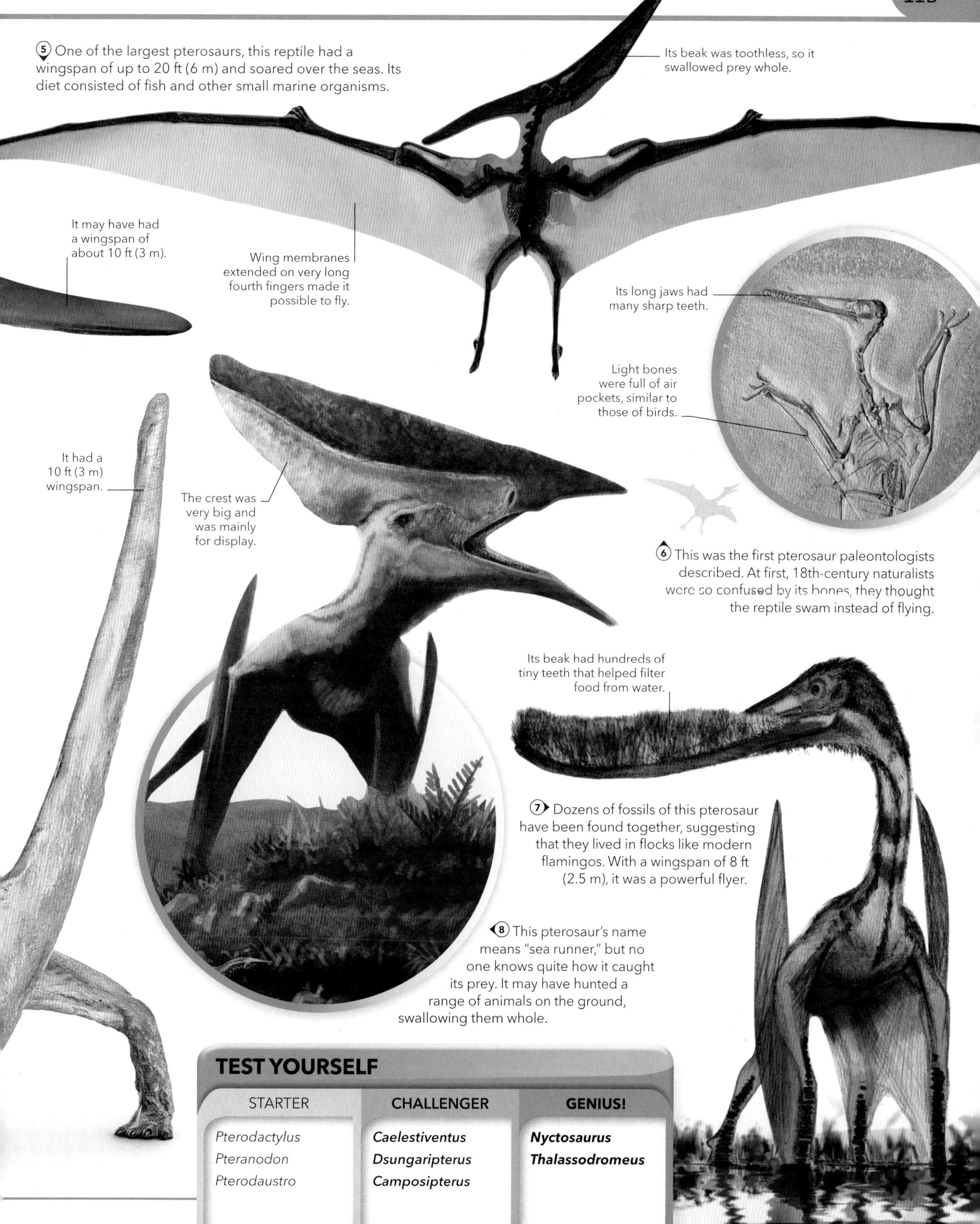

5 One of the largest pterosaurs, this reptile had a wingspan of up to 20 ft (6 m) and soared over the seas. Its diet consisted of fish and other small marine organisms.

6 This was the first pterosaur paleontologists described. At first, 18th-century naturalists were so confused by its bones, they thought the reptile swam instead of flying.

7 Dozens of fossils of this pterosaur have been found together, suggesting that they lived in flocks like modern flamingos. With a wingspan of 8 ft (2.5 m), it was a powerful flyer.

8 This pterosaur's name means "sea runner," but no one knows quite how it caught its prey. It may have hunted a range of animals on the ground, swallowing them whole.

TEST YOURSELF

STARTER	CHALLENGER	GENIUS!
Pterodactylus	***Caelestiventus***	***Nyctosaurus***
Pteranodon	***Dsungaripterus***	***Thalassodromeus***
Pterodaustro	***Camposipterus***	

1 *Hatzegopteryx* belonged to a group of pterosaurs called azhdarchids. The word comes from the Persian word *azhdar*. What does it mean?

A. Fish
B. Lizard
C. Dinosaur
D. Dragon

2 During the Late Cretaceous period, *Hatzegopteryx* lived on an island in the Tethys Sea that no longer exists. What is the island known as and what country is it now part of?

A. Hațeg Island, Romania
B. Bell Island, Canada
C. Seymour Island, Antarctica
D. Rusinga Island, Kenya

3 How do paleontologists believe *Hatzegopteryx* and other azhdarchids hunted?

A. Stalking the ground like hornbills and storks
B. In the air like falcons
C. Out at sea like gulls
D. Probing the mud like ibises

4 The size of its skull should have made flying impossible for *Hatzegopteryx*. What feature made it able to fly with such a large skull?

A. Strong neck muscles
B. Short neck
C. Small pits and hollows in the skull bone
D. Small brain

ANSWERS: 1-D, 2-A, 3-A, 4-C, 5-D, 6-A, 7-B, 8-B

5 In what kind of habitat did *Hatzegopteryx* live?

A. Tropical rainforests
B. Deserts
C. Marshlands
D. Subtropical woodlands

6 The wingspan of *Hatzegopteryx* almost matched that of a Cessna Skyhawk propeller plane. How wide were its wings?

A. 33 ft (10 m)
B. 98 ft (30 m)
C. 164 ft (50 m)
D. 230 ft (70 m)

Hatzegopteryx

Pterosaurs included the largest creatures to ever fly, and *Hatzegopteryx* may have been the largest of all. This winged giant ate small dinosaurs. It was so large that, on the ground, it stood as tall as a giraffe.

7 *Hatzegopteryx* had one of the biggest skulls of any land animal ever. How long could the skull be?

A. 3.9 ft (1.2 m)
B. 8.2 ft (2.5 m)
C. 9.8 ft (3.5 m)
D. More than 12.5 ft (3.8 m)

8 Scientists believe that *Hatzegopteryx* was the top predator on the island where it lived. Why would it not have been preyed upon by other animals?

A. *Hatzegopteryx* was too large to be preyed upon.
B. The island could not support large, carnivorous theropods.
C. Only fish-eating theropods lived on the island.
D. All the other animals on the island were herbivores.

Mesozoic mammals

The first mammals lived around the same time as the earliest dinosaurs. They were mostly furry, and nearly all of them laid eggs. Quite small in size, most of them were nocturnal, and many were excellent burrowers or climbers.

TEST YOURSELF

STARTER	CHALLENGER	GENIUS!
Didelphodon	***Kayentatherium***	***Durlstotherium***
Castorocauda	***Repenomamus***	***Volaticotherium***
Eomaia	***Fruitafossor***	***Zalambdalestes***

ANSWERS: 1. *Volaticotherium* 2. *Durlstotherium* 3. *Didelphodon* 4. *Eomaia* 5. *Zalambdalestes* 6. *Repenomamus* 7. *Castorocauda* 8. *Kayentatherium* 9. *Fruitafossor*

The dinosaur age ends

Around 66 million years ago, a massive asteroid crashed into Earth. The devastating impact created an intense blast of heat, followed by years of impact winter, which caused a mass extinction. More than 75 percent of species were wiped out, including all dinosaurs apart from birds.

Acid rain

The impact released sulfur vapor into the atmosphere, producing acid rain. This not only affected habitats but may have eroded the remains of dead creatures, destroying any trace of their existence.

End of an era

All dinosaurs except birds went extinct at the end of the Cretaceous period, but they were not the only animals to die out. Several groups experienced total extinction, and many reptile, bird, and mammal species suffered losses.

Ammonites
After nearly 400 million years on Earth, ammonites suffered catastrophic losses with the group totally disappearing.

Belemnites
These squidlike mollusks with hard internal skeletons disappeared, allowing other cephalopods to take over.

Pterosaurs
After thriving alongside dinosaurs for more than 150 million years, pterosaurs were unable to survive the rapid environmental changes.

Plesiosaurs
The last of this once abundant group of marine reptiles died out after the disastrous asteroid strike.

Mosasaurs
Top predators of the Late Cretaceous seas, these giant aquatic lizards perished with the collapse of ocean ecosystems.

How to go out with a bang!

01. An asteroid 6 miles (10 km) across hurtles toward Earth at a speed faster than 44,000 mph (70,000 kph) and a deadly angle.

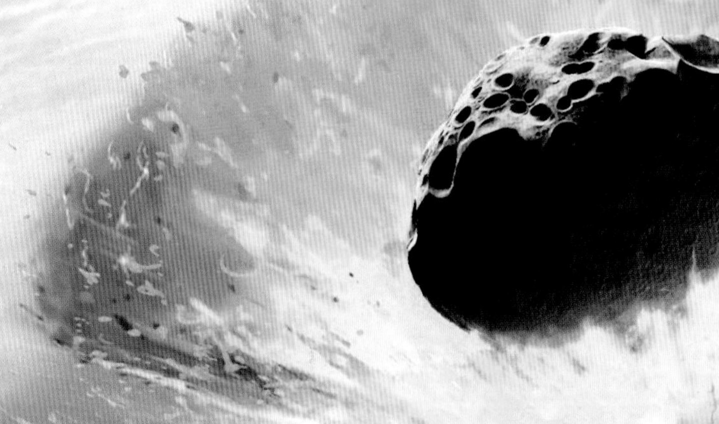

Almost all dinosaurs died out within three years of the extinction event.

02. The asteroid crashes into an area of land and sea near Chicxulub in what is now Mexico's Yucatán Peninsula. The force of the impact creates shockwaves as tall as skyscrapers and forms a crater 12 miles (20 km) deep.

03. The rock and debris from the crater is blasted into the atmosphere and begins to rain down all over Earth. An intense wave of heat raises the air temperature to 500°F (260°C), igniting fires that spread around the globe.

04. Volcanic activity and eruptions increase, leading to short-term climate change, acid rain, and depletion of oxygen in the oceans. This results in the mass extinction of dinosaurs and many marine reptiles and invertebrates.

The long winter

Following the sudden rise in temperature, the Earth slipped into 3-15 years of impact winter. Ash and debris blocked out the Sun, cooling the planet. With little sunlight, many plants could not make food using photosynthesis. With few plants, food chains on land and in the sea collapsed, and most animal life died out.

The dinosaurs that survived

A group of feathered theropods were the only dinosaurs to survive the effects of the impact. Today, we call them birds. Some of these birds were hard hit, too. Birds with teeth died out and only the beaked species lived on.

In numbers

30 minutes
The time it took for the debris to start falling back to Eartt after the asteroid hit

32,000 years
The period of time during which mass extinction took place at the end of the Cretaceous period

75%
The percentage of plant species that died out at the same time as the dinosaurs

A new life

Ferns often thrive after disasters. They grow well in habitats that have been disturbed and are often a first sign of recovery. Fern spores in rocks from 100,000 years after the impact indicate a fern spike that marked life's recovery from the extinction.

I don't believe it!

Some animals that survived the extinction did so because they were able to dig and get underground.

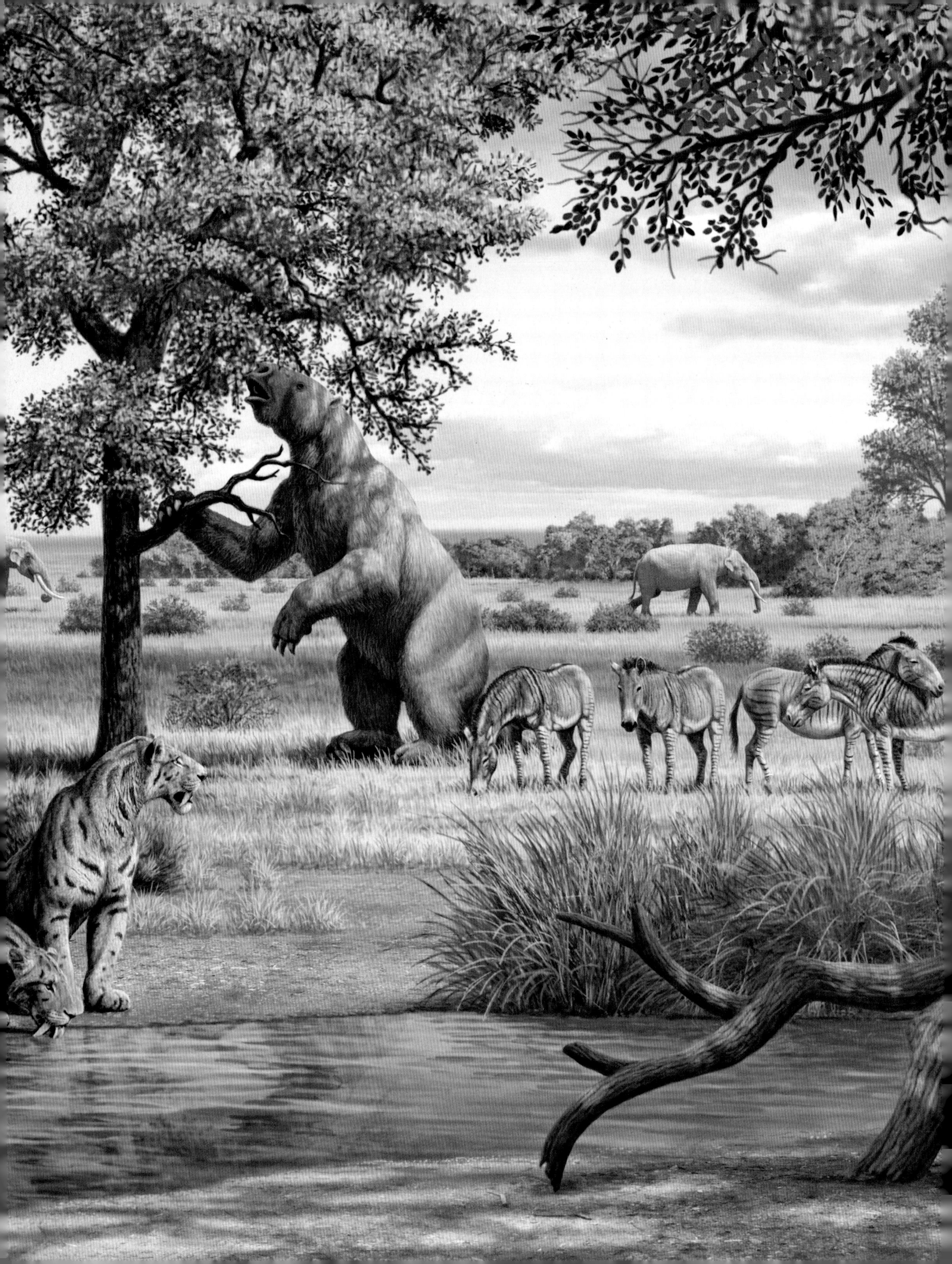

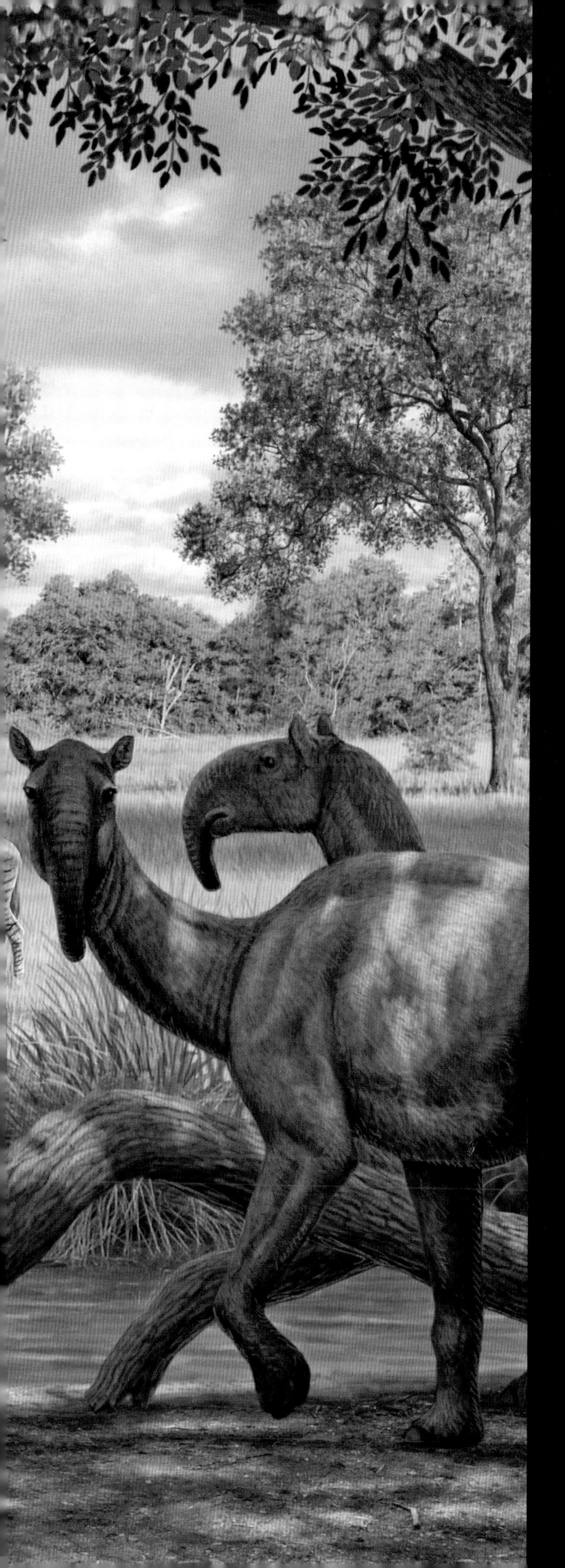

4 RISE OF THE MAMMALS

New life

When an asteroid crashed into Earth, wiping out all dinosaurs except birds, it changed everything. Mammals, birds, flowering plants, and other survivors of the catastrophe began to evolve in new ways and reshape the planet. The story of the Cenozoic is the origin of the world we live in today.

The Cenozoic Era

The asteroid strike 66 million years ago marked the dawn of the Cenozoic Era. Within a million years after the impact, flowering plants bloomed in warm forests, insects recovered their diversity, and beaked birds began to evolve in new ways. Mammals especially thrived during this time, so much so that the Cenozoic is sometimes called the "Age of Mammals."

Plant revival

Around 45 percent of plant species disappeared in the extinction. It took 6 million years for plant diversity to recover. Ferns and conifers continued to flourish during the Cenozoic while flowering plants began to spread, leading to the evolution of grasslands.

Conifers
Conifers that had been a source of food for dinosaurs survived into the Cenozoic and formed vast forests.

Flowering plants
Flowers blossomed following the extinction event, outcompeting older groups, such as cycads, and creating tropical rainforests.

Grasses
A cooling global climate favored grasses over tropical forests, and animals such as horses and elephants evolved to feed on this new source of greenery.

Human origins

The first humans originated only about 6 million years ago, late in the Cenozoic Era.

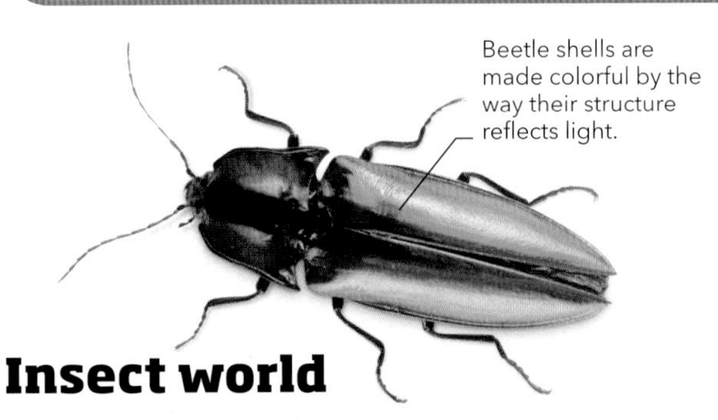

Insect world

Insects first appeared on Earth around 480 MYA, but many species went extinct at the end of the Cretaceous. Within 4 million years, however, insects reclaimed their diversity and their roles as pollinators, carrying pollen from flower to flower in exchange for nectar to eat. The spread of flowering plants was assisted by insects.

I don't believe it!

Early humans first left Africa around 2.1 MYA, while modern humans began to disperse around the world less than 150,000 years ago.

Shifting continents

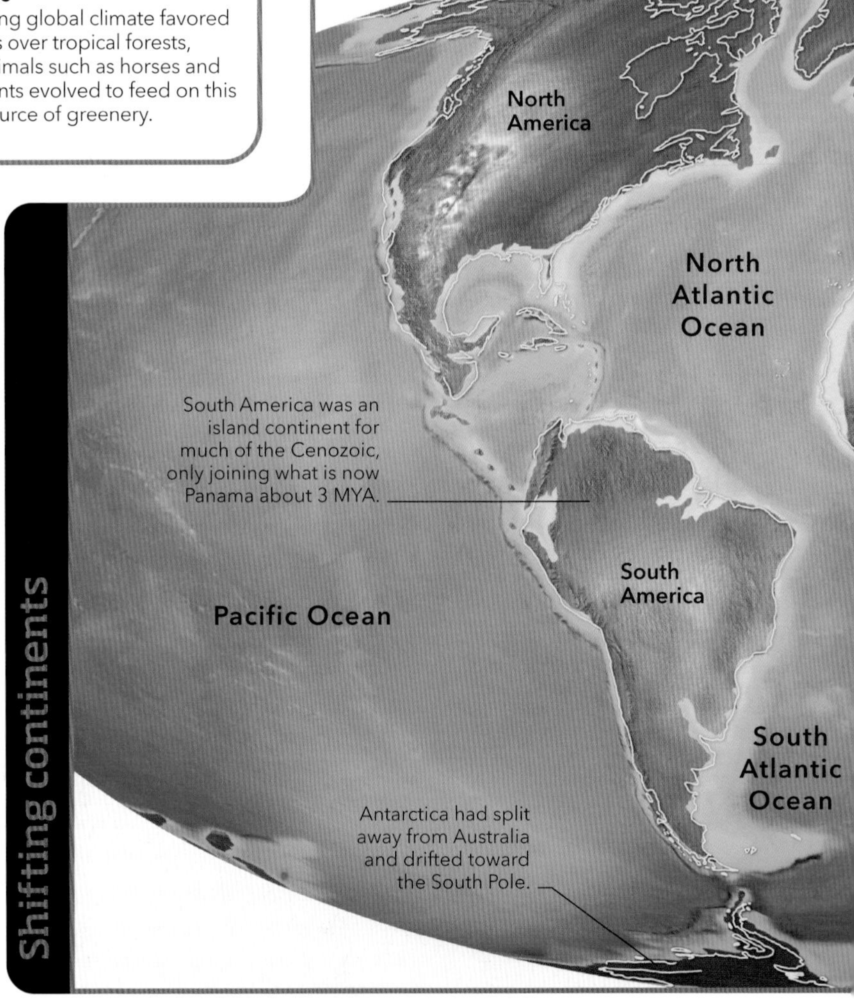

Petrified forests

Thick forests grew and were hotspots of evolution early in the Cenozoic. Their dense canopy created the perfect habitat for mammals, birds, and insects to evolve in new ways. Scientists know about this time from petrified forests, such as this one in South America, where massive tree trunks are preserved as fossils.

By 50 MYA, the world's continents had broken up into the landmasses we know today. However, they were different shapes and had not reached the positions they are in today. Parts of Asia and Africa were under a shallow sea, India was an island, and North and South America were not linked.

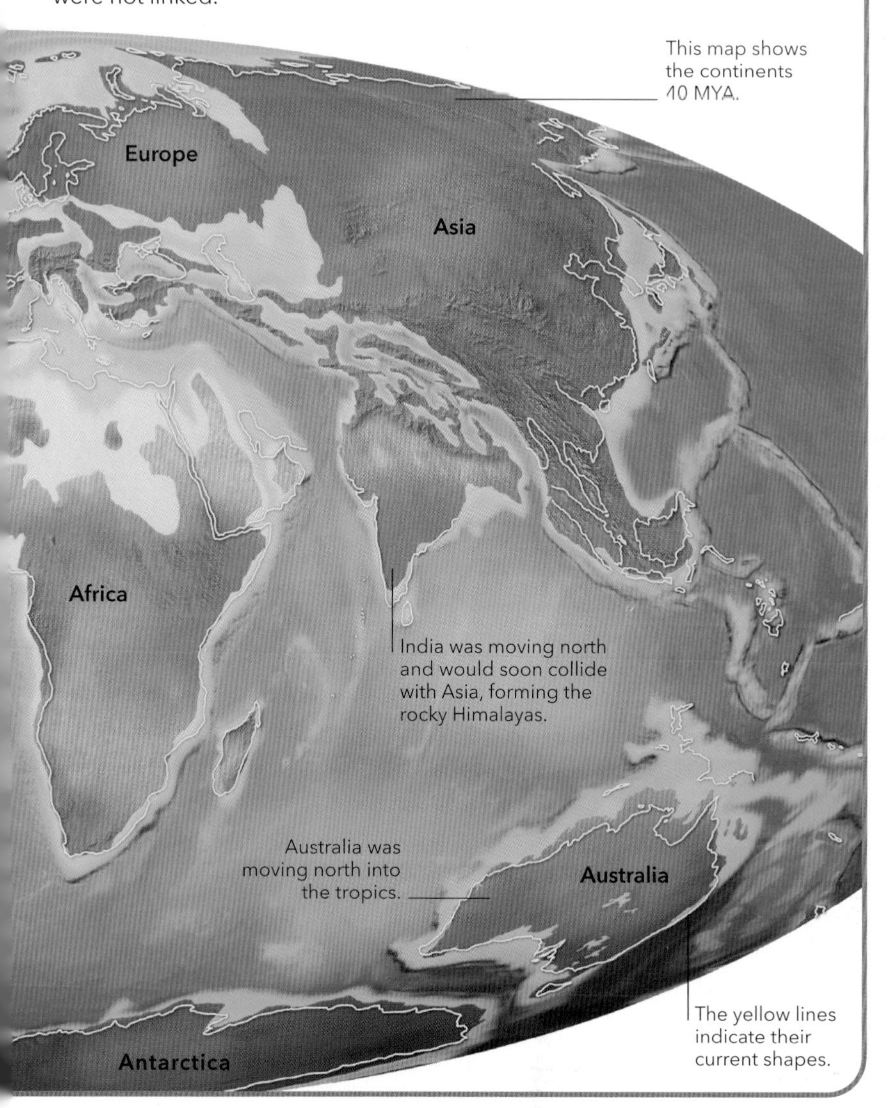

Through the Cenozoic

Paleogene Period

Paleocene (66-56 MYA)
In the first epoch (time period) of the Cenozoic, mammals were still small. One of the biggest, *Eoconodon*, was the size of a German shepherd dog.

Eocene (56-33.9 MYA)
The number of mammals began to increase—among them *Uintatherium*, an odd, horned plant-eater with saberlike fangs.

Oligocene (33.9-23 MYA)
Mammals such as cats, dogs, and rhinos evolved to become larger. *Paraceratherium* was possibly the largest land mammal of all time.

Neogene Period

Miocene (23-5.3 MYA)
New grasslands were the perfect habitat for primitive horses. The unusual *Moropus* was a slothlike cousin of horses and tapirs.

Pliocene (5.3-2.6 MYA)
The global climate became cooler and drier. *Pliohippus* was almost like today's horse except for two extra toes on each foot.

Quaternary Period

Pleistocene (2.5 million-11,700 years ago)
Large animals, or megafauna, thrived in this icy age. Giant wild cats, such as *Smilodon*, hunted horses and young mammoths.

Holocene (11,700-present)
Domestic dogs originated at the end of the Pleistocene but spread around the world alongside humans during the Holocene.

Titanoboa

An enormous constrictor that would have made today's anacondas look small, *Titanoboa* lived among some of the world's first tropical forests, just 8 million years after the time of *Tyrannosaurus rex*. How much do you know about the biggest snake to ever slither over the Earth?

1 *Titanoboa* could swallow fish and even small crocodiles with its massive jaws. How long was its skull?

A. 16 in (40 cm)
B. 24 in (60 cm)
C. 31 in (80 cm)
D. 39 in (100 cm)

2 In which present-day South American country have fossils of the giant *Titanoboa* been found?

A. Colombia
B. Bolivia
C. Ecuador
D. Venezuela

3 Paleontologists first discovered *Titanoboa* in 2009 in a coal mine. They collected hundreds of bones, which came from more than one snake. How many snakes did the bones belong to?

A. Seven
B. 16
C. 30
D. 99

4 *Titanoboa* lived in a swampy habitat. What creatures did it eat?

A. Birds
B. Smaller snakes
C. Insects
D. Fish and crocodiles

5 How did *Titanoboa* kill its prey?

A. By injecting venom
B. By swallowing it alive
C. By squeezing it in its coils and suffocating it
D. By tearing it apart with its teeth

6 A group of Canadian scientists have come up with an interesting way of studying *Titanoboa*'s movement. What is it?

A. Analyzing computer-generated graphics that recreate its movements
B. Watching movies about dinosaurs
C. Studying a robotic *Titanoboa*
D. Observing modern snakes

7 When the bones of *Titanoboa* were found, they were so big that they were mistaken for another animal. Which animal was it?

A. Another giant snake
B. Giant turtle
C. Crocodilian
D. Large fish

A single vertebra (neck bone) of *Titanoboa* is more than three times the size of that of a boa constrictor.

Boa constrictor vertebra

Titanoboa vertebra

8 *Titanoboa* belonged to an ancient group of snakes that is still around today and is known for squeezing their prey dead. *Titanoboa* was a:

A. Viper
B. Boa
C. Python
D. Grass snake

9 Fossils of *Titanoboa* show that it was one of the heaviest snakes that ever lived. Approximately how much did it weigh?

Titanoboa

Small car

A. 2,204 lb (1,000 kg) or as much as a Bactrian camel

B. 2,425 lb (1,100 kg) or as much as a water buffalo

C. 2,645 lb (1,200 kg) or as much as an American bison

D. 3,306 lb (1,500 kg) or as much as a Pacific walrus

ANSWERS: 1-A, 2-A, 3-C, 4-D, 5-C, 6-C, 7-C, 8-B, 9-B

1 Soaring over Argentina, this was one of the largest birds ever to have flown. Its wingspan was around 20 ft (6 m), which is almost double that of a modern Andean condor.
The wings of terror birds were tiny, likely to help keep them from being broken while the birds grappled prey with their feet.
2 One of the dominant land predators of South America, this flightless carnivore was as tall as an ostrich and weighed 290 lb (130 kg). It used its hooked beak and clawed feet to hunt prey.
TEST YOURSELF
Argentavis
Moa (Dinornithiformes)
Elephant bird (Aepyornithidae)
Brontornis
STARTER
Phorusrhacos
Pelagornis
Dromornis
CHALLENGER
Andalgalornis
Kumimanu
Haast's eagle (Harpagornis moorei)
GENIUS!
Hatchetlike beak for jabbing at prey
Large feet with four clawed toes
The trunklike neck of this heavy bird contributed to its 6-ft (1.8-m) height.
3 A powerful neck allowed this terror bird to strike downward at prey with its hooked beak.
The largest of these birds could reach 10 ft (3 m) tall.
4 Several species of this tall, flightless bird thrived in New Zealand because it had no predators. Hunting and loss of forest habitat drove them to extinction.
5 This large, flightless bird, sometimes called a "demon duck," was once thought to be a relative of modern emus and ostriches, but it has now been proven to be closely related to ducks and geese.

The beak of this toothless bird was serrated.

⑥ This prehistoric bird is thought to be the largest flying bird of all time. The biggest species had a wingspan over 24 ft (7.3 m), twice as wide as a wandering albatross.

⑦ The largest eagle ever, this raptor from New Zealand weighed more than 33 lb (15 kg). It is thought to have hunted flightless birds called moas.

Giant birds

The only dinosaurs to survive the mass extinction were the birds. They evolved into many types, some of which were huge! No one knows for sure why they got so big, but a lack of competition may have helped. In fact, some—known as "terror birds"—were top predators. Discover more about these giant birds from this quiz!

The deep, powerful beak may have been used to eat plants.

⑨ Discovered in Argentina, the fossils of this large bird have led paleontologists to suggest that it stood more than 9 ft (2.7 m) tall.

Its beak was longer than that of its modern cousins.

⑧ Some of the largest flightless birds of all time, these giants lived on Madagascar until recently. The last of them went extinct about 800 years ago.

⑩ Standing 5.2 ft (1.6 m) tall, this giant penguin flapped its flippers to chase after fish. The oldest fossil penguins are about 62 million years old.

ANSWERS: 1. *Argentavis* 2. *Phorusrhacos* 3. *Andalgalornis* 4. *Dinornithiformes* (Moa) 5. *Dromornis* 6. *Pelagornis* 7. *Harpagornis moorei* (Haast's eagle) 8. *Aepyornithidae* (Elephant bird) 9. *Brontornis* 10. *Kumimanu*

Gastornis

Big birds have evolved repeatedly during this era. *Gastornis* was one of the earliest. The flightless bird roamed over a wide area of the Northern Hemisphere, towering over the mammals of the time—the biggest of which would have been the size of a large dog.

1 When the first *Gastornis* fossil was discovered in the 1850s, it was believed to belong to a giant-sized species of another bird. Which bird was that?

A. Crane
B. Chicken
C. Emu
D. Ostrich

The beak of *Gastornis* was well-suited to crushing food.

2 Most *Gastornis* fossils have been found in North America and Europe, but paleontologists have found a single massive bone that shows the bird roamed prehistoric China, too. Which bone was it?

A. Thigh bone
B. Rib
C. Beak
D. Shin bone

3 The first known *Gastornis* fossil was discovered about 5 miles (9 km) away from the center of which major city?

A. Paris, France
B. Rome, Italy
C. Cairo, Egypt
D. Sydney, Australia

4 According to experts, what did *Gastornis* eat?

A. Fish and marine reptiles
B. Small mammals
C. Other birds
D. Fruits, seeds, and nuts

5 A chicken egg weighs around 2.5 oz (70 g). What was the estimated weight of *Gastornis*'s eggs?

A. 4 oz (100 g)

B. 18 oz (500 g)

C. 3 lb (1.4 kg)

D. 5 lb (2.3 kg)

Gastornis egg

Chicken egg

6 Initially, paleontologists believed that *Gastornis* was a carnivore. What made them change their minds about this?

A. Its beak was not hooked, like that of many meat-eating birds today

B. It had lightweight bones.

C. It was relatively large in size.

D. It had comparatively small eyes.

7 Which modern bird is *Gastornis* considered to be a relative of?

A. Vulture

B. Crane

C. Duck

D. Eagle

8 *Gastornis* was the biggest bird of its time. How tall was it?

A. 3 ft (1 m)

B. 6.5 ft (2 m)

C. 10 ft (3 m)

D. 13 ft (4 m)

ANSWERS: 1-A, 2-D, 3-A, 4-D, 5-C, 6-A, 7-C, 8-B

Early mammals

Mammals coexisted with the non-avian dinosaurs for millions of years, but most were very small. This helped them to survive the asteroid impact and over time they adapted to live in different ways. As some mammals became larger, they also evolved into many new forms.

What is a mammal?

While mammals are a large and diverse group, they all have certain characteristics in common. All mammals are vertebrates (they have a backbone and skeleton) and are warm-blooded (they can generate body heat from the food they eat). Most have fur or hair for warmth and all but a few bear live young that feed on their mother's milk.

Rise of the mammals

In the Cenozoic Era, after the dinosaurs became extinct, the number and diversity of mammals exploded. A variety of species can be seen in this North American grassland habitat.

Cats and dogs
Cats and dogs evolved about 30 million years ago. While dogs adapted to run after fleeing prey, most cats are ambush predators.

Extinct mammals

Many mammal groups survive and thrive today, but those below have gone extinct.

Pantodonts
With babies born already in possession of milk teeth, these mammals, including *Barylambda,* were among the first to grow bigger.

Mesonychids
These "wolves with hooves," such as *Ankalagon*, were some of the earliest mammals to become specialized meat-eaters.

Chalicotheres
These slothlike relatives of horses and rhinos, such as *Anisodon*, may have used their claws to pull down branches and strip trees.

Hyaenodonts
Some of these predators were the size of a household dog, while others—such as *Hyaenodon*—were larger than lions.

Protoceratids
Each species of these hoofed mammals, which included *Kyptoceras*, had a unique set of brow and nose horns.

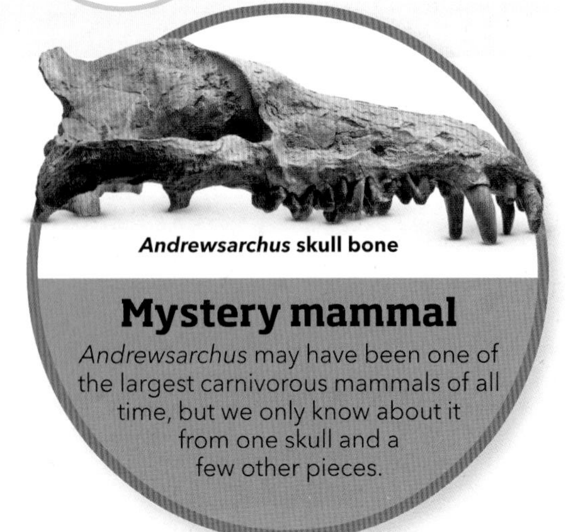

***Andrewsarchus* skull bone**

Mystery mammal

Andrewsarchus may have been one of the largest carnivorous mammals of all time, but we only know about it from one skull and a few other pieces.

Big and small

Some mammals evolved and increased in size during the Cenozoic Era. The giant rhino *Paraceratherium* stood over 15 ft (4.5 m) at the shoulder. However, most mammals have remained small in size. The smallest of all is the hog-nosed bat, which measures about 1 in (30 mm) long.

I don't believe it!

Whales evolved from hoofed mammals that lived on land, making them distant relatives of hippos and cows.

In numbers

1 million years
The average life span of a mammal species before becoming extinct.

22 months
How long a mammoth is thought to have carried a calf in its womb, based on studies of mammoths' close relatives, elephants.

Types of birth

Monotremes
There are very few egg-laying mammals today. Known as monotremes, they include the duck-billed platypus and echidnas.

Marsupials
Kangaroos and their relatives, opossums, and other marsupials, give birth to unformed young that develops inside a pouch.

Placentals
Rhinos and other placental mammals, such as humans carry babies in the womb for a relatively long time, giving birth to fully formed young.

Horses
The ancestors of horses evolved teeth suited to eating grass, grew larger, and became single-toed—which meant they could run faster.

Mammoths
Related to elephants, mammoths were some of the largest mammals on Earth for more than 50 million years. They evolved an array of different tusk and mouth shapes to help them eat, dig, and fight off predators.

Sloths
Many mammal groups moved around the world over time. Giant sloths evolved in South America before spreading into North America around 9 million years ago.

1. This ancient whale is named after one of the states of the US. Its long snout helped it snatch fish in the shallow seas.

2. This "king lizard" was one of the first prehistoric whales to be discovered. Growing to more than 49 ft (15 m) long, it fed on sharks and other whales.

3. This primitive whale takes its name from the beach in Australia where its fossil was found by a teenage surfer.

4. A prehistoric whale with no living relatives, this long-snouted sea creature lived in estuaries—an area where a freshwater river or stream meets the ocean—and hunted fish.

5. This giant is the largest animal alive today and possibly of all time. It uses its hairlike baleen, a series of small plates hanging from its upper jaw, to filter small morsels from the water. The oldest fossil is 1.5 million years old.

TEST YOURSELF

STARTER

Dorudon
Blue whale (*Balaenoptera musculus*)
Basilosaurus

CHALLENGER

Georgiacetus
Kutchicetus
Pakicetus
Ambulocetus

GENIUS!

Janjucetus
Maiacetus
Indohyus

ANSWERS: 1. *Georgiacetus* 2. *Basilosaurus* 3. *Janjucetus* 4. *Kutchicetus* 5. Blue whale 6. *Ambulocetus* 7. *Dorudon* 8. *Pakicetus* 9. *Maiacetus* 10. *Indohyus*

Whales

Recent fossil discoveries have shown that, around 50 million years ago, land-dwelling mammals moved into the water to become whales. As they evolved, their limbs became flipperlike, and they eventually lost their hind limbs. How much do you know about these hoofed mammals that returned to the water?

⑥ This early whale lived like a crocodile. Its eyes and nostrils were high on its head, so it could lie beneath the surface of the water and sneak up on prey.

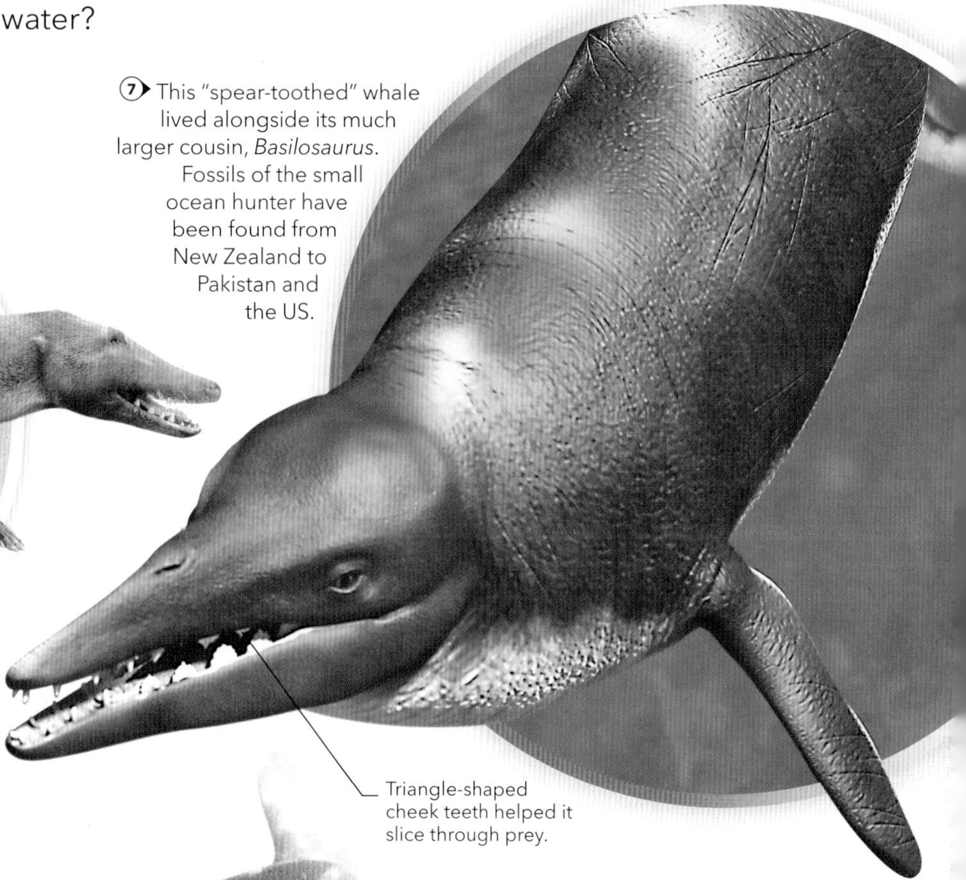

⑦ This "spear-toothed" whale lived alongside its much larger cousin, *Basilosaurus*. Fossils of the small ocean hunter have been found from New Zealand to Pakistan and the US.

⑧ This four-legged land mammal was actually one of the earliest whales. It had a thickened dome of bone around its ears. This feature is only found in whales.

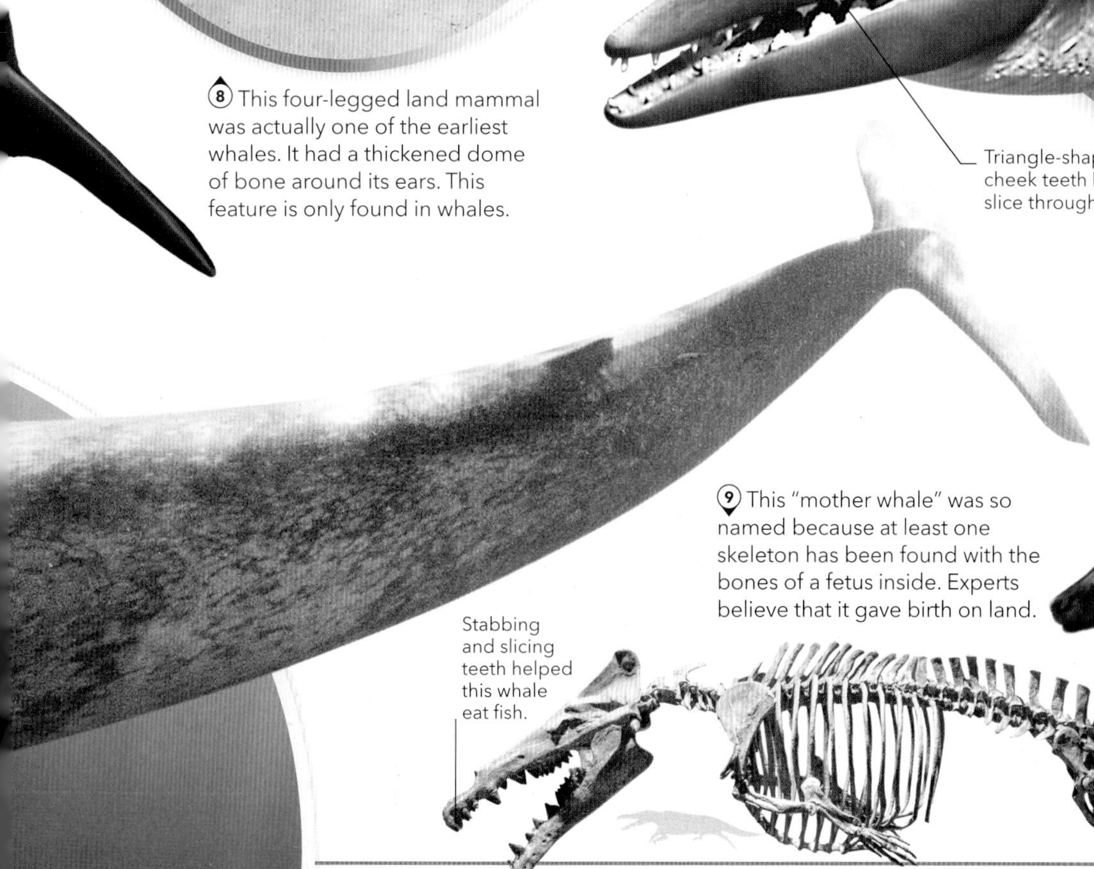

Triangle-shaped cheek teeth helped it slice through prey.

⑩ While not a true whale, this animal the size of a raccoon represents the hoofed mammals from which whales evolved. Its name means "India's pig."

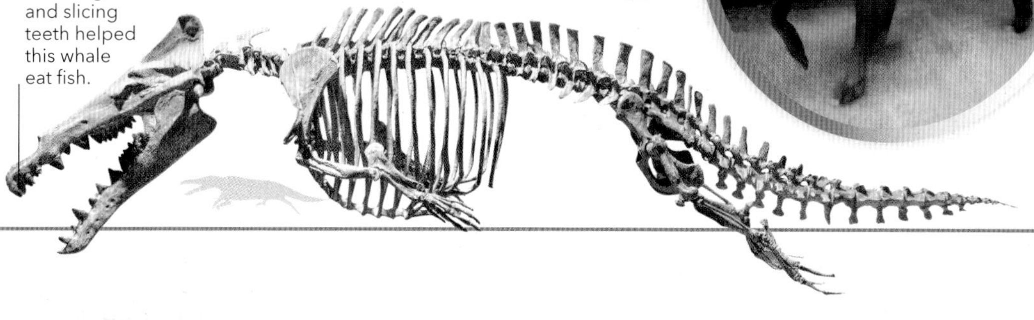

⑨ This "mother whale" was so named because at least one skeleton has been found with the bones of a fetus inside. Experts believe that it gave birth on land.

Stabbing and slicing teeth helped this whale eat fish.

1 Which modern-day whale is similar in size to *Livyatan*?

Livyatan

Modern whale

A. Blue whale **B.** Killer whale

C. Sperm whale **D.** Humpback whale

Livyatan's gigantic body weighed about 100,000 lb (45,000 kg).

Livyatan

One of the most impressive whales of all time lived around 9 million years ago. *Livyatan melvillei* was a toothy predator that swam in the same waters as smaller, filter-feeding baleen whales, which it hunted.

2 Which marine predator might have been the main rival of *Livyatan*?

A. *Sarcosuchus*

B. *Otodus megalodon*

C. *Pliosaurus*

D. *Ambulocetus*

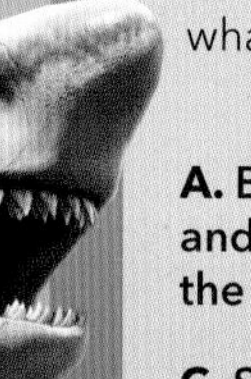

3 Scientists believe *Livyatan* might have hunted like an orca or killer whale. How did it attack its prey?

A. Bit the tail of the prey off and waited for it to sink to the ocean bed

B. Opened its mouth wide and swallowed its prey whole

C. Slapped the prey with its fins and then rammed it with its head

D. Rammed the prey with its head and body and then attacked with teeth

ANSWERS: 1-C, 2-B, 3-D, 4-B, 5-A, 6-A, 7-B

4 Many modern whales are filter feeders, but *Livyatan* was more closely related to the sperm whale, which has teeth on its lower jaw. How was it different from modern sperm whales?

A. It hunted in a different manner.

B. It had teeth on its upper jaw.

C. It did not have a breathing hole.

D. The shape of its skull was different.

5 A very famous story about a sperm whale, called *Moby Dick*, was written by American author Herman Melville in 1851. How is he connected to *Livyatan melvillei*?

A. *Livyatan melvillei* was named after him.

B. He was the first person to find *Livyatan* bones.

C. He was the first to predict that a prehistoric whale existed.

D. He based *Moby Dick* on the story of how *Livyatan*'s fossil was found.

6 What could have caused the extinction of *Livyatan*?

A. A global drop in temperature, reducing the population of animals that *Livyatan* preyed upon

B. Competition from other sharks hunting the same animals as *Livyatan*

C. Falling sea levels

D. A meteor strike

7 *Livyatan* had some of the largest biting teeth, excluding tusks, of any animal that ever lived. How long were its teeth?

A. 6 in (15 cm)

B. 12 in (30 cm)

C. 16 in (40 cm)

D. 22 in (55 cm)

① Paleontologists think this North American rhino's short height helped it munch on grasses that grew close to the ground.

It had a horn on its snout like a rhino, but its body was more like a hippo's.

Elephant tusks are actually elongated teeth.

② This "marine sloth" was the size of a large pig and evolved to swim in the shallows, eating algae and plants that grew close to the shore.

③ Its name means "shovel-tusked," but this elephant did not use its tusks in that way. Instead, its teeth helped saw and cut tree branches, which it plucked with its trunk.

A long, deep neck allowed it to browse high on trees.

TEST YOURSELF

STARTER

Megatherium
Glyptotherium
Steppe mammoth (*Mammuthus trogontherii*)

CHALLENGER

Teleoceras
Amebelodon
Shansitherium

GENIUS!

Moropus
Thalassocnus
Paramylodon
Paraceratherium

Skin-covered bones, called ossicones, similar to giraffes today

Its claws helped it grip rocks while feeding in the water.

④ Among the largest of the giant sloths, this "great beast" from South America was around 20 ft (6 m) long from head to tail.

⑤ This "beast of Shanxi," which lived in the region that is now China, was a prehistoric giraffe with a short neck, like the modern-day okapi.

Its claws were used for defense and to pull tree branches closer.

ANSWERS: 1. *Teleoceras* 2. *Thalassocnus* 3. *Amebelodon* 4. *Megatherium* 5. *Shansitherium* 6. *Glyptotherium* 7. *Paramylodon* 8. *Mammuthus trogontherii* 9. *Moropus* 10. *Paraceratherium*

Plant-eating giants

Ever since mammals first appeared, most have been small, but early in the Cenozoic Era, giant mammals began to emerge. Enormous elephants, super-sized sloths, and gargantuan giraffes evolved in astonishing ways as climates warmed.

Large ears helped it keep cool in warmer habitats.

Its shell was made of hundreds of interlocking bony plates (osteoderms).

⑥ This giant armadillo had a distinct shell that gives it its name, "carved beast." Unlike insect-eating modern armadillos, it was a herbivore.

Its tusks were versatile–used for clearing vegetation and in combat.

Under the thick fur, its skin was embedded with small bones (osteoderms).

⑦ One of many giant sloths that spread through the Americas, this sloth was a grazer, feeding on grasses and other low-growing plants.

⑧ This huge creature was one of the largest elephant relatives of all time. The biggest individuals could reach almost 15 ft (4.5 m) high at the shoulders.

⑨ This giant was related to a group of horses and rhinos that went totally extinct. These hoofed animals were given the name "sloth horses" due to their slothlike features.

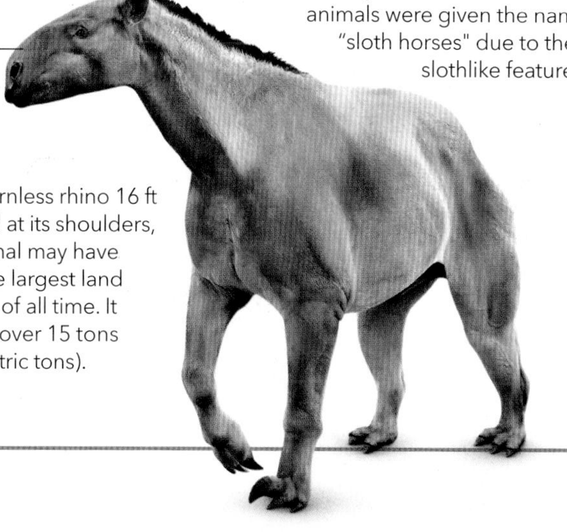

It could grow to be 8 ft (2.4 m) tall.

⑩ A hornless rhino 16 ft (5 m) tall at its shoulders, this animal may have been the largest land mammal of all time. It weighed over 15 tons (13.6 metric tons).

Body cover

As creatures in the Cenozoic Era evolved into an astonishing range of different groups and species, they also grew a variety of body coverings. Mammals grew fur that helped keep them warm, while the scales and scutes of reptiles provided a defense against predatory carnivores.

④ A lion of cold, Ice Age grasslands, this big cat had a thick undercoat—a layer of fur close to the skin that helped keep it warm in the chilly temperatures.

⑤ This alligator relative lived in what is now North America and Europe. It was covered in osteoderms—spongy bones that grew inside the skin.

Osteoderms covered the reptile's back, providing protection.

⑥ This primate was covered in a thick coat of fur, much like today's lemurs, trapping body heat, as well as protecting it from sunburn and injury.

TEST YOURSELF

STARTER

Darwinius

Big-horned bison (*Bison crassicornis*)

Panthera spelaea

CHALLENGER

Varanus

Nothrotheriops

Diplocynodon

GENIUS!

Megalochelys

Lepisosteus

Meiolania

⑦ This large turtle had a tough shell for protection. It also had horns on its head and a spiky tail for defense.

⑧ Pebbly scales on this early monitor lizard's body helped it resist bites during fights, also protecting it from scratches while moving through the undergrowth.

⑨ The shell of this giant tortoise could grow to be over 6 ft (1.8 m) long. Its shoulder blades were enclosed within the protective bones.

ANSWERS: 1. Big-horned bison 2. *Nothrotheriops* 3. *Lepisosteus* 4. *Panthera spelaea* 5. *Diplocynodon* 6. *Darwinius* 7. *Meiolania* 8. *Varanus* 9. *Megalochelys*

1 Paleontologists now know that *Deinotherium* is related to elephants, but which other mammal family did they incorrectly think it was linked to at first?

A. Pangolins
B. Sloths
C. Bisons
D. Koalas

2 How much did *Deinotherium* weigh?

A. Up to 13 tons (12 metric tonnes) or as much as one school bus
B. 26 tons (24 metric tonnes) or as much as two school buses
C. 39 tons (36 metric tonnes) or as much as three school buses
D. 52 tons (48 metric tonnes) or as much as four school buses

Deinotherium

Fossils show that elephant ancestors evolved tusks arranged in many different ways. But *Deinotherium* had one of the strangest—peculiar curved tusks jutting from its lower jaws. Quiz yourself on this early relative of elephants!

3 *Deinotherium* fossils were first found near the city of Lyon, France. What name was given to the site?

A. Home of monsters
B. Pit of bones
C. Field of giants
D. Valley of titans

4 The molar teeth of *Deinotherium* are similar to those of modern tapirs. This has led paleontologists to believe that it ate what food?

A. Fish
B. Insects
C. Plants
D. Meat

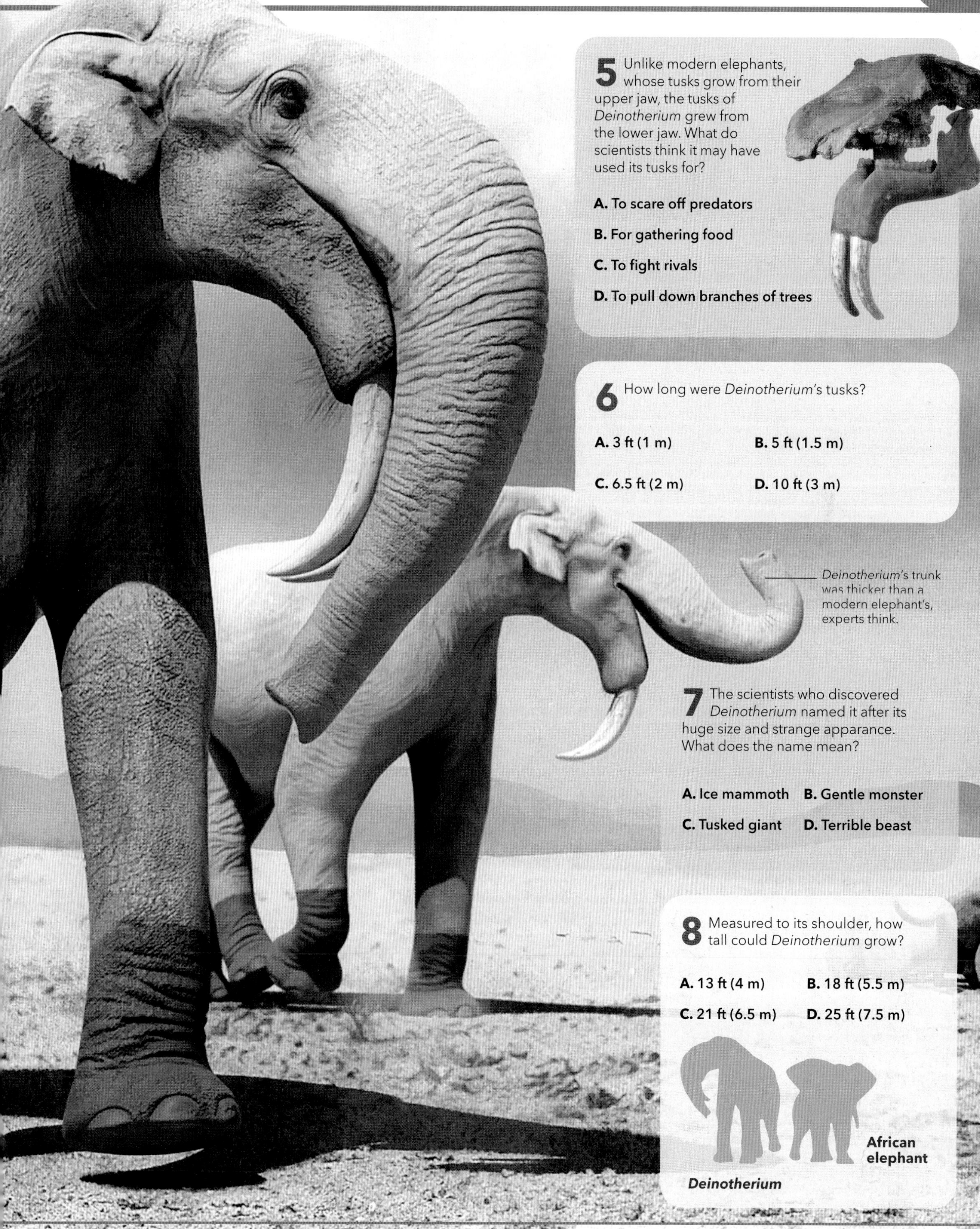

5 Unlike modern elephants, whose tusks grow from their upper jaw, the tusks of *Deinotherium* grew from the lower jaw. What do scientists think it may have used its tusks for?

A. To scare off predators

B. For gathering food

C. To fight rivals

D. To pull down branches of trees

6 How long were *Deinotherium*'s tusks?

A. 3 ft (1 m)

B. 5 ft (1.5 m)

C. 6.5 ft (2 m)

D. 10 ft (3 m)

7 The scientists who discovered *Deinotherium* named it after its huge size and strange apparance. What does the name mean?

A. Ice mammoth

B. Gentle monster

C. Tusked giant

D. Terrible beast

8 Measured to its shoulder, how tall could *Deinotherium* grow?

A. 13 ft (4 m)

B. 18 ft (5.5 m)

C. 21 ft (6.5 m)

D. 25 ft (7.5 m)

ANSWERS: 1-B, 2-A, 3-C, 4-C, 5-D, 6-A, 7-D, 8-A

Horns and antlers

Dinosaurs were not the only prehistoric animals to sport impressive headgear. Many Cenozoic mammals, from ancient giraffes to burrowing gophers, evolved stunning spreads of horns and antlers. Can you tell which animals the ones shown here belong to?

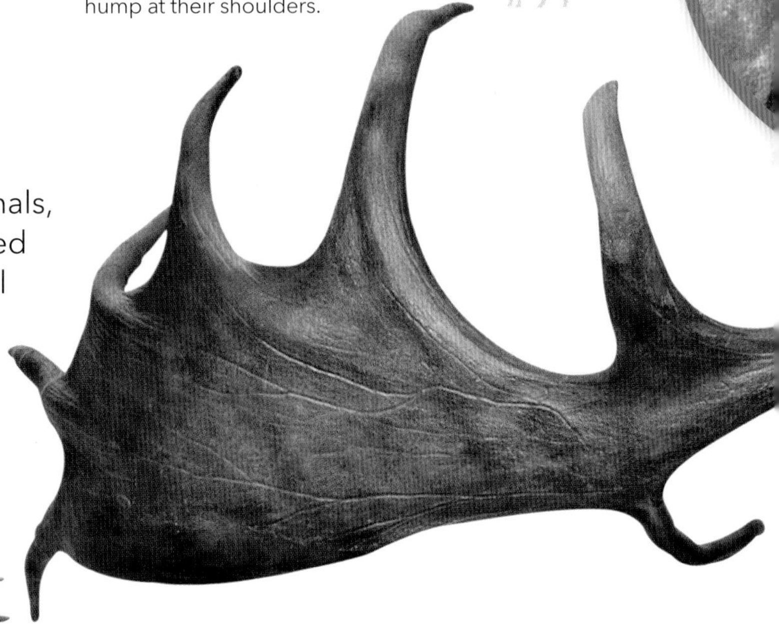

1 This giant deer species is also called the Irish elk. Cave paintings suggest males had a rust-colored hump at their shoulders.

2 Not all giraffes had long necks. This giant giraffe had a short neck and four horns. It had two large, wide horns that looked like upturned palms on its head and a second pair above its eyes.

The horns, known as ossicones, were covered with furry skin like those of a modern-day giraffe.

Antlers were shed every year, like those of deer today.

3 This bush-antlered deer was almost as big as a present-day moose. Its antlers branched into two parts, giving this deer its distinctive look.

4 Paleontologists are still stumped as to why this rodent, also known as a "horned gopher," had horns. Digging, defense, and impressing mates are all possibilities.

The horns on its nose were like those of a rhinoceros.

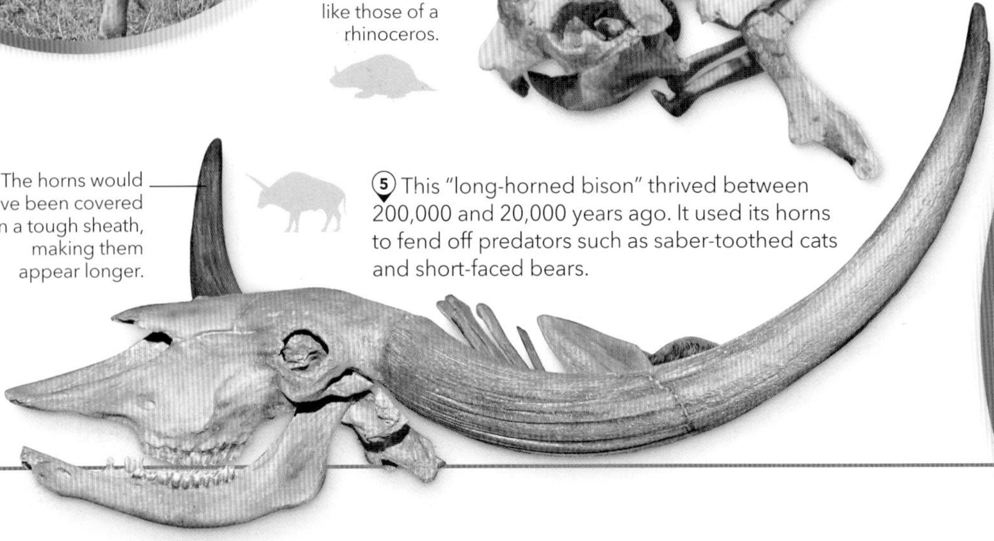

The horns would have been covered in a tough sheath, making them appear longer.

5 This "long-horned bison" thrived between 200,000 and 20,000 years ago. It used its horns to fend off predators such as saber-toothed cats and short-faced bears.

⑥ This "thunder beast" was a brontothere—an extinct family of rhinoceroslike mammals. A large hollow nose helped it communicate or control body temperatures.

Its nose horn may have helped it make deep sounds.

The antlers had a span of up to 12 ft (3.5 m).

TEST YOURSELF

STARTER

Megaloceros
Long-horned bison (*Bison latifrons*)
Megacerops

CHALLENGER

Arsinotherium
Embolotherium
Sivatherium

GENIUS!

Ceratogaulus
Eucladoceros
Kyptoceras

It used its horns to fight with rival males and scare away predators.

⑦ This small animal was one of an extinct group of hoofed mammals that often evolved slingshot-shaped horns on their snouts.

⑧ Even though it resembled a rhino, this mammal was more closely related to elephants, manatees, and hyraxes.

Both males and females had massive horns.

The skull of the male sported a pair of horns.

⑨ Only males of this "crescent-horned" prehistoric rhino had horns. Fossils found together hint that it may have lived in a herd.

ANSWERS: 1. *Megaloceros* 2. *Sivatherium* 3. *Eucladoceros* 4. *Ceratogaulus* 5. *Bison latifrons* 6. *Embolotherium* 7. *Kyptoceras* 8. *Arsinotherium* 9. *Megacerops*

① This prehistoric carnivore, often referred to as "dire wolf," was about the same size as modern wolves and hunted in packs over long distances.

Carnivorous mammals

The Cenozoic Era saw the rise of meat-eating mammals. Many of them belonged to the group Carnivora, which includes dogs, cats, bears, hyenas, weasels, and even seals. These were not the only flesh-eaters, though—other mammals, including whales, had carnivorous diets.

② Despite its name, "great lion," this animal was really a hyaenodont—a group of carnivorous mammals that thrived before cats and dogs. Its long jaws were lined with teeth for shearing the flesh of its prey.

The size of a grizzly bear, it was the largest canid ever known.

③ Fossilized poop suggests "bone-crushing dogs" like this one broke up and ate skeletons, in the same way spotted hyenas do today.

④ This carnivore was one of the largest bear dogs—predators related to both bears and dogs. Tracks found in California show it had long claws on each paw.

ANSWERS: 1. *Aenocyon* 2. *Simbakubwa* 3. *Epicyon* 4. *Amphicyon* 5. *Dinocrocuta* 6. *Hoplophoneus* 7. *Arctotherium* 8. *Barbourofelis* 9. *Ankylorhiza*

⑤ Bite marks of this massive predator and scavenger have been found on the bones of *Chilotherium*, an early rhino. Its name means "terrible hyena."

⑥ A "false saber-toothed cat," this cat relative could grow to the size of a leopard. Fossils found with damaged skulls suggest that they fought by biting each other on the face.

⑦ This huge relative of the spectacled bear from South America may have been an omnivore. It is the largest known bear.

⑧ One of the largest and last "false saber-toothed cats," this carnivore could grow to be as massive as a modern-day jaguar.

⑨ The adults of this toothed whale—related to today's orcas and dolphins—could grow to be 16 ft (5 m) long.

TEST YOURSELF

STARTER

Arctotherium
Amphicyon
Dinocrocuta

CHALLENGER

Simbakubwa
Epicyon
Hoplophoneus

GENIUS!

Ankylorhiza
Barbourofelis
Aenocyon

1 Because of it huge canines, *Smilodon* had to open its jaws at an extremely wide angle to bite its prey. What was the angle?

A. 120° **B.** 150°

C. 160° **D.** 200°

2 *Smilodon* cubs had milk teeth, which were replaced by adult teeth. How old were they when their full fangs appeared?

A. Two months **B.** Five months

C. 11 months **D.** Two years

3 By studying clues from its teeth, what do scientists think some North American *Smilodon* populations preyed upon?

A. Mammoths and giant sloths **B.** Fish and crocodiles

C. Humans and other apes **D.** Tapirs and deer

4 What kind of habitats did North American populations of *Smilodon fatalis* seem to prefer?

A. Open plains **B.** Coasts

C. Forests **D.** Riverbanks

The canines had sharp, saw-toothed edges for slicing through meat.

5 *Smilodon*'s canines were long and extended well below its lower jaws. How long were they?

A. 4 in (10 cm) **B.** 11 in (28 cm)

C. 20 in (52 cm) **D.** 30 in (75 cm)

Smilodon

Among the last of the saber-toothed cats, *Smilodon* is also one of the best known. From about 2.5 million to 11,000 years ago, several *Smilodon* species prowled the ancient Americas, preying upon the large mammals of their time.

Thick fur covered *Smilodon* to keep it warm in freezing-cold conditions.

Smilodon probably made sounds that were deeper than present-day lions and tigers.

Retractable claws protected by sheaths, like those of modern cats, helped *Smilodon* catch prey.

6 *Smilodon* was one of the largest saber-toothed cats. How much did it weigh?

A. 330 lb (150 kg) **B.** 395 lb (180 kg)

C. 440 lb (200 kg) **D.** 615 lb (280 kg)

7 *Smilodon* had front legs that were powerful, thick, and muscular—helpful for pinning prey down. What does this suggest about its way of hunting?

A. It usually hunted at night.

B. It usually hunted during the day.

C. It swam after its prey.

D. It ambushed and wrestled its prey before biting it.

8 Which of these is NOT one of the possible reasons for *Smilodon*'s extinction?

A. Decrease in the number of large herbivores

B. Landscape changes caused by wildfire

C. Climate change

D. Meteorite strike

ANSWERS: 1-A, 2-C, 3-D, 4-C, 5-B, 6-D, 7-D, 8-D

Otodus megalodon

There has never been a bigger shark than *Otodus megalodon*. Related to today's fast-swimming mako sharks, this marine predator cruised oceans all around the world for almost 20 million years, dying out 3.6 MYA. The thick layer of fat called blubber on the bodies of marine mammals, such as whales and seals, provided the food this voracious ocean giant needed to fuel its astonishing size. Learn more about this notorious hunter!

1 What is the estimated volume of *Otodus megalodon*'s stomach?

A. 1,300 gallons (4,800 liters, about 48 bathtubs)

B. 1,700 gallons (6,400 liters, about 64 bathtubs)

C. 2,500 gallons (9,600 liters, about 96 bathtubs)

D. 2,700 gallons (10,300 liters, about 103 bathtubs)

2 *Otodus megalodon*'s skin was covered with tiny, toothlike scales that acted as a form of protection. What were these called?

A. Cycloid scales
B. Keratinoids
C. Placoid scales
D. Denticles

3 Paleontologists think that a modern-day ocean predator competed with *Otodus megalodon* for food. Which predator was it?

A. Hammerhead shark
B. Great white shark
C. Colossal squid
D. Orca

4 *Otodus megalodon*'s teeth were three times the size of the teeth of a modern great white shark. How long was each tooth?

A. 4 in (12 cm)

B. 5 in (15 cm)

C. 7 in (18 cm)

D. 8 in (20 cm)

5 *Otodus megalodon* had a bite stronger than that of a great white shark—the most powerful shark alive. How much stronger was it?

A. Five times stronger

B. Six times stronger

C. Eight times stronger

D. 10 times stronger

6 *Otodus megalodon* had hundreds of teeth, which were continuously replaced with new ones. What was the number of teeth in its mouth at any one time?

A. 200

B. 256

C. 276

D. 305

7 What does the species name "megalodon" mean?

A. Big body

B. Fastest swimmer

C. Big tooth

D. Fierce predator

8 *Otodus megalodon* swam in warm waters. Its fossils have been found along the coastlines of all continents but one. Which is it?

A. Africa

B. Antarctica

C. Europe

D. Asia

9 *Otodus megalodon* had a gigantic bite. Which of these modern animals could it have eaten in just five bites?

A. Komodo dragon, 10 ft (3 m)

B. Hippopotamus, 13 ft (4m)

C. Great white shark, 20 ft (6m)

D. Orca, 26 ft (8m)

ANSWERS: 1-C, 2-D, 3-B, 4-C, 5-B, 6-C, 7-C, 8-B, 9-D

① This animal belonged to a family of civetlike mammals that could climb trees. These mammals were related to the first cats and dogs.

② One of the earliest dogs, this "western dog" had a long, civetlike body and was an omnivore that ate plants as well as small prey.

③ Only a single skull fossil has been found of this animal, which lived around 5 MYA. It is a distant relative of today's leopards, jaguars, and panthers.

④ Found in Africa, Eurasia, and North America, this saber-toothed cat could weigh more than 300 lb (136 kg).

⑤ A large dog found throughout North America, this "gluttonous eater" with an incredible bite force could crack open bones in a similar manner to spotted hyenas today.

TEST YOURSELF

STARTER

Canis lepophagus
Panthera blytheae
Megantereon

CHALLENGER

Xenocyon
Borophagus
Proailurus

GENIUS!

Hesperocyon
Aelurodon
Tapocyon

Small prey, such as rabbits, may have been hunted by this slightly built canid.

6 Paleontologists suggest this "cat-toothed" member of the dog family hunted in a pack, just like wolves today. It lived in North America between 16 and 5 MYA.

7 This "rabbit-eating dog" lived in North America during the early part of the Ice Age. It was related to both coyotes and gray wolves.

It walked on its toes, like a modern dog.

Cats and dogs

8 Slightly larger than a house cat, this animal was one of the earliest cats, living in the forests of the region that is now Spain about 30 million years ago.

The second half of the Cenozoic Era saw the rise of cats and dogs—the two main carnivore groups of this time. Both were specialized hunters, but in different ways. While most cats evolved to hunt by ambush, dogs usually chased down their prey alone or in packs.

9 This dog was similar in size to the modern gray wolf and its diet consisted of mostly meat. It was probably the ancestor of the African wild dog found today.

ANSWERS: 1. *Tapocyon* 2. *Hesperocyon* 3. *Panthera blytheae* 4. *Megantereon* 5. *Borophagus* 6. *Aelurodon* 7. *Canis lepophagus* 8. *Proailurus* 9. *Xenocyon*

Going strong

Some Ice Age animals survived the end of the Ice Age and are still around us today, possibly as close as your backyard.

Jaguar
Once roaming widely across the Northern Hemisphere, jaguars still live in the Americas.

White-tailed deer
White-tailed deer are one of the oldest living deer species. Their bones have been found in Ice Age deposits in Mexico.

Gray wolf
Gray wolves migrated to North America during the Ice Age. They became more common after dire wolves died out.

Golden eagle
This raptor once soared over the heads of saber-toothed cats. At La Brea Tar Pits fossil site in the US, their bones are found in the hundreds.

Where did they go?

Although some large Ice Age mammals (such as moose) are still alive today, other mammals (such as the mammoths and the giant sloth *Megatherium*) went extinct. Experts believe climate change, changes in vegetation, and hunting by humans may have been to blame.

Megatherium

Mammoth materials

Few trees grew on the Ice Age grasslands. Humans hunted bison, deer, wild horses, and mammoths and used their hides to make clothes and their bones and tusks to make tools and huts. This is a reconstruction of a 20,000-year-old Ice Age shelter found in Ukraine. The frame of mammoth bones would have been covered with hides to keep out the rain.

I don't believe it!

The last woolly mammoths only died out about 4,000 years ago. They were an isolated group on Siberia's Wrangel Island.

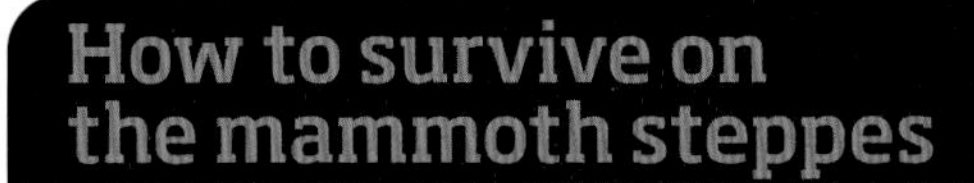

How to survive on the mammoth steppes

01. Keep close to the herd as you roam the cold mammoth steppe. Travelling in a group of up to 15 females offers some safety from the many predators that roam these cold grasslands. Living in a herd also helps to protect vulnerable young, Males leave the herd at the age of 10.

The Ice Age

Ice ages happen when global temperatures drop and thick sheets of ice build up on land and sea. The last ice age began around 2.6 million years ago and has seen Earth's climate swing between freezing and warmer phases. The last big freeze peaked around 20,000 years ago. This is what we call the Ice Age, when large mammals—megafauna—thrived on open, treeless landscapes known as the mammoth steppe.

In numbers

14 ft
(4.2 m) The longest woolly mammoth tusk found so far

4,000
The number of dire wolf fossils that have been found in La Brea, California

23,000 years
The age of the oldest human footprints in North America

3 ft
(1 m) The shoulder height of the smallest mammoth species, which lived on the Greek island of Crete

Walls of ice

Colder temperatures in the Ice Age led to large ice sheets forming on continents. Walls of ice extended from the North Pole to as far south as what is now New York City. When the ice receded, it dropped large boulders, called glacial erratics, which can be seen in Central Park.

03. If under threat, the largest female in the herd will intimidate even the fiercest prey with her large size and sharp tusks.

Two layers of fur, including a shaggy outer layer up to 20 in (50 cm) long, help conserve warmth.

02. Tusks are handy tools. You can use them to dig for food and, in winter, sway them from side to side to clear snow and reveal the vegetation beneath.

Ice Age giants

Many large beasts, known as megafauna, lived on land during the Ice Age. These mammals evolved to be bigger than most mammals are today, although none of them were as large as the dinosaurs. While many of them went extinct at the end of the Pleistocene around 12,000 years ago, some are still living with us today.

① Named for the shaggy coat that covered its body, this rhino had a hump on its back that supported its head and probably also acted as a fat reserve.

Its legs were relatively shorter than those of the modern rhino.

② This cat has been around for about 1 million years and is still prowling the Americas. The species today are a little smaller than their Ice Age ancestors.

A spotted coat helps it hide in the thick vegetation of its forest habitat.

Its shell was very heavy and weighed about 2 tons (2 metric tonnes).

③ One of many giant armadillos covered by a shell made of bone, this herbivore even had rings of bone covering its tail.

Its three hand claws may have been used for defense.

④ This giant animal was among the largest known ground-sloths. It was the size of a modern elephant, reaching a height of 20 ft (6 m).

ANSWERS: 1. Woolly rhinoceros 2. Jaguar 3. *Glyptodon* 4. *Eremotherium* 5. *Chasmaporthetes* 6. American mastodon 7. *Miracinonyx* 8. *Homotherium serum* 9. Columbian mammoth

⑤ The only hyena that ever lived in the Americas, this "running hyena" had teeth that were more adapted to slicing meat than crushing bone, unlike its modern cousins.

⑥ This elephantlike animal preferred forests in warmer periods, ripping branches off tough shrubs and trees. Some males had short tusks on their lower jaw, too, but these were absent in females.

⑦ Also known as the American cheetah, this prehistoric relative of cougars had a lean build. Its bones are usually found in caves, suggesting the cats hunted in steep and rocky habitats like some cougars do today.

⑧ This scimitar-toothed cat had shorter canines and longer limbs than those of a saber-toothed cat. Remains at one fossil site suggests it often preyed on baby mammoths.

⑨ Measuring almost 13 ft (4 m) at the shoulder and weighing 11 tons (10 metric tons), this was the largest of all mammoth species. It was well-adapted to the warmer climates it lived in and did not have thick fur.

TEST YOURSELF

STARTER	CHALLENGER	GENIUS!
Jaguar (*Panthera onca*)	***Glyptodon***	***Chasmaporthetes***
American mastodon (*Mammut americanum*)	**Columbian mammoth (*Mammuthus columbi*)**	***Miracinonyx***
Woolly rhinoceros (*Coelodonta antiquitatis*)	***Eremotherium***	***Homotherium***

Mega marsupials

The Ice Age world was teeming with megafauna—some of the largest animals ever to have lived on land and in water. Not all of them gave birth to live young, such as mammoths. In Australia and South America, a variety of impressive marsupials, which gave birth to partially developed young, evolved through the Cenozoic Era.

1 This "strong-tailed" kangaroo stretched 10 ft (3 m) from nose to tail. It was so big, it evolved a unique way of walking on its hind legs instead of hopping like its modern relatives.

2 A meat-eating cousin of wombats, this "little lion" was about the size of a Labrador retriever but could take down prey larger than itself.

3 This marsupial was not a true kangaroo but a relative of musky-rat kangaroos. It used a serrated cheek tooth for slicing.

4 This saber-toothed marsupial relative from South America looked like a cat, but its jaws were not as strong. It may have scavenged as much as hunted prey.

ANSWERS: 1. *Sthenurus* 2. *Wakaleo* 3. *Ekaltadeta* 4. *Thylacosmilus* 5. *Diprotodon* 6. *Mukupirna* 7. *Ektopodon* 8. *Procoptodon* 9. Tasmanian tiger (*Thylacinus*) 10. *Thylacoleo*

TEST YOURSELF

STARTER

Ektopodon
Diprotodon
Procoptodon

CHALLENGER

Sthenurus
Mukupirna
Ekaltadeta

GENIUS!

Wakaleo
Thylacosmilus
Tasmanian tiger (*Thylacinus*)
Thylacoleo

1 Woolly mammoths traveled long distances. Studies of one mammoth in Alaska shows that they traveled far enough in their lifetime to circle the Earth:

A. Once
B. Twice
C. Three times
D. Five times

2 How long did woolly mammoth fur grow?

A. 20 in (50 cm)
B. 1 ft (60 cm)
C. 2 ft (80 cm)
D. 4 ft (100 cm)

3 Paleontologists have found degraded genes from woolly mammoths. DNA degrades at death and decomposes by half every

A. 100 years
B. 250 years
C. 521 years
D. 1,100 years

4 How long were the tusks of an adult woolly mammoth?

A. 10 ft (3 m), the length of a small car
B. 20 ft (6 m), the length of a van
C. 26 ft (8 m), the length of a truck
D. 36 ft (11 m), the length of a school bus

Woolly mammoth

With their thick, shaggy fur and curved tusks, woolly mammoths were the best known of Ice Age animals. Herds of them ranged over much of the Northern Hemisphere, living in a cold, grassy habitat called the mammoth steppe.

5 Around 100,000 years ago, woolly mammoths crossed a stretch of land between Eurasia and North America. Today, that area is covered by water because the sea level has risen. What is it called?

A. Dead Sea
B. Bering Strait
C. Red Sea
D. Mediterranean Sea

6 In 1977, paleontologists found a woolly mammoth they nicknamed Dima. It was so well preserved that its fur retained its original color. What color was it?

A. Light brown
B. Black
C. Gray
D. Blonde

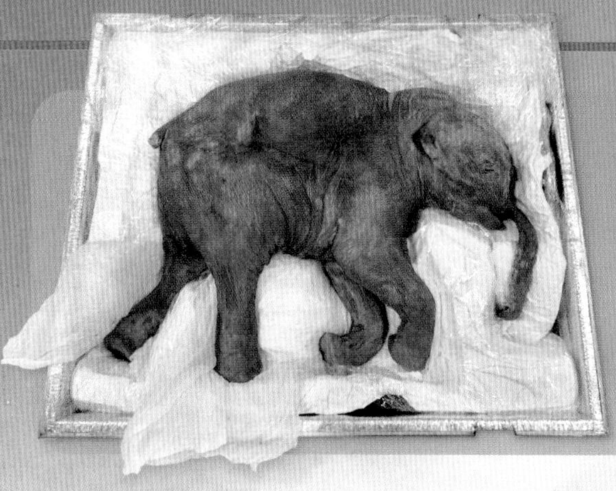

7 The best-preserved woolly mammoth remains ever found were 42,000 years old. They were of a calf, discovered in 2007 in Siberia. What was it named?

A. Ivory **B.** Lyuba
C. Misha **D.** Mamut

8 When did woolly mammoths go extinct?

A. About 4,000 years ago
B. About 8,000 years ago
C. About 9,000 years ago
D. About 10,000 years ago

9 Why did woolly mammoths have smaller ears than modern elephants?

A. They had exceptionally good hearing and did not need big outer ears.

B. Big furry ears would be too heavy when covered in snow.

C. Small ears helped them avoid losing body heat.

D. Big ears were not practical in the windy conditions where they lived.

10 How many layers of fur did woolly mammoth have?

A. One **B.** Two
C. Three **D.** Four

ANSWERS: 1-B, 2-A, 3-C, 4-A, 5-B, 6-D, 7-B, 8-A, 9-C, 10-B

The first humans

Scientists trace the evolution of humans to 6 million years ago, based on fossil finds in eastern Africa. Even though we are the only surviving humans today, hundreds of thousands of years ago, many more species lived alongside each other. They began spreading around the world long before the origin of our own species *Homo sapiens*.

In numbers

206
The number of bones in the average human skeleton

3.5 ft
(1.06 m) The height of "Lucy," the famous fossil of *Australopithecus afarensis*, our prehistoric cousin with ape and human features

3.3 MYA
When the oldest known stone tools used by humans—simple choppers—were created

Cave painters

Humans through time have used caves for shelter, but these prehistoric homes were also places to play and invent. Ice Age cave paintings are the first art and depict the animals early humans lived among. This horse from Lascaux, in France, was painted 16,000 years ago.

How to make fire

01. Place an upright stick in a notch on a piece of wood on top of a nest of dry grasses, which will catch fire easily. Rotate the stick quickly to create friction.

Other early primates

Humans are just part of a much broader primate family tree. Lemurs, monkeys, apes, and other extinct primate groups all thrived alongside human species during the Cenozoic Era.

Plesiadapis
An ancient relative of modern primates that lived in forests about 58 MYA, it had rodentlike teeth with long incisors.

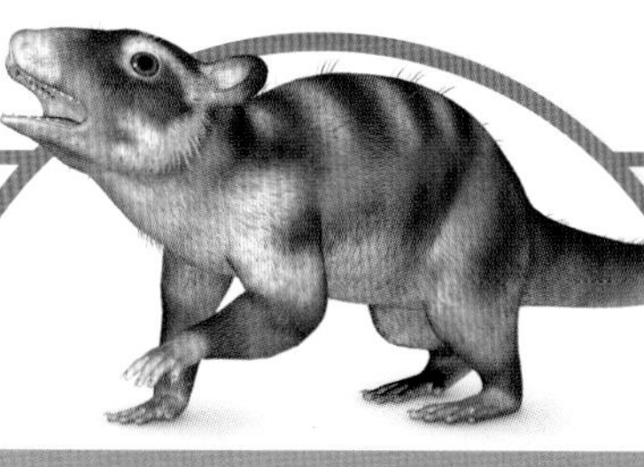

The ancient one

The earliest known primate relative, *Purgatorius* was a tree-shrew-like insectivore. It evolved just after the end Cretaceous mass extinction.

I don't believe it!

Around 300,000 years ago, there were nine different human species on Earth.

02. Friction produces hot dust, then a glowing ember, which drops onto the dry material below. When this begins to smoke, pick up the nest of grasses and gently blow on it until it bursts into flames.

03. When the flames are strong enough, build up the fire using smaller sticks first, then larger pieces of wood.

04. Use the fire, like *Homo erectus* first did, to scare away predators at night. keep warm, and cook food.

Walking upright

Around 3.6 MYA, a small group of early humans walked through volcanic ash at what is now Laetoli, Tanzania. The tracks, together with skeletons found in this region, suggest that humans walked upright very early in their evolutionary history.

Eosimias
A relative of the very first monkeys, this "dawn monkey" lived in what is now China around 45 MYA.

Danuvius
Living in central Europe about 11.6 MYA, this primate could stand up and use its arms to move between trees.

Megaladapis
About the size of a gorilla, this lemur from Madagascar went extinct only 600 years ago.

Meet the family

Our species is part of a diverse family tree. These are our closest relatives, some of whom lived at the same time as each other. Only *Homo sapiens* survived.

***Sahelanthropus tchadensis* (7-6 MYA)**
One of the oldest hominins, *Sahelanthropus* is primarily known from a crushed skull found in western-central Africa.

***Ardipithecus ramidus* (4.4 MYA)**
Though *Ardipithecus* could stand upright, this hominin from eastern Africa moved in a different way than we do and climbed trees.

***Australopithecus afarensis* (3.85-2.95 MYA)**
One of the earliest hominins to walk fully upright, *Austraopithecus afarensis* still had long arms and curved fingers to help them climb.

***Homo habilis* (2.4-1.4 MYA)**
One of the earliest human bones of *Homo habilis* were found in Africa alongside stone tools and give the species its name—handy man.

***Homo erectus* (1.89 MYA-110,000 years ago)**
Homo erectus were skilled hunters who spread around the world. Their remains are found from Africa to the island of Java.

***Homo floresiensis* (100,000-50,000 years ago)**
One of the smallest humans, *Homo floresiensis* lived on the island of Flores in modern-day Indonesia among small elephants and giant storks.

***Homo neanderthalensis* (400,000-40,000 years ago)**
Our closest relatives, Neanderthals lived in Eurasia. They used stone tools, made cave paintings, and wore shell necklaces.

***Homo sapiens* (300,000 years ago-present)**
Our species, the oldest fossils of whom date to about 300,000 years ago in Africa.

1 Neanderthals were named after the Neander Valley, where their fossilized bones were first found. In which present-day country is this?

A. Jordan
B. Canada
C. Germany
D. Japan

2 Three of the discoveries below are true evidence that some Neanderthals made their homes in caves. Which one is the false clue?

A. Red and ocher cave paintings
B. Remains of meals including seafood and birds
C. Traces of fire
D. Wooden beds

Neanderthals

Neanderthals (*Homo neanderthalensis*) were prehistoric humans who were our closest relatives and thrived until relatively recently. They inhabited much of Europe and West Asia between 430,000 and 40,000 years ago. Researchers have learned a great deal about Neanderthals not only from fossils, but also from their tools, cave paintings, and food remains.

Neanderthals wore fur capes probably made of deer, bison, and bear skins.

European bison roamed the plains of Europe at the same time as Neanderthals.

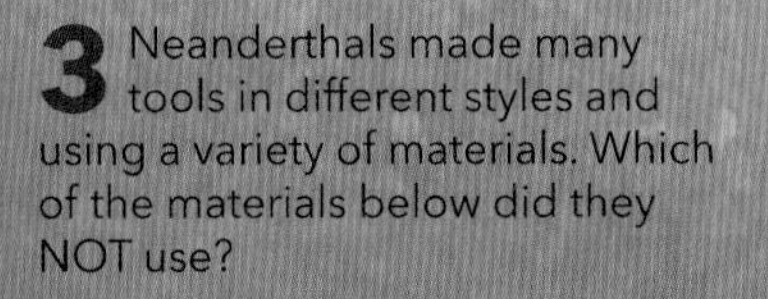

3 Neanderthals made many tools in different styles and using a variety of materials. Which of the materials below did they NOT use?

A. Stone
B. Bone
C. Wood
D. Iron

Scraper used to clean animal hides

4 Neanderthals sometimes decorated their bodies by painting them with colored patterns. What are the common pigment colors found at Neanderthal sites?

A. Reddish brown (copper)
B. Black (manganese dioxide)
C. Blue (woad leaves)
D. Red ocher (iron oxide)

5 Scientists in Iraq recently found 70,000-year-old leftovers of meals made by Neanderthals. This is the oldest cooked food ever found. What food did they find?

A. Small pots of berry jam
B. Pancakes made from pounded seeds
C. A salad of foraged leaves
D. A cake made with dried fruit

The large antlers of male *Megaloceros* made it formidable prey.

Wooden spears were thrust into prey.

6 How were Neanderthal's brains different from those of modern humans?

A. **Their brains were much smaller.**

B. **Their brains were the size of modern human brains.**

C. **Their brains were larger and longer.**

D. **Their brains got smaller with age.**

Neanderthal

Modern human

7 In 1995, archaeologists found an instrument that could have been made out of prehistoric animal remains and used by Neanderthals. What was that instrument?

A. **A guitar**

B. **Drums**

C. **A flute**

D. **A whistle**

8 Neanderthals hunted and foraged for different kinds of food. At Cueva de los Aviones on the Spanish coast, experts found evidence that Neanderthals ate and used parts of which animal?

A. **Giant squid**

B. **Spiny oyster**

C. **Bear**

D. **Shark**

ANSWERS: 1.C, 2.D, 3.D, 4.D, 5.B, 6.C, 7.C, 8.B

Glossary

3D imaging
Using computer software to create a 3D model of an object, such as a fossil. This can be used to study fossils or create replicas of them.

Air sac
A little growth of lung tissue filled with air. Air sacs help **saurischians** and pterosaurs breathe and keep their bodies light.

Amber
Sticky resin that has oozed from a tree and become hardened over many millions of years.

Ammonite
A marine **mollusk** with a coiled shell and squidlike tentacles that was common until the end of the Mesozoic Era.

Amphibians
A group of cold-blooded **vertebrates** that appeared more than 100 million years before the dinosaurs. They were the first back-boned animals to spend much of their time on land.

Ankylosaurid
A type of ankylosaur with a bony tail club for defense.

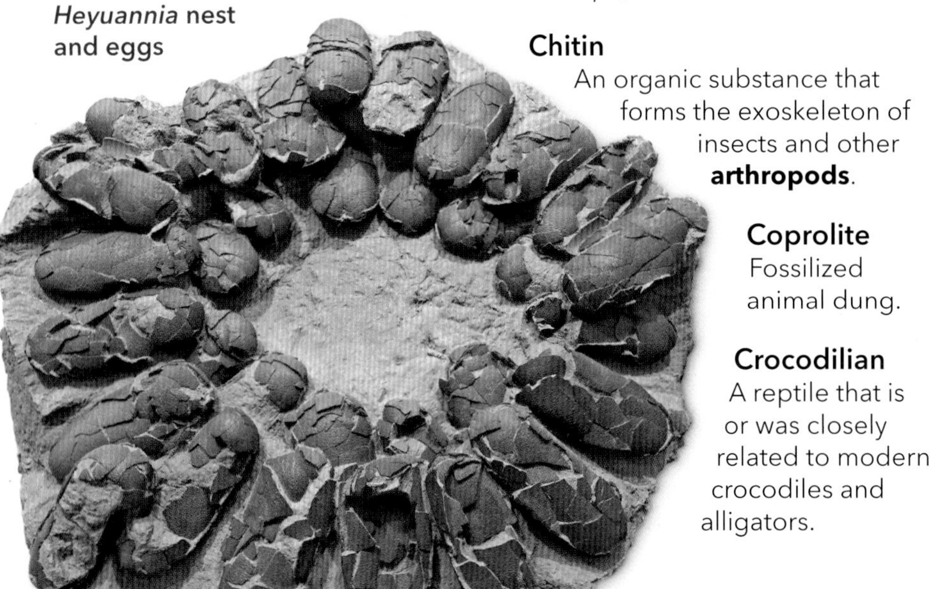
Heyuannia nest and eggs

Archosaurs
A group of related reptiles that includes extinct dinosaurs and pterosaurs, as well as birds and **crocodilians** living today.

Arthropod
An **invertebrate** with a segmented body and a hard outer covering (exoskeleton). Includes insects.

Asteroid
A rocky lump orbiting the Sun. Asteroids are smaller than planets but can measure hundreds of miles (kilometers) across.

Azhdarchid
A giant Late Cretaceous pterosaur.

Belemnite
An extinct **mollusk** with a cone-shaped internal skeleton that often forms bullet-shaped fossils.

Brooding
Keeping eggs or young warm using feathered wings and body heat.

Ceratopsians
Plant-eating dinosaurs with a deep beak and a bony frill at the back of the skull. Many, including *Triceratops*, had facial horns.

Chitin
An organic substance that forms the exoskeleton of insects and other **arthropods**.

Coprolite
Fossilized animal dung.

Crocodilian
A reptile that is or was closely related to modern crocodiles and alligators.

Cycad
A tropical plant that appeared 280 MYA. It has a broad crown of leaves and looks like (but is not related to) palm trees.

Epoch
A span of geological time that is part of a **period**—for example, the Middle Jurassic.

Era
A very long span of time. Eras are divided into shorter spans called **periods**. The Mesozoic Era, for example, is divided into the Triassic, Jurassic, and Cretaceous periods.

Evolution
The gradual change of species over many generations as they adapt to their changing environment.

Ginkgo
A plant that evolved 200 MYA and grows into a tall tree with more or less triangular leaves.

Gondwana
The southern landmass that formed as a result of the division of the **supercontinent Pangea**.

Hadrosaurs
Large plant-eaters from the Cretaceous **period**.

Ichnite
A fossilized footprint. It is a type of **trace fossil**.

Invertebrate
An animal with no backbone.

Keratin
A tough substance found in hair, nails, feathers, scales, claws, and horns.

Laurasia
The northern landmass that formed after being split from the **supercontinent** of **Pangea**.

Liliensternus

Maniraptorans
Literally "hand-snatcher"—a group of theropod dinosaurs with long arms and claws, which gave rise to the birds.

Marsupials
A group of mammals in which offspring are born in an undeveloped state and typically continue to grow inside a pouch on the mother.

Mass extinction
A disaster that causes the disappearance of many types of life forms.

Mollusks
Snails, clams, squid, and their relatives. **Ammonites** belonged to a group of mollusks called cephalopods.

Monotreme
Egg-laying mammals, including the platypus and the echidnas (spiny anteaters). This egg-laying habit is thought to be how mammals originally reproduced.

Nodosaurids
A family of ankylosaurs that did not have a heavy club on the end of its tail.

Ornithischian
One of the two main divisions of dinosaurs. Ornithischians were "bird-hipped" and mostly herbivores, but some were omnivores.

Osteoderms
Bony plates that form within the skin of various **vertebrates** and often form the basis of defensive armor.

Pachycephalosaurs
A group of **ornithischian** dinosaur. Pachycephalosaurs were possibly omnivores with a thick, bony dome on the skull.

Paleontologist
A scientist who specializes in the study of fossils.

Pangea
A **supercontinent** that formed at the end of the Paleozoic Era.

Period
A span of geological time that is part of an **era**—for example, the Jurassic period is part of the Mesozoic Era.

Primate
One of a group of mammals that includes monkeys, apes, and humans.

Pseudosuchians
A group of ancient **archosaurs** that were closely related to modern crocodiles.

Saurischian
One of the two main divisions of dinosaurs, which typically had "lizardlike hips."

Serrated
Saw-toothed, like a bread knife.

Supercontinent
A huge landmass made up of many continents that have joined together.

Trace fossil
Indirect evidence of prehistoric life—instead of their actual fossils—preserved in rock. Trace fossils can be footprints, bite marks, droppings, or eggshells.

Track
A footprint left by a dinosaur or other animal.

Trackway
A series of **tracks**.

Trilobite
A kind of extinct **arthropod** with a body divided into three sections or lobes.

Tyrannosaurids
Dinosaurs including and closely related to *Tyrannosaurus*.

Vertebrate
An animal with a backbone and a skeleton.

Wingspan
The measurement from the tip of one wing of an animal to the tip of the other when the wings are outstretched.

Insect in amber
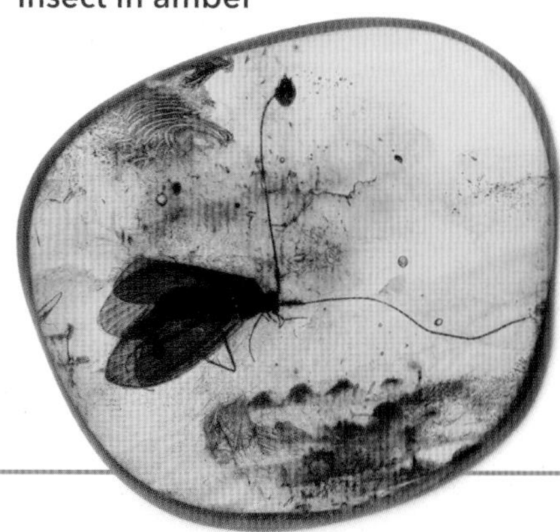

Index

Main topics are shown in **bold** page numbers.

Muttaburrasaurus

A

B

C

D

Scelidosaurus

E

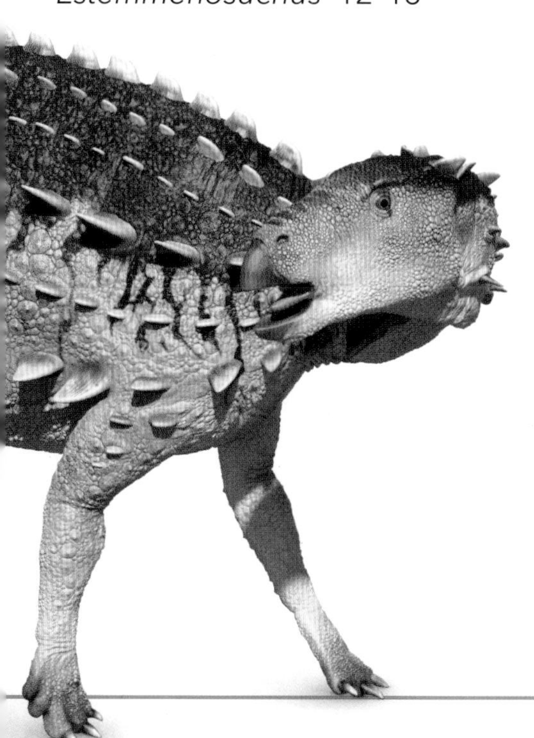

F

G

H

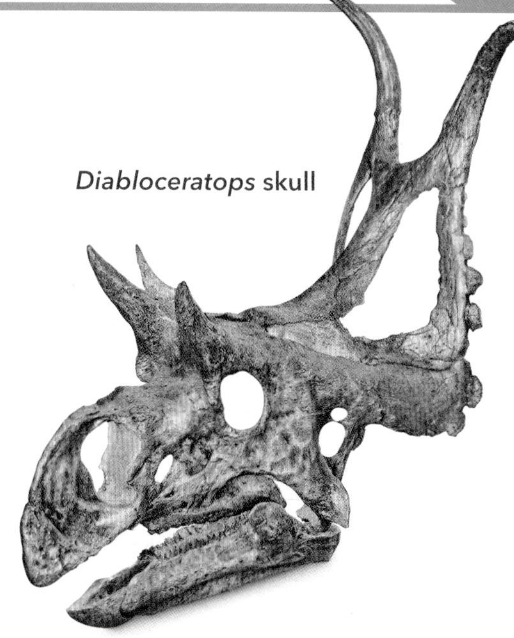

Diabloceratops **skull**

I

JK

L

Torosaurus

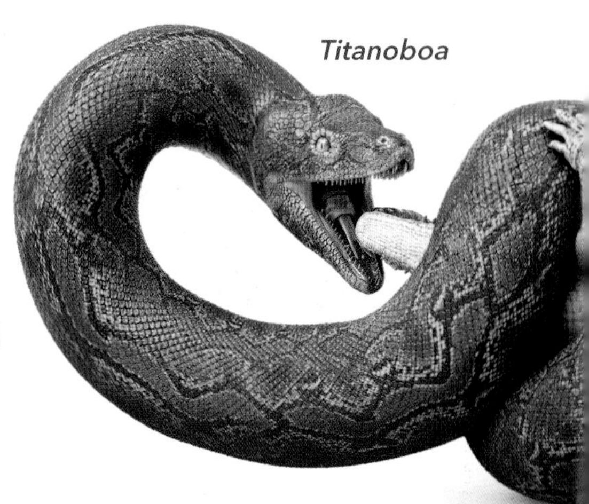
Titanoboa

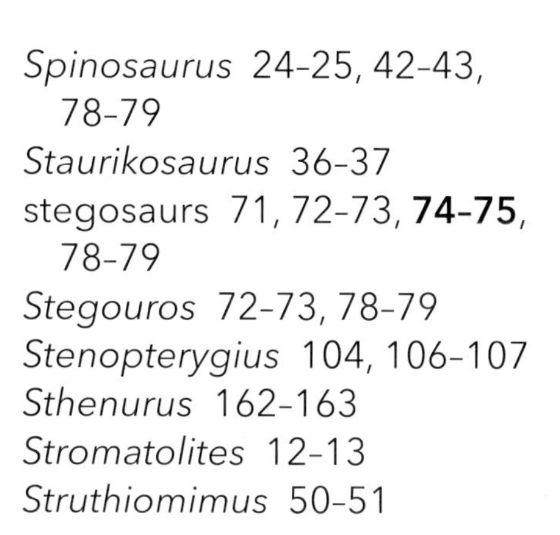

Gastornis

Acknowledgments

The publisher would like to thank the following people for their help with making this book: Laura Dean for proofreading; Elizabeth Wise for indexing; Simon Mumford for cartography; Simon Tegg for illustrations; Abhimanyu Adhikary, Adarsh Tripathi, Ragini Rawat, and Prateek Maurya for design assistance; Manpreet Kaur and Sam Rajkumar for picture research assistance.

Picture Credits

The publisher would like to thank the following for their kind permission to reproduce their photographs:

(Key: a-above; b-below/bottom; c-center; f-far; l-left; r-right; t-top)

2 Alamy Stock Photo: Mohamad Haghani (bl). **Dorling Kindersley:** James Kuether (cla, clb). **Dreamstime.com:** Rodho (bl/palm tree); Mark Turner (cb). **James Kuether:** (tl, tc). **Science Photo Library:** Claus Lunau (cla). **3 Dreamstime.com:** Linda Bucklin (cla); Kitti Kahotong (br). **Science Photo Library:** Ja Chirinos (tc). **Shutterstock.com:** Herschel Hoffmeyer (tr). **4 Alamy Stock Photo:** Mohamad Haghani (tl); Suzanne Long (bl); Natural Visions / Heather Angel (br). **James Kuether:** (cra, bc). **Science Photo Library:** James Kuether (tr). **5 Alamy Stock Photo:** Stocktrek Images / Sergey Krasovskiy (tl). **Depositphotos Inc:** warpaintcobra (bc). **Dreamstime.com:** Ken Backer (bl). **Shutterstock.com:** Adwo (tr). **8-9 James Kuether**. **10 Alamy Stock Photo:** Auscape International Pty Ltd / Jean-Paul Ferrero (cra/forest). **Getty Images:** Ralph White (tl). **Science Photo Library:** Richard Bizley (cb); Masato Hattori (c); Mark P. Witton (clb); James Kuether (crb, fcrb). **Shutterstock.com:** Daniel Eskridge (cra). **11 Alamy Stock Photo:** Elena Elenaphotos21 (crb); Edo Loi (tl); Science Photo Library / Steve Gschmeissner (cra). **Dreamstime.com:** Winzworks (cla). **James Kuether:** (cl). **Science Photo Library:** Marco Anson (cb); Steve Gschmeissner (cra/Archaea); Dr David Furness, Keele University (cr); James Kuether (c). **12 Alamy Stock Photo:** Album (br); Mint Images Limited (tl); The Natural History Museum (tc). **Dreamstime.com:** Victor Zherebtsov (clb). **Science Photo Library:** James Kuether (bl). **13 Alamy Stock Photo:** All Canada Photos / Stephen J. Krasemann (clb). **Dreamstime.com:** Planetfelicity (br). **Science Photo Library:** Science Stock Photography (tr). **14 James Kuether:** (cl). **Science Photo Library:** James Kuether (cr, cb); Mark P. Witton (clb, crb). **15 123RF.com:** Andrejs Pidjass / NejroN (c). **Alamy Stock Photo:** RooM the Agency / Kristianbell (tl). **Science Photo Library:** Richard Bizley (cb, clb); Mikkel Juul Jensen (crb). **16-17 James Kuether**. **16 Dorling Kindersley:** Colin Keates / Natural History Museum, London (bl). **17 Science Photo Library:** Millard H. Sharp (cr). **18 Alamy Stock Photo:** Natural Visions / Heather Angel (crb). **Dorling Kindersley:** Colin Keates / Natural History Museum, London (clb); Colin Keates / Natural History Museum (cb). **18-19 Dreamstime.com:** 7xpert (c). **19 Alamy Stock Photo:** Rosanne Tackaberry (clb). **Ardea:** © Francois Gohier (tc). **Science Photo Library:** Pascal Goetgheluck (cr, crb/3D imaging); Philippe Psaila (crb). **Shutterstock.com:** Breck P. Kent (cb). **20 Alamy Stock Photo:** Jeff Rotman (cr); The Natural History Museum (br). **Dreamstime.com:** Viter8 (tc). **Science Photo Library:** Pascal Goetgheluck (ca); Mark A. Schneider (bl). **20-21 Alamy Stock Photo:** The Natural History Museum (tc). **21 Alamy Stock Photo:** The Natural History Museum (tr). **Science Photo Library:** Frank Fox (br); Javier Trueba / MSF (clb). **SuperStock:** Albert J. Copley / Age Fotostock (cr). **22 Alamy Stock Photo:** Incamerastock / ICP (tr). **Dorling Kindersley:** Gary Ombler / Oxford Museum of Natural History (clb). **22-23 Universidade de Lisboa:** Pombal Municipality, Grupo de Biologia Evolutiva-UNED and Instituto Dom Luiz / Faculdade de Cincias (c). **23 Alamy Stock Photo:** CPA Media Pte Ltd / Pictures From History (crb); Natural History Library (cra). **Dreamstime.com:** Martingraf (r). **24 James Kuether:** (ca). **Shutterstock.com:** Herschel Hoffmeyer (bc); SciePro (crb). **25 Science Photo Library:** James Kuether (tl, crb). **26 123RF.com:** Athikhun Boonrin (bl). **Alamy Stock Photo:** National Geographic Image Collection / Robert Clark (tc). **26-27 Image Courtesy of the Royal Tyrrell Museum, Drumheller, AB:** (c). **27 Alamy Stock Photo:** Stocktrek Images / Nobumichi Tamura (b). **30 Dorling Kindersley:** Colorado Plateau Geosystems Inc (cl, cra). **Science Photo Library:** James Kuether (clb, crb); Mark P. Witton (bc). **30-31 Science Photo Library:** James Kuether (c). **31 Alamy Stock Photo:** NPS (tr); Stocktrek Images / Sergey Krasovskiy (bl). **Dorling Kindersley:** Colorado Plateau Geosystems Inc (c). **Dreamstime.com:** Corey A Ford (bc/Cronopio). **Science Photo Library:** James Kuether (cr); Dr Keith Wheeler (bc). **32 Science Photo Library:** Mark P. Witton (cl, c, cb, bl, cr, br). **32-33 Science Photo Library:** Mark P. Witton (tc, cb). **33 Dreamstime.com:** Planetfelicity (tr). **Science Photo Library:** Mark P. Witton (crb, br). **34-35 James Kuether:** (b). **35 Alamy Stock Photo:** Mohamad Haghani (br); Stocktrek Images / Sergey Krasovskiy (bc). **Dorling Kindersley:** James Kuether (cra). **Science Photo Library:** James Kuether (crb). **36 James Kuether:** (br). **36-37 Dorling Kindersley:** James Kuether (c). **37 Alamy Stock Photo:** Nobumichi Tamura / Stocktrek Images (cb). **Dorling Kindersley:** James Kuether (bl). **James Kuether:** (t, br). **38-39 James Kuether**. **38 Alamy Stock Photo:** agefotostock / Tolo Balaguer (bc). **39 Science Photo Library:** Millard H. Sharp (tr). **40 Dorling Kindersley:** James Kuether (ca/Baronyx, cra, fcra). **James Kuether:** (ca). **40-41 Science Photo Library:** James Kuether (b). **41 Alamy Stock Photo:** Stocktrek Images / Emily Willoughby (ca). **Dreamstime.com:** Alicenerr (tr); Shutterfree (fcra). **Royal Saskatchewan Museum (RSM/ R.C. McKellar):** (cla). **42-43 James Kuether:** (c). **42 Dorling Kindersley:** James Kuether (br). **James Kuether:** (tl, ca). **43 Dorling Kindersley:** James Kuether (tr). **James Kuether:** (crb). **44-45 James Kuether**. **44 Shutterstock.com:** Andrea Izzotti (bc). **46 Alamy Stock Photo:** Mohamad Haghani (bc). **James Kuether:** (tc). **Science Photo Library:** James Kuether (clb); Mark P. Witton (c). **Velizar Simeonovski:** under the direction of Julia Clarke and Chad Eliason (tr). **46-47 Shutterstock.com:** Rodos Studio Ferhat Cinar (bc). **47 Alamy Stock Photo:** imageBROKER.com GmbH & Co. KG / Martin Siepmann (tc). **Dreamstime.com:** Dave Newman (br). **Gabriel Ugueto:** (tr). **48-49 Dreamstime.com:** Jaume Juncadella (Background). **James Kuether**. **49 Getty Images:** Christian Masnaghetti / Stocktrek Images (br). **50-51 James Kuether:** (t). **50 Dorling Kindersley:** Oxford Museum of Natural History / Gary Ombler (cl). **Dreamstime.com:** Fabio Iozzino (ca); Rodho (tl); Irochka (bl). **Getty Images:** The Washington Post (crb). **51 Alamy Stock Photo:** REDA &CO srl / Andrea Innocenti (clb); Science Photo Library / Sciepro (tr); The Natural History Museum (cl). **52-53 James Kuether**. **53 Alamy Stock Photo:** Martin Shields (tr). **Dorling Kindersley:** Natural History Museum, London / Harry Taylor (bc). **54 Alamy Stock Photo:** Mohamad Haghani (tl); The Natural History Museum (bc). **Dorling Kindersley:** Andy Crawford Courtesy of Dorset Dinosaur Museum (cra). **Dreamstime.com:** Ken Backer (clb); Fabio Iozzino (c); Huating (c/Sand). **Getty Images:** Mohamad Haghani / Stocktrek Images (crb). **55 Alamy Stock Photo:** Mohamad Haghani (cla). **Getty Images:** Christian Masnaghetti / Stocktrek Images (cra). **Science Photo Library:** Natural History Museum, London (tl); Dirk Wiersma (ca). **Shutterstock.com:** Adwo (tr). **56-57 James Kuether**. **57 Alamy Stock Photo:** The Natural History Museum (cra). **58-59 Alamy Stock Photo:** Martin Shields (tc). **58 Dorling Kindersley:** James Kuether (br). **Science Photo Library:** Millard H. Sharp (tl); Mark P. Witton (cl). **59 Alamy Stock Photo:** The Natural History Museum (cr). **Dorling Kindersley:** Colin Keates / Natural History Museum, London (cl); James Kuether (bl). **Getty Images:** Sergey Krasovski (tc). **60-61 James Kuether**. **61 Dorling Kindersley:** James Kuether (ca, cb/Titanosaurs). **Dreamstime.com:** Corey A Ford (clb); Mr1805 (ca/Mamenchisaurids); Lina Moiseienko (bc). **Getty Images:** Science Photo Library / Mark Garlick (cb). **62-63 James Kuether**. **62 Dorling Kindersley:** Senckenberg Gesellschaft Fuer Naturforschung Museum / Gary Ombler (clb). **63 Getty Images:** Stocktrek Images / Nobumichi Tamura (ca). **64 Alamy Stock Photo:** © Chrisstockphotography (tl); Peter van Evert (cr); Science Photo Library / Sciepro (br); dpa picture alliance archive (cb). **Dorling Kindersley:** James Kuether (cla, c). **Dreamstime.com:** Elena Duvernay (bl). **65 Depositphotos Inc:** warpaintcobra (c). **Dreamstime.com:** Sebastian Kaulitzki (tr); Mark Turner (tc). **Science Photo Library:** James Kuether (b). **66-67 James Kuether**. **67 Dorling Kindersley:** Nigel Hicks / Museo Paleontologico Egidio Feruglio (cra). **68 Alamy Stock Photo:** Hemis / Sudres Jean-Daniel (ca). **Science Photo Library:** James Kuether (cl). **68-69 Alamy Stock Photo:** Travelscape Images (c). **69 Science Photo Library:** Adam Hart-Davis (cb). **70-71 James Kuether:** (b). **70 Dorling Kindersley:** Andy Crawford / Royal Tyrrell Museum of Palaeontology, Alberta, Canada (ca). **71 Choi Yusik:** Digital Painting, 2021 (br). **72 Alamy Stock Photo:** Mohamad Haghani (cla). **73 Alamy Stock Photo:** Mohamad Haghani (cb). **Dreamstime.com:** Alxyago (tl/Forest). **James Kuether:** (tl, cla, cra, bc). **74 Alamy Stock Photo:** dpa picture alliance / Peter Steffen (bl). **Science Photo Library:** Millard H. Sharp (tc). **74-75 Science Photo Library:** James Kuether. **76-77 James Kuether**. **Science Photo Library:** James Kuether (Background). **76 WitmerLab at Ohio University:** (tr). **77 Ryan Somma:** (bc). **78 Alamy Stock Photo:** All Canada Photos / Stephen J. Krasemann (cla, c). **Dorling Kindersley:** James Kuether (cra). **Getty Images:** Mohamad Haghani / Stocktrek Images (bl). **Shutterstock.com:** Herschel Hoffmeyer (tl). **78-79 Dorling Kindersley:** James Kuether (cb). **79 Alamy Stock Photo:** Mohamad Haghani (cl). **Dorling Kindersley:** Jon Hughes (crb); James Kuether (cla). **80-81 Science Photo Library:** James Kuether. **81 Alamy Stock Photo:** Sergey Krasovskiy / Stocktrek Images (cb/Chaoyangsaurids). **Dorling Kindersley:** James Kuether (cb). **Dreamstime.com:** Ken Backer (cra). **Getty Images / iStock:** leonello (c). **Shutterstock.com:** YuRi Photolife (cb/Udanoceratops). **82-83 James Kuether**. **82 Dreamstime.com:** Ken Backer (br). **83 James Kuether:** (tr). **84-85 James Kuether:** (b). **84 Alamy Stock Photo:** Jim Lane (cra). **Dreamstime.com:** Jaroslav Moravcik (bl). **James Kuether:** (clb). **Science Photo Library:** James Kuether (cl). **85 Bridgeman Images:** Novapix / Julius Csotonyi (cl). **Dorling Kindersley:** James Kuether (br). **James Kuether:** (tl, tr). **Science Photo Library:** Science Source / Millard H. Sharp (cb). **86 Science Photo Library:** James Kuether (cl, tr); Millard H. Sharp (cr). **86-87 Science Photo Library:** James Kuether (ca). **87 Dorling Kindersley:** Andy Crawford / Royal Tyrrell Museum of Palaeontology, Alberta, Canada (cra). **Shutterstock.com:** Herschel Hoffmeyer (br); SciePro (tr); Reimar (clb). **88-89 James Kuether**. **88 Dorling Kindersley:** James Kuether (bl). **90 Alamy Stock Photo:** Mohamad Haghani (cl). **Science Photo Library:** James Kuether (clb, tr); Mark P. Witton (cla). **Shutterstock.com:** SciePro (bl). **91 Alamy Stock Photo:** The Natural History Museum (cla). **James Kuether:** (cra). **92 Dorling Kindersley:** James Kuether (cra). **James Kuether:** (tr, clb, tl, cb). **Science Photo Library:** Richard Jones (cra/forest). **93 James Kuether:** (tl, cr, tr). **Science Photo Library:** Richard Jones (tr/forest). **94-95 James Kuether**. **94 Dorling Kindersley:** Colin Keates / Natural History Museum, London (cra). **95 Dorling Kindersley:** Colin Keates / Natural History Museum (bl). **96 Science Photo Library:** Millard H. Sharp (cla). **96-97 Science Photo Library:** James Kuether (bc). **97 Alamy Stock Photo:** Steve Vidler (br). **Dorling Kindersley:** Andy Crawford Courtesy of Dorset Dinosaur Museum (tl); Peter Minister, Digital Sculptor (cr). **Science Photo Library:** Millard H. Sharp (tc). **98 Louie Psihoyos ©psihoyos.com:** (bl). **98-99 Dreamstime.com:** Dave Newman (Background). **James Kuether:** (Citipati). **100 Alamy Stock Photo:** The Natural History Museum (clb, cb). **Science Photo Library:** Philippe Psaila (crb). **WitmerLab at Ohio University:** (c). **101 James Kuether:** (cr, crb). **Science Photo Library:** Julius T Csotonyi (br); James Kuether (bl). **WitmerLab at Ohio University:** (cl). **104 Alamy Stock Photo:** Mohamad Haghani (ca/Elasmosaurus). **Dreamstime.com:** Andreykuzmin (fcla/sea); Planetfelicity (fcla); Ozspzone2 (cla/sea, cra); Mr1805 (cla). **Science Photo Library:** Ja Chirinos (ca, fcra). **104-105 Science Photo Library:** James Kuether (cl). **105 Alamy Stock Photo:** Mohamad Haghani (cla, fcrb); The Natural History Museum (cr). **Dreamstime.com:** Grafner (cb); Oleksandr Prykhodko (cla/sea). **Science Photo Library:** James Kuether (tc). **106 Alamy Stock Photo:** Mohamad Haghani (c). **Science Photo Library:** Ja Chirinos (tc, cra); James Kuether (cla). **106-107 Alamy Stock Photo:** Mohamad Haghani (tc). **James Kuether:** (b). **107 Alamy Stock Photo:** The Natural History Museum (bl). **Science Photo Library:** James Kuether (tc). **108 Alamy Stock Photo:** Alessandro Zocchi (bl). **James Kuether**. **108-109 Dreamstime.com:** Rangizzz (Background). **109 Alamy Stock Photo:** Biosphoto / Pascal Goetgheluck (tr); Dorset Media Service (crb). **Science Photo Library:** John Sibbick (c). **110 Alamy Stock Photo:** R Kawka (clb). **Dreamstime.com:** Linda Bucklin (ca, fcra). **Ohio University College of Osteopathic Medicine:** (cb). **Science Photo Library:** Millard H. Sharp (fclb). **Cerian Thomas:** (cra). **110-111 Alamy Stock Photo:** National Geographic Image Collection / Raul Martin (r). **111 Alamy Stock Photo:** Fve Media (tl). **112 Shutterstock.com:** Herschel Hoffmeyer (cla). **112-113 Dreamstime.com:** Mr1805 (Background). **Shutterstock.com:** Herschel Hoffmeyer. **113 University of Chicago Fossil Lab:** (tr). **114 Alamy Stock Photo:** CNMages (cb); Stocktrek Images / Nobumichi Tamura (tl); Mohamad Haghani (bl). **Dreamstime.com:** Corey A Ford (tr); Grafner (fbl). **114-115 Science Photo Library:** Ja Chirinos (c). **115 Alamy Stock Photo:** Melba Photo Agency (ca); Stocktrek Images / Nobumichi Tamura (tl). **Dreamstime.com:** Grafner (bc). **Getty Images / iStock:** Barbaraaaa (br). **Gabriel Ugueto:** (cb). **116-117 Chase Stone:** (br). **116 Alamy Stock Photo:** Stocktrek Images / Sergey Krasovskiy (cla, cl, clb, bl). **Science Photo Library:** Mark P. Witton (ca). **117 Alamy Stock Photo:** Stocktrek Images / Sergey Krasovskiy (cra). **Science Photo Library:** Carlton Publishing Group (fcra); Mark P. Witton (fcla, ca). **Vitor Silva:** (cla). **118 Dreamstime.com:** Alinamd (bc); Kitti Kahotong (bl). **Paleostock.com:** Lucas Lima (tr). **Science Photo Library:** Carlton Publishing Group (cl). **Gabriel Ugueto:** (bl). **119 Alamy Stock Photo:** The Natural History Museum (cra). **Dreamstime.com:** Wei Huang (t). **Science Photo Library:** Mark P. Witton (cl, br). **120-121 James Kuether**. **122 Alamy Stock Photo:** Stocktrek Images / Nobumichi Tamura (cl). **Dreamstime.com:** Jessicahyde (tl). Masato Hattori: (cla). **Science Photo Library:** Mark P. Witton (tr). **122-123 Science Photo Library:** Mark P. Witton (bc). **123 Dreamstime.com:** Chansom Pantip (cra). **Masato Hattori:** (bc). **Paleostock.com:** Sergey Krasovskiy (c). **Science Photo Library:** Mark P. Witton (cla). **124 Alamy Stock Photo:** Mohamad Haghani (cb/platyurus, bc); RGB Ventures / SuperStock / Brad Lewis (tr). **Science Photo Library:** Mark P. Witton (cb). **124-125 Alamy Stock Photo:** Science Photo Library / Mark Garlick (c). **125 Getty Images / iStock:** Sstop (br). **Science Photo Library:** James Kuether (tr). **126-127 Science Photo Library:** Mauricio Anton. **128 Dreamstime.com:** Orawan Atthi (c). **Science Photo Library:** Philippe Psaila (cra); Barbara Strnadova (cb). **128-129 Dorling Kindersley:** Colorado Plateau Geosystems Inc / Simon Mumford (bc). **129 ©Denver Museum of Nature & Science:** EAS2019-5-7 (tr). **Dorling Kindersley:** Tracy Morgan (br). **Science Photo Library:** Phil Degginger (tl); James Kuether (cra). **Roman Uchytel:** (cra/Uintatherium, crb, cr). **130-131 Alamy Stock Photo:** Holger Kleine (Background). **132 Alamy Stock Photo:** Stocktrek Images / Christian Masnaghetti (cr); The Natural History Museum (bl). **Science Photo Library:** Ja Chirinos (tc, bc). **132-133 Science Photo Library:** Ja Chirinos (tc); Roman Uchytel (bc). **133 Paleostock.com:** Andrey Atuchin (bc). **Science Photo Library:** Mark P. Witton (tr, crb). **Roman Uchytel:** (ca). **134-135 Alamy Stock Photo:** Auscape International Pty Ltd / Jean-Paul Ferrero (Background). **134 Science Photo Library:** Millard H. Sharp (bl). **135 123RF.com:** Aaron Amat (br). **136-137 James Kuether**. **136 Alamy Stock Photo:** The Natural History Museum (bl). **Bridgeman Images:** Novapix (clb). **Roman Uchytel:** (cla, cla/Ankalagon). **137 Alamy Stock Photo:** Dave Watts (tr). **Dreamstime.com:** John Casey (cra); Wayne Marinovich (cr). **138 Alamy Stock Photo:** Stocktrek Images, Inc. / Sergey Krasovskiy (tl); Stocktrek Images / Nobumichi Tamura (cr). **Dorling Kindersley:** James Kuether (tr). **Paleostock.com:** Lucas Lima (c). **138-139 Alamy Stock Photo:** Nature Picture Library / Alex Mustard (b). **139 Alamy Stock Photo:** Stocktrek Images / Nobumichi Tamura (tr); Torontonian (bc). **Paleostock.com:** Lucas Lima (br). **Science Photo Library:** James Kuether (cr); Roman Uchytel (cl). **140-141 Dreamstime.com:** Donfiore. **Science Photo Library:** James Kuether (whale). **140 Dreamstime.com:** Mark Turner (bl). **141 Alamy Stock Photo:** Minden Pictures / Lex van Groningen / Buiten-beeld (br). **142 Science Photo Library:** Ja Chirinos (tr); Roman Uchytel (c). **Roman Uchytel:** (tl, bl). **142-143 Science Photo Library:** James Kuether (bc). **143 Dreamstime.com:** CrailsheimStudio (fcla). **Sergio De La Rosa:** (cla). **Science Photo Library:** Roman Uchytel (cra). **Roman Uchytel:** (br, crb). **144 Science Photo Library:** Herve Conge, ISM (cb); Tom Mchugh (cla). **Roman Uchytel:** (tr). **144-145 Alamy Stock Photo:** Design Pics Inc / Peter Langer (c). **Science Photo Library:** Roman Uchytel (bc). **145 Alamy Stock Photo:** Suzanne Long (cb); Martin Shields (tr). **Roman Uchytel:** (tl, br). **146-147 Paleostock.com:** Julio Lacerda. **146 Dorling Kindersley:** Colin Keates / Natural History Museum, London (bc). **147 Dorling Kindersley:** Harry Taylor / Natural History Museum, London (tr). **148 Science Photo Library:** Millard H. Sharp (bc); Roman Uchytel (cl). **Shutterstock.com:** Danny Ye (cb). **148-149 Dorling Kindersley:** Natural History Museum, London / Harry Taylor (ca). **Science Photo Library:** Ja Chirinos (bc). **149 Alamy Stock Photo:** The Natural History Museum (cr). **Dreamstime.com:** Elena Duvernay (cla). **Science Photo Library:** Roman Uchytel (tl, bc). **150 Science Photo Library:** Roman Uchytel (tc, bl). **Roman Uchytel:** (cl, crb). **150-151 Roman Uchytel:** (tc). **151 Alamy Stock Photo:** Joseph Creamer (b); Smilodon Producciones (cb). **Dreamstime.com:** Puwadol Jaturawutthichai (tr). **Science Photo Library:** Roman Uchytel (cl). **152 Dreamstime.com:** Suljo (tr). **152-153 Dreamstime.com:** Pawel Cichonski. **Shutterstock.com:** Rob Crandall (Bison). **154 Alamy Stock Photo:** Aaron Parker (bc). **154-155 Dreamstime.com:** Willyambradberry (Background). **155 Alamy Stock Photo:** Arterra Picture Library / Clement Philippe (tc). **156 Alamy Stock Photo:** Erberto Zani (bl). **Getty Images:** Stocktrek Images / Nobumichi Tamura (tl). **Science Photo Library:** Roman Uchytel (crb). **Roman Uchytel:** (c). **156-157 Roman Uchytel:** (tc). **157 Science Photo Library:** Roman Uchytel (cl). **Roman Uchytel:** (tr, crb, bc). **158 Alamy Stock Photo:** Daniel Dempster Photography (cla/Deer); The Print Collector / CM Dixon / Heritage Images (tr). **Dreamstime.com:** Valeriy Kalyuzhnyy / Dragoneye (cl); Martin Schneiter (cla). **158-159 Alamy Stock Photo:** John Lambing (b/Background). **Roman Yevseyev:** (b). **159 Dreamstime.com:** Linda Harms (c). **160 Alamy Stock Photo:** The Natural History Museum (cr). **Science Photo Library:** Paul Becx, The Netherlands (cla). **Roman Uchytel:** (bl). **160-161 Science Photo Library:** Millard H. Sharp / Science Source (bc). **Roman Uchytel:** (tc). **161 Dreamstime.com:** Tyler Olson (fcr). **Sergio De La Rosa:** (cr). **Science Photo Library:** Mauricio Anton (crb); Roman Uchytel (tc). **Roman Uchytel:** (cl). **162-163 Science Photo Library:** Roman Uchytel (tc). **162 Dreamstime.com:** Shargaljut (bl). **Science Photo Library:** Ja Chirinos (crb). **Roman Uchytel:** (cl, ca, c). **163 Alamy Stock Photo:** World History Archive (clb). **Science Photo Library:** Roman Uchytel (bl). **Roman Uchytel:** (tr, ca). **164-165 Shutterstock.com:** Dotted Yeti. **165 Getty Images:** AFP / Aaron Tam / Stringer (tl). **166-167 Alamy Stock Photo:** Images of Africa Photobank / David Keith Jones (cl). **166 Alamy Stock Photo:** Universal Images Group North America LLC / DeAgostini (br). **Shutterstock.com:** Charbonnier Thierry (bl). **167 Alamy Stock Photo:** Friedrich Saurer (tl). **Science Photo Library:** Marco Anson (clb); John Reader (c); Claus Lunau (fclb). **Roman Uchytel:** (cb). **168-169 Paleostock.com:** Julio Lacerda. **168 Alamy Stock Photo:** The Natural History Museum (bl). **170-171 James Kuether:** (t). **170 Science Photo Library:** Millard H. Sharp (bl). **171 Science Photo Library:** Frank Fox (br). **173 Science Photo Library:** Science Source / Millard H. Sharp (tr)

WHAT WILL YOU DISCOVER NEXT?